THE COMING BALKAN CALIPHATE

THE COMING BALKAN CALIPHATE

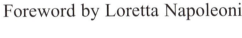

The Threat of Radical Islam to Europe and the West

Christopher Deliso

Foreword by Loretta Napoleoni

PRAEGER SECURITY INTERNATIONAL

Westport, Connecticut · London

Library of Congress Cataloging-in-Publication Data

Deliso, Christopher, 1974–
   The coming Balkan caliphate : the threat of radical Islam to Europe and the West / Christopher
Deliso ; foreword by Loretta Napoleoni.
      p. cm.
   Includes bibliographical references and index.
   ISBN-13: 978–0–275–99525–6 (alk. paper)
1. Terrorism — Balkan Peninsula. 2. Islam — Balkan Peninsula — History. 3. Islam and politics —
Balkan Peninsula. 4. Balkan Peninsula — Ethnic relations. I. Title.
HV6433.B35D45 2007
305.6'9709496—dc22   2007014360

British Library Cataloguing in Publication Data is available.

Library of Congress Catalog Card Number: 2007014360
ISBN-13: 978–0–275–99525–6
ISBN-10: 0–275–99525–9

First published in 2007

Praeger Security International, 88 Post Road West, Westport, CT 06881
An imprint of Greenwood Publishing Group, Inc.
www.praeger.com

Printed in the United States of America

The paper used in this book complies with the
Permanent Paper Standard issued by the National
Information Standards Organization (Z39.48–1984).

10 9 8 7 6 5 4 3 2 1

Every reasonable effort has been made to trace the owners of copyright materials in this book, but
in some instances this has proven impossible. The author and publisher will be glad to receive
information leading to more complete acknowledgments in subsequent printings of the book and in
the meantime extend their apologies for any omissions.

Contents

Foreword

The Balkans is the cultural and historical bridge between East and West. It is a region where the seeds of many civilizations have been sown, as well as a land that has witnessed endless wars fought to enhance different visions of history. It is the geographical divide between two worlds, which at times have merged, as during the Roman Empire, and at others have collided violently with each other, as during the Crusades. Historically and strategically, the Balkans are today as important for the future of Europe as they were a century ago, when an anarchic fanatic in Sarajevo offered the *casus belli* for World War I. This is the message encrypted in Christopher Deliso's seminal work, in his detailed reconstruction of the genesis of jihadist and fundamentalist movements in the region.

Right from the beginning the author shows how major political mistakes have boosted the spreading in the region of the most reactionary and backwards interpretations of Islam, particularly Wahhabism. Since the fall of the Berlin Wall, the former Yugoslavia has disintegrated, being replaced by several small states, all seeking independence from one another and all eager to compete with each other over territorial enclaves. To legitimate such claims, religion became synonymous with ethnicity and nationality. In a region where races and creeds had mixed for centuries, this phenomenon triggered new strife. Ethnic cleansing became the appalling weapon to clear the way to territorial conquest. Neighbors killed each other, and families were torn apart.

Deliso superbly and almost scientifically unveils the political mistakes and blindness that fostered the most recent Balkan wars. As early as the 1980s, the peculiar geography and history of Yugoslavia appealed to emerging Islamic powers. Saudi Arabia and Iran saw in the Balkans an ideal hub from where to challenge Europe. They targeted the region, which became part of a master plan to proselytize radical Islam in areas where Muslim minorities lived. Thus Wahhabi religious colonization was planned across a wide frontier stretching from Central Asia to the Balkans. As with the Caucasus during the Chechnya conflict, the Balkans became a region where the type of fighting that led to the victory of the Afghan-Arab jihad could be reproduced. The religious fervor that legitimized the vicious war against the Soviet "nonbelievers" was transplanted, after Afghanistan, to Chechnya, other Russian Caucasus republics, and the Balkans. For the jihadis, Russian and Serb nationalists became replicas of the Soviets, people without a God.

Paradoxically, President Clinton's schizophrenic foreign policy facilitated such a process. Mujahedin who fought in the anti-Soviet Jihad flocked to the Balkans and ended up fighting on the same side as U.S. and European troops. This should not come as a surprise considering that a decade earlier the United States and Saudi Arabia had bankrolled the mujahedin in Afghanistan in the first place. The key question that Christopher Deliso poses is this: "Did the West believe that another war by proxy could be fought along the Adriatic Sea, just a few miles from the coast of a founding member of the European Union?" Using language accessible to a general readership, and presenting a wealth of shocking recent examples, the author answers such an uncomfortable question. No, the West was simply dragged into the conflict, hence its schizophrenic behavior.

Today, new emerging powers are eager to promote the proliferation of conflicts in areas where Muslims live. The aim is simple: Religion is the ideological cloth that disguises wars of economic conquest. Deliso explains how, during the 1990s, Saudi charities bankrolled the jihadi brigades that acted as the vanguards of the Wahhabi ideological colonization movement in the Balkans. Their task was to conquer new territories, wielding Arab money and religious ideals to do so. Funds flooded the region to build mosques and madrasahs where young Muslims especially could be indoctrinated. However, while until the 1990s such indoctrination was aimed at strengthening the jihadi fight in distant lands, such as Kashmir or Afghanistan, since 1998 the target has changed. With methodical vigor, Christopher Deliso reconstructs the links between al Qaeda and the Balkans. He shows the importance that the region played prior to and leading up to the 9/11 plot, as well as in the tragic transition of Europe from just a financial hub of al Qaeda to a main target in and of itself.

What is next? This is the question that the author addresses at the end of the book. Having presented the background and revised the main strategies pursued by the West and the East on the Balkan chessboard, he attempts to outline the possible outcomes. Above all, the Balkans should not be ignored or erased from the world's political agenda. Current media indifference projects the wrong conclusion; Western publics remain under the false impression that the region has been pacified. Far from it, it is instead brewing more violence. If Europe continues to turn away from and ignore this threat, fundamentalist movements, such as the Wahhabis and jihadist followers of Osama bin Laden and Ayman al-Zawahiri, will succeed in transforming the region into a hub for radical activity and even terrorist plots against Europe and the West. Their growing network has already forged key alliances with Italian organized crime, and has entered strategic joint ventures with local Balkan criminal organizations. It is only a matter of time until an attack on European soil will be launched from Balkan enclaves controlled by the foreign-directed fundamentalists, the author warns. To back up this warning, Deliso lists in his book several plots, some of them major, which have been foiled since 9/11. He also cites whistle-blowers and other informed sources from within the Western security apparatus in the Balkans, who reveal an apparent lack of fortitude and even a lack of interest on the part of Western governments at really getting to the heart of the emerging Islamic extremist threat in the region. The final message to our leaders encrypted in this important book is simple: For once, let us be proactive and clean up the mess we have made in the Balkans.

Loretta Napoleoni

Preface

Doubtless there will be readers who pick up this book and, after a cursory glance, wonder just what "Balkans" the author is talking about. Certainly not the Sarajevo where Muslims drink beer, nor scantily clad Pristina, nor modernizing Tirana and Tetovo, and, indeed, the entire tradition of "liberal" Islam inherited from the long centuries of former Ottoman Turkish rule. Thus, we should define from the outset what this book does and does not contend.

I am not arguing that the future Balkan Peninsula will revert to a borderless empire ruled by Sharia law (though bits and pieces of it are certainly headed in that direction). What I do lay out is a factually supported unfolding situation in which small groups of local but globally connected fundamentalists, supported by wealthy foreign organizations and state sponsors, gravitate towards existing and newly forming terrorist entities abroad, while at the same time making strong and unprecedented challenges to the social order in Balkan areas with Muslim populations, thus introducing a whole new dimension to political issues and social policy—one that will have ramifications for the significant Balkan Christian populations as well.

Demographic trends indicate that indigenous Muslim populations in the Balkans are growing much more rapidly than non-Muslim ones, meaning that in one or two decades the religious balance will have changed irrevocably in key areas, and that various political parties will increasingly reassess their priorities to better exploit the "Muslim vote." Also, the ongoing process of denationalization from previous Communist regimes has seen Islamic organizations make increasingly strong claims to their former properties—even in places where no Muslims currently live.

The political and cultural issues that will begin to take precedence in the regional discourse will, of course, not take place in a vacuum; they will be affected by larger world issues, such as Western military campaigns in Islamic countries and the perceived closeness of America with the hated Israelis. Then there is the emotional issue of Turkey and the European Union; the Union's only Muslim candidate country has left a huge historical footprint on the Balkans.

Already, the aggressive moves of foreign Islamic groups supported by Saudi Arabia, Kuwait, Iran, and Pakistan, and by groups from these and other Islamic states have had a disruptive effect, resulting in infighting and schisms within the Muslim communities of several Balkan countries, as various factions stake their claims to legitimacy. The fact that the overwhelming majority of Balkan Muslims have no interest in terrorism does not diminish the danger that small radical groups can (and already do) find safe havens within larger Muslim communities, for a complex set of reasons that I explain further in this book.

Nevertheless, the Western media has distracted public attention from this threat. It continues to overemphasize the narrative of Balkan political actors and populations as being fueled entirely by the quixotic obsession with reviving the nineteenth century nation-state—something increasingly irrelevant in the global age, yet which the Western powers not accidentally have sought to give them as some sort of sovereign remedy against destabilization. The truth is that they have nothing else to offer, and destabilization is occurring regardless.

However, despite the lingering national ethnic narratives, the real future shaping force in the Balkans, as everywhere else in Europe, will be not ethnicity but religion. What radical Islamists in the Balkans seek to do is to use all the communicative and technological tools of globalization to advance their cause by persuasion and by force. Their ultimate goals are to spread the faith as widely as possible and to eliminate those deemed to be enemies of Islam—that is, Islam as they see it.

The prevailing narrative of the media and Western governments, which predicts that once the last territorial disputes are settled, the Balkan states will all fall into line, becoming well-behaved, compact, and pro-Western countries, is shortsighted. While there have seemingly been enough recent wars and political rhetoric to support this thesis, it is contradicted by visible trends on the ground. For the Islamists, the desirable future political order is not one of cozy nation-states, but rather a religious commonwealth, a sort of revived Ottoman Empire distinguished by Saudi mosques, Afghan clothes, and fundamentalist mores.

While the Islamists cannot realistically achieve such a goal, at least not everywhere, hope, fanaticism, and money are powerful forces, and it is highly likely that, because of their activities, the Balkans will increasingly come to be identified as a spawning ground for terrorists, dotted with no-go areas and concealed urban command centers, together comprising a series of interconnected nodal points in a global network of terrorist and fundamentalist organizations. This is a sort of virtual caliphate, one appropriate to its epoch. And Western governments ignore it at their own peril.

That said, it is my hope that the critique of Western policies and the evaluation of Western intelligence and counterterrorism operations presented in this book might, in some small way, help Western governments and their Balkan allies to learn from mistakes made, and so develop a more nuanced approach to a fight that looks likely to be with us for many years to come.

Finally, I would like to make a brief mention of spellings, transliterations, and abbreviations. Since the names and terms mentioned in this book come from a wide variety of different languages and alphabets, there are in some cases different, and equally correct, renditions used. As a rule of thumb, I have tried to follow the spellings that are most often encountered in English language media.

The same rule of commonality of usage applies when it comes to abbreviations. Thus, in some cases a group is referred to by its original-language acronym rather than by the relevant English translation, if that is how it is more frequently encountered in media citations. I hope the reader will forgive the occasional and unavoidable inconsistencies that occur because of the complexity of the present task.

Acknowledgments

Books about terrorism and security issues are quite often enhanced by the testimony of people who, for reasons of their personal security or because of their line of work, inevitably cannot be named, and in this respect this book is no exception. I trust that the many nameless individuals who fall into this category will all know who they are and will thank me for remembering to forget them here. I do thank them wholeheartedly for their valuable testimony.

That said, there are several indispensable sources who can be named, and they have made the experience of writing this book infinitely easier and more enjoyable. It is important, therefore, to take a moment to mention them.

Sibel Edmonds, who contributed many valuable insights, is a very brave and tenacious woman whose decision to go public about the incompetence, corruption, and espionage that she witnessed firsthand while working as an FBI translator in 2002 has brought her endless hassles, threats, and even personal danger. Yet despite great adversity and pressure, she has continued speaking out, in order to bring attention to serious national security problems that need to be addressed.

Another whistle-blower motivated by the desire to create a safer world, Thomas Gambill, has since 1999 given constant attention to the security and terrorism challenges faced by the international community in Kosovo. The firsthand accounts and moral support he has provided over the years have been greatly appreciated by this author.

The compelling foreword to this book was contributed by Loretta Napoleoni, a first-rate economist who has presented numerous groundbreaking ideas about the confluence of economics, terrorism, and globalization in her books, in the process displaying a remarkable ability to synthesize them in a way that is comprehensible for those of us less economically gifted. Like Tom and Sibel, Loretta has also made herself available for my frequent questions. This book has benefited greatly from her insights.

I would also like to thank Eric Garris, managing editor of Antiwar.com, for his good humor, patience, and wise counsel over the past six years. Eric has always been more than fair with me and has encouraged me to provide good and original work. I am very lucky to have had a supporter such as him.

Web designer Mike Ewens did a great job of redesigning the Balkan-interest Web site I direct (www.balkanalysis.com), and I am grateful for his consistent aid in fixing technical glitches and so on, allowing me to spend more of my time on necessary research when I was facing looming deadlines. Greek analyst Ioannis Michaletos also made significant contributions to this Web site and to my research, for which I am grateful.

Then we have the heroic Scott Taylor, a good friend and journalistic colleague, whose love of adventure and wry Canadian sense of humor livened up some of the fieldwork that went into researching this book. Scott has been covering the Balkans since the early 1990s, and I look forward to many more years of work with him.

The experts on terrorism who have selflessly lent me their time and testimony (those ones who can be named anyway) include Darko Trifunovic, Philip Giraldi, Anes Alic, and Claude Moniquet. Darko's frenetic work schedule makes it sometimes hard to track him down, and even harder to keep up with him when you do, but his wealth of knowledge more than makes up for it. Phil Giraldi's consummate professionalism and insights have also greatly enhanced this work, and I especially thank him for taking time out of his busy schedule to answer my numerous questions. The same goes for Anes Alic in Sarajevo and Claude (better late than never!) Moniquet in Brussels. I also benefited tremendously from the input of Mr. Zoran Mitevski, whose many tales from a 25-year career in senior positions in every branch of Macedonian intelligence were revelatory, to say the least. Other experts whose insights cannot go unmentioned include Dusan Janjic, Sladjana Djuric, Zoran Dragisic, Professor Peter Maher, and Igor Jovanovic.

I am also thankful for those who shared their gripping personal testimony with me—people like Emre Yilmaz, Blagoja Samakoski, Goran Stojkov, and Michael Harrison. Jason Miko is another person who fits into this category; though his name pops up only a couple of times in this book, he has been a great source of wisdom and comaraderie for a long time. Cheers to him!

Life in the Balkan wilds often makes it impossible to find necessary books. So I thank Marko Lopusina, Jürgen Elsässer, and especially Professor Emeritus Robert Collins for making their works directly available to me; Professor Collins also graciously made time to personally answer further questions regarding his work.

I would also like to thank my editor at Praeger Security International, Hilary Claggett, who made the tough task of bringing this book to fruition less arduous in numerous ways, and who mercifully allowed me to take more time than usually allowed to finish my research.

Now, I could certainly not conclude here without first giving a huge thanks to Dr. Marty Klein, whose thoughtful assistance made this whole book possible.

Finally, of course, I would like to thank my family for their constant love and support, without which none of this would ever have been possible in the first place.

Abbreviations

The following abbreviations appear at least once throughout the text. Where there are English and other language versions of the same name, the abbreviation most often used is listed first.

AIO	Aktivna Islamska Omladina (Active Islamic Youth)
ANA (AKSH)	Albanian National Army (Armata Kombëtare Shqiptare, Kosovo)
BBC	British Broadcasting Corporation
BIF	Benevolence International Foundation; Bosanska Idealna Futura
BND	Bundesnachrichtendienst (Foreign Intelligence Service, Germany)
CIA	Central Intelligence Agency
CNN	Cable News Network
DBK	Direkcija za Bezbednost i Kontrarazuznavanjke (Directorate for Security and Counterintelligence, Macedonia)
DIGOS	Divisione Investigazioni Generali e Operazioni Speciali (Division of General Investigations and Special Operations, Italy)
DPA (PDSH)	Democratic Party of Albanians (Partia Demokratike Shqiptare, Macedonia)
DUI (BDI)	Democratic Union for Integration (Bashkimi Demokratik për Integrim, Macedonia)
EIJ	Egyptian Islamic Jihad
ESISC	European Strategic Intelligence and Security Center
EU	European Union
FBI	Federal Bureau of Investigation
GRF	Global Relief Foundation
G7	Group of Seven
HAI	Human Appeal International
HRCA	Human Relief and Construction Agency

HUM	Harkat-ul-Mujahideen
IBV	Islamic Balkan Center
IDB	Islamic Development Bank
IIRO	International Islamic Relief Organization
IOM	International Organization for Migration
ISI	Directorate for Inter-Services Intelligence (Pakistan)
IVZ	Islamska Verska Zajednica (Islamic Community, Macedonia)
KFOR	NATO Kosovo Force
KLA (UCK)	Kosovo Liberation Army (Ushtria Çlirimtare e Kosovës, Kosovo)
KPC (TMK)	Kosovo Protection Corps (Trupat Mbrojtëse të Kosovës, Kosovo)
KSK	Kommando Spezialkräfte (Special Forces Unit, Germany)
MAB	Muslim Association of Britain
MFA	Muslim Forum of Albania
MHP	Milliyetçi Hareket Partisi (Nationalist Movement Party, Turkey)
MI6/SIS	Military Intelligence Directorate (Secret Intelligence Service, Great Britain)
MIT	Milli Istihbarat Teskilati (National Intelligence Organization, Turkey)
MOK	Muslimanski Omladinski Klub (Muslim Youth Club, Sandzak)
MPRI	Military Professional Resources Incorporated
MTCR	Missile Technology Control Regime
MWL	Muslim World League
NATO	North Atlantic Treaty Alliance
NGO	Non-Governmental Organization
NLA (UCK)	National Liberation Army (Ushtria Çlirimtare Kombëtare, Macedonia)
OIC	Organization of the Islamic Conference
OSCE	Organization for Security and Cooperation in Europe
PKK	Partiya Karkerên Kurdistan (Kurdistan Workers Party, Turkey)
PROXIMA	European Union Police Mission in the former Yugoslav Republic of Macedonia
RIHS	Revival of Islamic Heritage Society
RPG	Rocket-Propelled Grenade
SAS	Special Air Service (Great Britain)
SAVAMA	Sazman-e Ettela'at va Amniat-e Melli-e Iran (Ministry of Intelligence and National Security, Iran)
SHIK	Sherbini Informative Kombetare (State Information Service, Albania)
SHRC	Saudi High Relief Commission
SISMI	Servizio per le Informazioni e la Sicurezza Militare (Military Intelligence and Security Service, Italy)
SJCRKC	Saudi Joint Committee for the Relief of Kosovo and Chechnya
SRCS	Saudi Red Crescent Society
TWRA	Third World Relief Agency
UMSA	Udruzenje Muslimana Sjeverne Amerike (Association of Muslims of North America)
UN	United Nations

UNHCR	United Nations High Committee for Refugees
UNMIK	United Nations Mission in Kosovo
VMRO-DPMNE	Vnatresno-Makedonska Revoluciona Organizacija–Demokratska Partija za Makedonsko Nacionalno Edinstvo (Internal Macedonian Revolutionary Organization–Democratic Party for Macedonian National Unity, Macedonia)
WAMY	World Assembly of Muslim Youth
ZDF	Zweites Deutsches Fernsehen (National Public Television, Germany)

Introduction

It was a normal winter's day, and Hassan Mustafa Osama Nasr was strolling Milan's Via Guerzoni on his way to his usual noontime prayers at the mosque. Then something came up.

Two CIA agents jumped in front of the bearded cleric. Muttering orders in Italian, they splashed his face with chemicals. Passersby gaped as the Egyptian was hauled into a white van that then sped off to an Italian-American air base. Transferred to a waiting Learjet, Nasr caught a connecting flight to a military base in Germany, from where he was flown to Egypt. There the torture began.

The audacious kidnapping of the radical, refugee cleric also known as Abu Omar is something of a parable for the entire post-9/11 war on terror, offering in homeopathic doses everything that has characterized the Western response to the Islamic terrorist threat, from incompetence and subterfuge to flawed cooperation and needless distrust among allies. And, as we will see below, Abu Omar's curious Balkan connections bring a whole new dimension to the story of how these themes have played out in this pivotal part of southeastern Europe—a forgotten front in the war on terror.

Conducted barely weeks before the U.S. invasion of Iraq, the Milan kidnapping was a dramatic example of the Bush administration's policy of "extraordinary renditions," in which suspected terrorists the world over have disappeared, been sent to secret CIA prisons, and been put into the clutches of "friendly" Arab regimes. By mid-2005, the number of such renditions had reached more than 100 since September 11, 2001.[1]

Such operations have been criticized for their apparent violation of human rights and state sovereignty. From a counterintelligence point of view, they are often self-defeating. The Milan operation certainly was. Italian police had long been tracking the Egyptian cleric, a firebrand who denounced the West in his sermons, and were uncovering further connections to terrorist-linked individuals in Milan's Muslim immigrant community through these efforts. But the Americans' cowboy kidnapping, carried out in broad daylight, ruined their sensitive surveillance operation, and a key link to the extremist underbelly of Milan vanished into thin air.

As a smokescreen, the CIA sent the Italian antiterrorist police an "urgent message" that the cleric had gone to ground in the Balkans—not entirely implausible, considering the Egyptian's previous years in Albania. However, it was just a ruse that kept Italian authorities in the dark for more than a year.[2] In reality, the CIA had actually handed over Abu Omar to the Egyptian authorities. They had been seeking him for years due to his membership in an Islamic group dedicated to replacing the pro-American government there with an Islamist one.

When the Italians finally found out the truth, there was hell to pay. After careful research into the movements of the suspected agents, Milanese Judge Chiara Nobili put together a case in June 2005 calling for the arrest of 13 CIA operatives. An uproar ensued from the Italian public, already angry with the government of then-Prime Minister Silvio Berlusconi for its participation in the disastrous American adventure in Iraq. Italians decried the American disrespect for their state sovereignty, and the police lamented that their counterterrorism investigation had been destroyed precisely at a time when they were preparing to arrest Abu Omar—ironically, on the charge of supplying fighters for the anti-American insurgency in Iraq.

The Abu Omar kidnapping was disturbing not only because of its implications for human rights and botched cooperation with allies. More alarming, from the point of view of counterintelligence professionalism, the careless profligacy of the operatives involved made it easy for them to be tracked, while also bleeding American taxpayers of tens of thousands of dollars.

The tallies were astonishing indeed. As the *Washington Post* put it, "The mission was equal parts James Bond and taxpayer-financed Italian holiday."[3] Both before and after the kidnapping, the team of 19 agents splurged at luxurious five-star hotels and Mediterranean seaside resorts, spending up to $500 a day in expenses and making "dozens of calls from unsecure phones in their rooms."

This disregard for operational secrecy did not end there. As London's *Guardian* reported in July 2005, "Italian investigators put names to the abductors by matching their calls to the phone contracts they had signed. And they could be sure of the team's movements because they could see when the calls had been made and from which mobile phone."[4] More embarrassing was the "intimate links" discovered between male and female agents. The CIA team "made several, apparently recreational, trips within Italy as they waited to seize Abu Omar and, on at least two occasions, couples booked into double rooms."[5]

Worst of all, perhaps, was why the kidnapping went down in the first place. A U.S. intelligence official told the *Washington Post* in December 2005 that it was "definitely not a favor to the Egyptians"; rather, the operation was simply a result of the "inspiration" of the CIA station chief in Rome, who apparently wanted to kidnap someone just for the hell of it.[6]

However, this sordid adventure was not completely unknown to the Italian security apparatus at the time it happened. In July 2006, deputy head of military intelligence Mauro Mancini was arrested, and his predecessor, Gustavo Pignero, was placed under house arrest. The Italian government's spin on the arrests was that, while "rogue agents" may have been involved, the Military Intelligence and Security Service (SISMI) as an institution was not.[7] Yet according to four CIA veterans surveyed by the *Washington Post,* "the CIA station chief in Rome briefed the Italian intelligence service on the operation before it was carried out and obtained approval for it."[8]

Italian police also discovered "a massive secret archive of surveillance on journalists, judges and businesspeople in Italy," part of SISMI's desperate efforts to limit the political damage of the Abu Omar kidnapping, both to itself and to its American allies.[9] In the end, therefore, the whole lurid saga was a colossal waste of time, resources, and money that encouraged infighting and distrust within and between the Italian and American governments. Instead of fighting the war on terror, they were fighting each other, squandering precious time and treasure in the process.

For the remit of the present book, Abu Omar's career as a Muslim extremist resonates in many ways. Long before his Italian period the cleric had set up shop in the Balkans, where he worked with terrorist groups, some sponsored by Osama bin Laden himself. The ease with which they operated and the difficulties weak Balkan governments had in shutting them down remain as persistent challenges today. Finally, the rendition of this Egyptian extremist in Italy has also been duplicated, with similar damaging political fallout, in several Balkan countries allied with the United States. Yet the murkiness of these operations in the shadows has blurred the line between fact and fiction so often that any real evaluation of the quality of counterterrorism work becomes a difficult task. Nevertheless, such an evaluation is of critical importance to any discussion of the West's counterterrorism policies and operational success.

All of these dimensions have import for Western governments' understanding of the motivations, plans, and movements of today's budding terrorists, decentralized and autonomous groups inspired by the examples set by al Qaeda, Hezbollah, and the Iraqi resistance, groups that seek to intensify their holy war in Europe and America. More and more, the unpredictable and increasingly Muslim region of the Balkans is emerging as a critical, though still overlooked theater of operations for extremists in Europe.

CHAPTER 1

Bosnia: Clinton's Gift to Fundamentalist Islam

The 300 or so retired mujahedin gathered outside Sarajevo's parliament were clearly not in a good mood. A few days earlier, on September 5, 2006, the Muslim-dominated Bosnian government had declared, under heavy pressure from the United States, that it would revoke the passports that had been granted these foreign fighters and deport them to their home countries, where they would most probably face the kind of torture and executions that they had so excelled in handing out to Christian Serbs and Croats just over a decade earlier. In all, the citizenships of some 1,500 foreigners were to be scrutinized by the government.[1]

Recruited by the government of now deceased president Alija Izetbegovic to fight Bosnian Serbs and Croats in the early 1990s, the foreign jihadis had afterwards settled down to become solid and upstanding members of the fundamentalist family in Sarajevo and especially in the rural "triangle" between Tuzla, Zenica, and Travnik in central Bosnia, their main wartime headquarters. The irony of the whole situation, however, was that these holy warriors would never have reached Bosnia in the first place had it not been for the Clinton administration's determination to defeat the Bosnian Serbs at all costs. In comparison to achieving this goal, allowing several thousand Muslim fanatics to establish themselves in the heart of Europe seemed a small price to pay indeed.

It would not be until the watershed events of September 11, 2001, that the role of Bosnia as an incubator and catalyst for international terrorism would become impossible to ignore. This embarrassing truth had long been suppressed by the many Western diplomats, journalists, and public relations hacks who had built large fortunes and careers on protecting this myth of their own making. Controlling and simplifying the historical interpretation of the complex civil war that ravaged Bosnia and Hercegovina between March 1992 and November 1995 remains essential for those whose credibility and integrity depends on how that war is remembered. Preliminary to any historical debate, therefore, it must be acknowledged that high-powered Washington lobbyists and much of the Western media purposefully distorted, omitted, and concealed key facts on the ground. This actually prolonged and intensified the conflict, while also reinforcing wildly exaggerated stereotypes of the Bosnian Muslims as innocent victims and the Serbs as genocidal maniacs.[2]

While U.S. President George W. Bush has described the West's terrorist adversary today in sweeping and figurative speech as "Islamic fascism," the man who brought the terrorists to Bosnia, the late Alija Izetbegovic, had a proven weakness for fascist movements. During the Nazi occupation of Yugoslavia in World War II, Izetbegovic had been a recruiter for the Bosnian Muslim Handzar ("Dagger") Division, which swore loyalty to Hitler and his "New Europe," and was committed to killing Christian Serbs and Yugoslav Jews. After the defeat of the Axis and its Croat, Bosnian, and Albanian Balkan collaborators, some Handzar Division veterans volunteered in Arab armies fighting the nascent Israeli state.[3] The Muslim fascist brigade would be resurrected in the 1990s, during the presidency of Izetbegovic. A journalist at the time stated that the Handzar "glories in a fascist culture" and that the fighters "see themselves as the heirs of the SS Handzar division formed by Bosnian Muslims in 1943 to fight for the Nazis."[4]

Indeed, Izetbegovic's early affiliations could not be passed off merely as mistaken youthful zeal. His *Islamic Declaration,* published three decades after the Second World War, praised Pakistan as a model for Bosnian society and decreed that "there can be no peace or co-existence between the 'Islamic faith' and non-Islamic societies and political institutions." Along with this paean to multiculturalism, Izetbegovic spelled out a key concept of expansionist Islam: that it "should and must start taking over the power *as soon as it is morally and numerically strong enough* to not only overthrow the existing non-Islamic, but also to build up a new Islamic authority."[5] From 1939, when he founded a Muslim youth society modeled on Egypt's Muslim Brotherhood until his death on October 19, 2003, Alija Izetbegovic's single dream was the creation of an Islamic state in Europe. This vision was honored in December 2001, when he was awarded a one million dirham ($272,480) prize for his services to Islam by the Crown Prince of Dubai.[6] Only two months earlier, however, the terrorist attacks on America had revealed how complicit he and his government had been in allowing al Qaeda to expand in Europe, through the Bosnian jihad.

As it turned out, a number of key figures associated with the 9/11 plot, both planners and some of the hijackers themselves, were veterans of the Bosnian jihad. At the time of the most spectacular terrorist attacks in American history, scores of charities, "humanitarian" organizations, and militant groups associated with international terrorist syndicates continued to flourish in Bosnia. As the smoke was still rising from the rubble in New York and Washington, government investigators and journalists alike quickly discovered a fact long evident to non-partisan observers: that Bosnia had become one of al Qaeda's most important European assets, as both the staging post that proved the viability of jihad in its global sense and the place where Europe's first Islamic state might someday be established. While the Bush administration has sought to repair the damage by shutting down charities and rounding up fugitives, the task remains enormous. Terrorist funding structures are notoriously resilient, while charity names and individual identities are easily changed. Further, the radicalization of Islam in Bosnia due to the war has also bred a new generation of homegrown jihadis—the so-called "white devils" whose European features make them precious commodities for infiltrating Europe without being suspected.

Indeed, for Osama bin Laden and other terrorist masterminds, the strategic value of Bosnia lies in its "human resources" capacity for becoming a net exporter of jihad in the never-ending struggle to establish a global caliphate. In this respect, says terrorism expert Darko Trifunovic of the University of Belgrade's Faculty of Security Studies, "the biggest achievement of al Qaeda in Bosnia was not military. It was ideological: when they created Samir al-Bosnari, the first Bosnian who died as a mujahedin in a foreign country, in Chechnya in 1994."[7] The first suicide bombing in Europe, carried out the next year in Rijeka, Croatia, was also organized and prepared in Bosnia, maintains Trifunovic.

Just as the Bosnian connection with 9/11 tends to be overlooked, so, too, has the Afghan-Soviet war been forgotten in its relationship to the Bosnian jihad. However, testimony from veterans of both campaigns indicates the perceived continuity of the operation for global Islam. Abu Abdel Aziz, a Saudi commander of the foreign-staffed El Mujahid unit in Bosnia, revealed in a 1994 interview the mind-set of the mujahedin who had started streaming into Bosnia early in 1992. For these jihadis, Bosnia represented the seamless continuation of a single holy war, simply the next front in a long war to spread Islam by the sword. As Aziz put it:

> We were looking for Jihad (after Afghanistan). We found it in the Philippines, and in Kashmir. Only fifteen days lapsed (after the conquest of Kabul) and the crisis of Bosnia begun. This confirmed the saying of the Prophet (of Islam), peace and blessings be upon him, who said, "Indeed Jihad will continue till the day of Judgment." A new Jihad started in Bosnia, (we moved there), and we are with it, if Allah wills.[8]

It was not to be a holy war organized merely by a few ragged, cave-dwelling jihadis, however. The most powerful and respected leaders of the Islamic world, led by Saudi King Fahd himself, pledged their support to the Bosnian Muslim war effort. In December 1992, King Fahd met with Izetbegovic and promised to open Saudi coffers wide; a special board was soon established (the Supreme Committee for the Collection of Donations for the Muslims of Bosnia) and overseen by Riyadh's governor, Prince Salman bin Abdul Aziz. The Supreme Committee funneled money to the mujahedin through seven major Islamic charities: the Muslim World League, Al Haramain, the International Islamic Relief

Organization, the World Assembly of Muslim Youth, Saudi Arabia Red Crescent Society, the Islamic Waqf Organization, and the Makkah Humanitarian Organization. Osama bin Laden had influence over several of these organizations. Between 1992 and February 1996, the Supreme Committee provided some $356 million to the Bosnian Muslims, of which $103 million came from King Fahd himself.[9]

The billions of dollars pouring in from Saudi Arabia, Kuwait, the United Arab Emirates, and other countries were either handed over directly to Bosnian officials or, more often, siphoned through a charity network that took root all over Europe, but especially in Germany, Austria, and Croatia. Vienna and Zagreb became the strategic centers of operations through which money, weapons, logistical support, and foreign mujahedin were funneled. Of course, the operation could not have flourished without the tacit support of the Western secret services and their "friendly" partners in the Balkans, such as Croatia and Slovenia—as was shown in May 1993, when UN officials discovered a major Iranian weapon shipment bound for Bosnia coming in at Maribor Airport in Slovenia, well within the Austro-German sphere of influence.

The weapons had come via Sudan. This confirmed that the African country, run by the radical National Islamic Front and then hosting Osama bin Laden, was playing a major role in the Bosnian jihad. At the same time, the discovery also "implicated members of the Slovenian secret service and indirectly the Austrian Ministry of Interior. . . both Slovenian security agents and the Austrian Ministry of Interior were providing funds for the Muslim government of Alija Izetbegovic in Sarajevo."[10] Austria's long historical relations with Bosnia included the annexation of the province from the Ottoman Empire by the Austro-Hapsburg Empire in the dying days of both powers, in 1908, a move that provoked Serbia and Turkey and indirectly led to the First World War. Similarly, Germany had deep attachments to the Balkans. Both Croatia and Muslim Bosnia had served as fascist puppet states for the Nazis, during the Second World War, and committed some of the worst atrocities of that conflict. The strong historical animosity that both Austria and Germany had for Serbia, the only regional rival that had ever stood up to their invasions, had by the early 1990s added a vicious element to an interventionist policy driven by economic interests and the resurgent German presence on the world stage following the demolition of the Berlin Wall.

According to German journalist Jürgen Elsässer, German and Austrian intelligence groups were running large amounts of weapons to the Bosnians through a private company owned by an Austrian named Dieter Hoffman. His company reportedly "delivered more than 100 tons of weapons" flown into Maribor from Khartoum, and were "directly delivered to the fronts in Tuzla, Zenica and Visoko." Radical Islamic charities based in Germany, such as Merhamet, also cooperated with the German secret services to deliver weapons. When Hoffman was arrested in Budapest in 1993, Hungarian officials "accused him of delivering weapons purchased with Arab money to Bosnia and Herzegovina." At one point,

Germany's foreign intelligence service, the BND (Bundesnachrichtendienst) escorted "at least five" truckloads of weapons disguised as humanitarian aid to the western Bosnian enclave of Bihac.

BND spies and gunrunners were inserted into Bosnia under diplomatic cover, as EU monitors.[11] A BBC report disclosed the "key man" in the weapons smuggling operation as being one Christoph von Bezold, ostensibly in charge of the 24 German EU monitors in Zagreb, but actually a covert operative for "BND section 12D, responsible for Balkan affairs." Former EU monitors recalled one major operation of March 27, 1994, in which von Bezold tricked the Bihac hospital director into storing an ammunition shipment of 17,280 bullets; the Germans claimed it was powdered milk. "The BND's delivery, one of many smuggled across Serb lines, was then collected at night by Bosnian troops," reported the *Sunday Telegraph* in 1997.[12]

Austria was also the home of a notorious Muslim organization, the Third World Relief Agency (TWRA), which "eventually became the principal humanitarian front for moving arms to Bosnia."[13] The TWRA had been established in 1987 by a Sudanese native, Al-Fatih Ali Hassanein, who had collaborated with Alija Izetbegovic since the late 1970s, when the former was a medical student in Belgrade. After war broke out in 1992, Hassanein through his Vienna-based TWRA was able to move huge amounts of money for al Qaeda into Bosnia; "some $80 million were remitted on a Vienna account in the First Austrian Bank in 1992 and $231 million the following year."[14]

A key figure on the TWRA board of directors was Hasan Cengic, a veteran of the World War II SS Handzar Division who reincarnated the unit while serving as Bosnia's deputy defense minister in the early 1990s. He became the most influential middleman in arms and cash transfers from Iran and Afghanistan to Bosnia, moving during the war throughout Turkey, Iran, Bosnia, and Croatia. Cengic had extensive contacts in the Muslim world and was an adept terrorist deal maker, "known as the 'godfather' to Afghan-Arab mujahedeen."[15] A second major al Qaeda-linked charity, also operating through Zagreb, was the Muwafaq Foundation of Saudi businessman Yassin al-Qadi. This wealthy mogul, some of whose assets were frozen by the U.S. government after September 11, 2001, denied any links with terrorism. However, numerous sources indicated that the Zagreb base of al Muwafaq, which had branches in Germany, Austria, Albania, and Bosnia as well, was, in fact, an al Qaeda front. Another major Sudanese organization utilized by Cengic in Zagreb was the Islamic Relief Agency, based in Khartoum.[16] According to a former Sudanese intelligence agent, Osama bin Laden's operations in Sudan during the early 1990s involved an "advisory council" made up of some 43 separate Islamic groups, contraband arms depots, and several terrorist training camps.[17]

Since the Saudi government preferred to keep its hands clean, supplying mostly money and logistical supplies, Iran would play the key role in importing the fighters and military equipment through the Iranian Revolutionary Guard and the national intelligence service, SAVAMA (Sazman-e Ettela'at va

Amniat-e Melli-e Iran, or Ministry of Intelligence and National Security of Iran). By fall 1992, Iran was sending huge consignments of arms and supplies via Zagreb airport, on Air Iran Boeing 747 aircraft. According to the Croat defense minister at the time, the now deceased Gojko Susak, the Clinton administration "never protested" about the escalating flow of arms to Bosnia during 1992 and 1993.[18] Weapons shipments from Iran via Sudan, overseen by intelligence officials of both countries and utilizing al Qaeda-linked charities like the TWRA, also picked up in 1993 and 1994. And while the United States had blacklisted Sudan as a state sponsor of terrorism in August 1993, it adhered to its overriding policy goal—that is, to defeat the Serbs—and thus took no action to stop the TWRA's flow of arms to the Bosnian Muslims.[19]

Indeed, the "Iranian pipeline" had the firm support of Washington. It became policy for President Clinton, who in his first presidential campaign in 1992 sought to end the September 1991 UN arms embargo on the warring Yugoslav republics, so as to tip the military balance in favor of the Muslims and Croats. Then-National Security Advisor Anthony Lake was an eager supporter of the plan. On April 27, 1994, President Clinton directed Peter Galbraith, Ambassador to Croatia and son of the famous economist Kenneth Galbraith, to inform the Zagreb government that he had "no instructions" regarding the resumption of Iranian arms shipments to Bosnia via Croatia. This laissez-faire policy was decided by the very highest leaders in Washington; the CIA and the Departments of State and Defense were reportedly consulted only after the fact.[20] Some 14,000 tons of weapons, valued at over $200 million, were funneled through Croatia to Bosnia (the former kept 30 percent of the total as a "tax").[21]

On the receiving end, the Bosnian Muslim government of Alija Izetbegovic also got the "green light" to use the Iranian weapons however it saw fit, and in similarly tacit fashion. In private, Galbraith bragged that he had told Bosnian government officials to "don't listen to what I say—listen to what I *don't* say," according to Jason Miko, an American who worked on contracts for the Bosnian and Croatian governments with the Washington lobbyist Ruder-Finn in the early 1990s. From the context, it was clear that Galbraith was referring to the Bosnian government's Iranian adventure.[22]

For President Izetbegovic, the foreign mujahedin enhanced Bosnian military capabilities, but had an even greater significance as "the conduit for funds from the Gulf and the Middle East."[23] Once inside Bosnia, the mujahedin were put to work, first of all building roads and strategic installations, and then they were sent into combat. On August 13, 1993, some 750 of the jihadis were organized into the El Mujahid, a division that was loosely attached to the Bosnian government army based in the Travnik-Zenica area of central Bosnia. The unit was created by Rasim Delic, supreme commander of the Bosnian Muslim government's armed forces (Delic would later be indicted by the Hague Tribunal for atrocities carried out by the foreign jihadis) and led by the Algerian Abdelkader Mokhtari, also known as Abu El Mali. U.S. officials would later call El Mali "a junior Osama Bin Laden."

Zenica was also the base of other related mujahedin groups, such as the Egyptian Jamaat al Islamiya. Leaders of the Egyptian group posed as humanitarian workers, "using UN High Commissioner for Refugees (UNHCR) credentials to move freely throughout the Balkans." There was considerable sympathy and assistance from the Islamic humanitarian and medical relief agencies working in Bosnia, and the mujahedin were actually helped by international peacekeeping troops, such as the Malaysians. Yet Western countries as well saved the holy warriors. A rarely seen video taken in 1994 by the mujahedin themselves clearly shows blue-helmeted British soldiers relieving Bosnian Serb soldiers of foreign Islamists they had captured and releasing the delighted jihadis unscathed in the central Bosnian town of Travnik to cheers of "*Allah Akbar!*"[24]

The intervention of the Western powers against the Serbs often helped the mujahedin to live and fight another day. This seems particularly perverse in light of the fact that the mujahedin indulged in some of the most horrific atrocities ever witnessed in war, as they rampaged unchecked across Christian Serb and Croat villages. Decapitations, amputations, and "non-surgical circumcisions" were standard procedure, as were electrical shock, sexual abuse, and other forms of torture. Serbian prisoners were starved to death or thrown into pits and ordered to attack one another with knives; if they did not die, the jihadis would move in with chain saws.[25] Their cruelty knew no limits and sometimes shocked the native Bosnian fighters. Most incredibly, the holy warriors on at least one occasion even impaled and roasted people alive on spits.[26] Today, the markets and mosques of Bosnia and other Balkan countries do a brisk business in commemorative videos and DVDs that capture the mujahedin in action.

The Dayton Agreement of July 1995, which ended the war in Bosnia and created a tripartite ethnic federation, stipulated that the former mujahedin leave at once. No doubt in expectation of such a decree, the Izetbegovic government had by then been busily supplying hundreds of mujahedin with Bosnian passports for some time, in an effort to remove the heroes of Bosnian liberation from the pool of "foreigners" expected to leave. While some mujahedin did go, between several hundred and one thousand stayed. Many married local women and began to raise families, creating bizarre pockets of Afghanistan-in-Europe in Sharia-run villages like Bocinja Donja, which had been ethnically cleansed of its Christian Serbian inhabitants by the mujahedin and handed over to them thereafter as a "reward" for their services.[27]

After the Bosnian war, the relationship between the mujahedin and their former Western enablers turned sour. The Clinton administration hastily reappraised its behavior in Bosnia and pressured the Izetbegovic government to deport the mujahedin. NATO peacekeeping troops from the Stabilizing Force delegation occasionally arrested small numbers of foreign jihadis or even killed them in firefights. However, the Clinton administration was planning for a second war to save yet another allegedly endangered Balkan Muslim population, this time the Albanians of Kosovo, and thus could not openly admit that it had already made a huge mistake in Bosnia—despite a reality of increasingly spectacular Islamic terrorist attacks against American interests globally, like the June 1996 Khobar Towers bombing in Saudi Arabia and the East Africa embassy bombings of August 1998.

Critics, however, blasted the government's mujahedin-friendly policies: "to state that the Clinton Administration erred in facilitating the penetration of the Iranians and other radical elements into Europe would be a breathtaking understatement," concluded a January 16, 1997, report from the Senate Republican Policy Committee. Privately, officials from the U.S. intelligence community also expressed concern. In a classified deposition before the U.S. Congress, a senior CIA officer testified:

> There is no question that the policy of getting arms into Bosnia was of great assistance in allowing the Iranians to dig in and create good relations with the Bosnian government...And it is a thing we will live to regret because when they blow up some Americans, as they no doubt will before this...thing is over, it will be in part because the Iranians were able to have the time and contacts to establish themselves well in Bosnia.[28]

By that time, it was well known that the mastermind of the 1993 bombing of the World Trade Center, radical Egyptian Sheikh Omar Abdel Rahman, was intimately cooperating with the Sudanese Third World Relief Association, bin Laden's front charity for Bosnian jihad.[29] In September 1999, the world would learn that Osama bin Laden himself had been given a Bosnian passport, though the Sarajevo government had furiously tried to cover it up.[30] Prior to 9/11, a major warning sign that indicated something was wrong with the picture came on December 14, 1999, when U.S. border police in Washington state arrested Ahmed Ressam, a young Algerian planning to blow up Los Angeles International Airport on the eve of the millennium. Ressam was part of a sophisticated Montreal terrorist cell made up of North African and French "graduates" of Bosnia, led by a crafty El Mujahid veteran, Fateh Kamel.[31]

The Bosnian connection had made European investigators aware of Kamel since 1994, though their requests for Canada to take action were unsuccessful until the failed millennium plot. On March 28, 1996, just a few months after the Bosnian jihad had officially ended, French police in the town of Roubaix near the Belgian border stumbled across a bomb-laden car, which revealed a plot to attack the upcoming Group of Seven (G7) conference in nearby Lille the following month. The next night, police shot up a terrorist safe house in the town, causing a massive explosion as munitions stored inside went up in flames. Two survivors tried to escape in a getaway car filled with rocket launchers, automatic weapons, ammunition, and grenades. They were killed, and in the car police found an electronic organizer belonging to a French convert to Islam and Bosnia veteran, Christophe Caze. One official later described it as "the address book of the professional terrorist." Among many other incriminating contacts, it included "direct lines to El Mali's Zenica headquarters" and to Fateh Kamel. "Five years before the sophisticated terrorist assault on the U.S.," the *Los Angeles Times* would conclude, "the French were starting to uncover loosely linked violent networks spreading into several countries, all tied together by a common thread: Bosnia."[32]

Nevertheless, it would take the cataclysmic events of September 11, 2001, and the subsequent crackdown on Islamic radicals in Bosnia, to reveal just how deeply the Bosnian jihad had become interwoven with the whole fabric of international Islamic terrorism, in Europe, America, and elsewhere. The newly discovered facts, combined with others already known, led to a devastating conclusion: that Bosnia, the Muslim country America had so fervently supported during the previous decade, had also served as a finishing school for terrorists intent on killing Americans.

Indeed, the 9/11 attacks and the terrorist cell that had spawned them in Hamburg, Germany, had numerous links to Bosnia. Mohammad Haydar Zammar, an al Qaeda operative suspected of having recruited Mohammad Atta into the Hamburg cell, had fought there. Nawaf al Hazmi and Khalid al-Mihdhar, two hijackers on American Airlines Flight 77 that crashed into the Pentagon, were also veterans of the Bosnian jihad, as was Khalid Sheikh Mohammad, the plot's ultimate mastermind.[33] An al Qaeda video created in Afghanistan before the attacks shows bin Laden together with other terrorist leaders and two of the future hijackers, Hamza al-Ramdi and Wael el-Shemari. According to *Al Jazeera*, which aired the videotape only in September 2006, the hijackers ironically enough invoked the need "to avenge the suffering of Muslims in Bosnia and Chechnya" in justifying their suicide attacks on America.[34]

Most provocatively, high-ranking Bosnian government officials were even implicated in the 9/11 attacks. A 2003 *Defense & Foreign Affairs* report claimed that Hussein Zivalj, former Bosnian Ambassador to the United Nations, "arrived just before the attacks and left the post shortly thereafter," a fact that "was not coincidental." According to the report, this longtime Islamist agitator who had been imprisoned along with Alija Izetbegovic during Communist times had sat on the governing board of TWRA, the al Qaeda-linked charity based in Vienna. While serving at the Bosnian Embassy there in the mid-1990s, Zivalj allegedly issued passports to Safet Catovic and Osama bin Laden himself. In August 2001, Catovic, another Bosnian UN official and a key leader in a second terrorist-linked charity, the Global Relief Foundation, had just led an annual summer gathering of young Islamists in Pennsylvania called "Jihad Camp" (this embarrassingly blunt name was changed after the 9/11 attacks) and was later detained by the FBI "on suspicion of involvement in 'humanitarian organizations' propagating and supporting terrorism, namely the Global Relief Foundation and Benevolence International."[35] Curiously, according to the *Defense & Foreign Affairs* report, Zivalj has a U.S. Green Card, and his family lives in Florida; Catovic, for his part, turned up in Anaheim, California, on October 12, 2003, at an event for the so-called Internet Islamic University that brought together Muslim leaders from around the world.[36]

After the 9/11 attacks, under heavy American pressure, Bosnian authorities arrested an Egyptian and a Jordanian already wanted by Interpol. The arrests led them, one month later, to Bensayah Belkacem, a confidante of Abu Zubaydah, a Palestinian responsible for screening volunteers at mujahedin training camps in Afghanistan. Of course, both had been given Bosnian passports. American investigators were especially interested in Belkacem because he had repeatedly sought to get a travel visa to Germany before the 9/11 attacks.[37] At the same time, five Algerian ex-mujahedin were arrested while planning attacks against American troops, as well as against the U.S. Embassy in Sarajevo. Then, in spring 2002, a raid on several Islamic charities in Bosnia led to the closure of three charities: Al Haramain, the GRF, and Bosanska Idealna Futura (BIF), a branch of the Chicago-based Benevolence International Foundation. Both of these groups were major al Qaeda fundraisers long active in the Balkans. BIF was designated a terrorist sponsor by the U.S. Treasury on November 19, 2002, along with Benevolence International.[38]

Faced with this mountain of evidence implicating Bosnia's role in international terrorism, Western security services after 9/11 could appreciate how difficult a task it would be to sever the hydra-headed European terror networks that had sprung up all around to service the Bosnian jihad. Western intervening governments had not learned from the past, but rather had merely compounded the stupidity of the original anti-Soviet Afghan jihad in wrongly believing that their Islamic proxies could be controlled. This failure belied a stunning arrogance and shortsightedness on the part of the Clinton administration. Yet no less a champion of arming the Bosnian Muslims than Richard Holbrooke, chief negotiator at Dayton, was even forced to admit that the United States had made a "pact with the devil." Yet it is very rare that the devil loses in such dealings.

Clearly, for the Western security services it would be a race against time. Despite the shutdown of key wartime charities, the terrorist threat that had proliferated originally due to the Bosnian jihad simply metastasized, with new cells, umbrella organizations, funding channels, and personnel coming into existence. The dismemberment of large parts of the al Qaeda apparatus in Afghanistan and Pakistan had not killed the beast, but simply resulted in a new and decentralized structure, much harder to track down and much more fluid in design. It was clearly only a matter of time before the devil of the old Bosnian jihad, now radicalized by U.S. military action in Afghanistan and Iraq, came calling in European cities.

It happened soon enough. The first major terrorist attack on European soil after 9/11—the Madrid train bombing of March 11, 2004—had Bosnia's fingerprints all over it. According to the Belgrade University terrorism expert, Darko Trifunovic, "Bosnia is mentioned 300 times in the indictment issued by the Spanish investigators." The two men considered to be the top organizers of the bombings, Saud al-Otaibi and Abdel Karim al Meyati, had both fought for the Izetbegovic government in Bosnia during the 1990s, after the war regularly moving within "the triangle between Zenica, Sarajevo and Tuzla, under false identities." Further, the rogue's gallery of terrorist internationals, including Algeria's Armed Islamic Group and Islamic Salvation Front, al Qaeda and Hamas that had since 1994 been sheltered under an umbrella group, the Islamic Alliance, provided an essentially rear logistical base for the Bosnian jihad in Spain; the Alliance had "organized and financed medical treatment" for injured mujahedin, while also assisting some Bosnia jihadis financially and sheltering others wanted for unrelated common crimes by various governments.[39] In its investigation, the Spanish government soon petitioned Bosnia to turn over Bosnian citizens believed to have had knowledge of the attacks.[40]

Some went underground, however. Sixteen months after the Madrid bombings, Serbian police "accidentally" found one of the key suspects in that plot, Moroccan citizen Abdelmajid Bouchar, while he was transiting through the country by train, probably in search of a safe haven in Bosnia or Kosovo. Bouchar had narrowly escaped capture at the hands of the Spanish police after the bombings, and subsequently fled to Brussels. However, since his network there had been disrupted by police, the Moroccan headed south for the Balkans, spending time in Austrian and Hungarian jails along the way. However, police in these countries failed to take the basic step of doing an Interpol fingerprint check on the fugitive, and it would not be until their Serbian colleagues did so in July 2005 that the wanted terrorist was arrested and extradited back to Spain.[41]

At the same time, the vigilance, good detective work, and sheer luck of other Balkan governments eliminated serious plots in their planning stages. These investigations led to the inescapable conclusion that, by mid-2005, Bosnia's strategic value to major international terrorist groups was no longer merely as a logistical base and terrorist transfer zone. Bosnia had instead become both a staging post for terrorist attacks in Europe and a target for attacks itself. On October 19, 2005, after a complex eight-month operation involving the secret services of nine countries, Bosnian police raided an apartment occupied by young, homegrown terrorists allegedly planning to blow up the British Embassy in Sarajevo. They seized guns, explosives, and a videotape "pledging vengeance for the 'brothers' killed fighting Americans in Afghanistan and Iraq." A Western intelligence agent surveyed by the *Washington Post* attested that al Qaeda's Bosnian radicalization and recruitment drive was driven by a need for fresh, Caucasian radicals who would not arouse Western suspicions, unlike the darker-skinned Arab or Southeast Asian terrorist. "They want to look European to carry out operations in Europe," the agent confirmed.[42]

Western officials were taken aback to find that the arrested conspirators were not distempered ex-mujahedin left over from the war, but young, Internet-savvy Bosnians, the sort of people who would never pass across the radar as terrorist suspects. Using code identities on Internet chat Web sites, the Bosnian group had been in constant communication with other plotters throughout Europe as it devised and refined its destructive plan. When the Bosnian police finally moved in, 20 pounds of explosives were already waiting, near the home of one suspect arrested in Hadzici, a town near Sarajevo. Other arrested suspects had practiced hiding explosives inside lemons and tennis balls, and tried to establish training camps in the wooded hills outside the capital. They included two ethnic Bosnians, Bajro Ikanovic and Almir Bajric, Cesur Abdulkadir, of Turkish heritage, and 19-year-old Mirsad Bektasevic, a Bosnian with Swedish citizenship. Bosnian police officials claimed that Bektasevic "also ran a web site on behalf of Abu Musab Zarqawi, the Jordanian who heads the insurgent group al Qaeda in Iraq. He had pictures of the White House in his computer, they added." The arrests in Sarajevo led police in Denmark and Britain to quickly arrest other young Muslim radicals, most of them just teenagers, who were allegedly planning to carry out suicide bombings in Europe and who had been in contact with Bektasevic.[43]

A second, Bosnia-based terrorist plot had also been thwarted months earlier. While it received almost no media attention, this one was far more serious: a rocket attack on the major world leaders, as they assembled at the funeral of Pope John Paul II in Rome on April 8, 2005. To have eliminated Western leaders deemed to be "crusaders" in Muslim lands as they gathered round the casket of Christendom's greatest leader would have been a symbolic challenge to Europe and the West at least equivalent to the one made against America on September 11, 2001. Whereas the latter had taken aim at symbols of America's economic and military hegemony—the World Trade Center and the Pentagon—the former would have targeted the Western political order in its relationship to Christianity and best of all, in Rome, a historic seat of Western and Christian heritage.

Given the significance of this symbolic challenge and the fact that the would-be attack was planned in a backwater Bosnian village, it is surprising that the plot received hardly a mention in the international media. Quite possibly, the full story would have been highly embarrassing for the many Clinton-era holdovers in government and think tanks who had made careers on the myth of the Bosnian Muslims as benevolent victims and the Bosnian Serbs as bloodthirsty, anti-Western oppressors. Indeed, according to University of Belgrade terrorism expert Darko Trifunovic, despite the fact that Italy and Croatia took the credit for stopping the plot, "the intelligence originally came from the RS (Bosnian Serb Republic) services, which had their own sources in the area, and was given to the Italians in February 2005."[44]

According to Trifunovic, Bosnian Serb intelligence agents operating in the Muslim half of the federation discovered that terrorists in a small northeastern village, Gornja Maoca, were planning to attack the papal funeral with rocket launchers. The RS government shared this information with its Italian and Croatian colleagues, some two months before the event was to take place. However, the latter two countries only acted at the last minute. One day before the funeral, a Zagreb apartment was raided, yielding explosives; on the day of the funeral itself, two men were nabbed in Rome. According to Trifunovic, one of them, Said Rexhematovic, was a Bosnian and member of the radical group, Active Islamic Youth (Aktivna Islamska Omladina, AIO). The other man was an Italian convert to Islam, found in the possession of 11 rocket launchers, C-4 explosives, and detonation caps. Four months later, police in Croatia would arrest five more Bosnians involved with the plot, following a request from Italian military intelligence. For Trifunovic, "the fact that a village as small as Gornja Maoca could become a center for plotting major international terrorist attacks—this shows how dangerous is the international jihad network established in Bosnia during the war."

Indeed, what American policymakers in the Clinton administration failed to understand was that the military campaign was never the Islamists' real goal. While the United States sought to manipulate the wars in the Balkans in order to create democratic political entities around a negotiating table, the foreign sponsors of the mujahedin had an entirely different vision. For them, the war and its accompanying chaos and civilian suffering was just a handy excuse to get into the country and establish a presence. The Bosnian civil war was, in fact, just the prelude to a longer and entirely different battle, one that would not be conducted primarily against the Serbs, Croats, or Western peacekeepers, but against the Bosnian Muslims themselves. What the guardians of fundamentalist Islam, especially the Saudis, sought to do was to create a new religious infrastructure that would eventually become strong enough to make provocations against the accepted social and political order. With the creation of a small but growing Wahhabi fundamentalist population that has proved capable of causing chaos within Bosnia's Islamic community, while committing murders and threatening civilians with forceful imposition of Sharia law, this has come to pass.

The state religion of Saudi Arabia, Wahhabism is named after its reformist founder, Muhammad ibn Abd al Wahhab (1703–1792). Also known as *Salafi* ("the Pious"), the sect adheres to a puritanical, fundamentalist interpretation of Islam that considers the religious and social customs of the Prophet Muhammad's era (seventh century CE) to be most legitimate. Theologically, the Wahhabis claim to follow the teachings of early Muslim theologians such as Ibn Taymiyya and his student Ibn Al Qayyim. For the Wahhabis, the list of perceived impurities, innovations, and heresies to be stamped out in modern Islam is long. The fundamentalists' tendency to see creeping polytheism and idolatry in diverse forms of worship means that praying at tombs or venerating Muslim saints, such as is common in the Shiite Sufi tradition, is prohibited—a fact that has often brought the Wahhabis into violent confrontation with other Muslim groups in the Balkans, where they stand out conspicuously with their bushy beards, baggy, short-legged trousers, and fully veiled wives and daughters. For the most puritanical, it is forbidden even to listen to music, watch television, or take photographs.

The worldwide exporting of Wahhabism has been a major goal of Saudi Arabia for over two decades. With its infinite oil wealth, the kingdom is able to project power in the form of humanitarian organizations, educational institutions, cultural centers, orphanages, banks, businesses, and more, all serving the purpose of expanding the Saudi style of Islam. Everywhere Wahhabism has spread, it has

shown all the aspects of cult behavior, drawing in chiefly the poorer and less educated members of Muslim society, though plenty of promising young Balkan students have certainly embraced the doctrine through theological study in Saudi
Arabia and other Gulf states. Cynics scoff at the possibility of Wahhabism taking root in Bosnian society in any meaningful way, pointing out that the vast
majority of Bosnian Muslims are pro-Western and enjoy alcohol, night life,
Western fashions, and so on. While it is certainly true to say that most Bosnians
are not prepared to return to the mores of the early Middle Ages or live under
Taliban-style Sharia law, their opinion is not important to the movement's
deep-pocketed foreign funders, who can, and do, throw around millions without
a second thought. It is also irrelevant to the Wahhabis themselves, who have displayed extreme stubbornness and a determination to spread their religious views
as widely as possible, not only in Bosnia but in Kosovo, Serbia, Macedonia, and
Albania as well.

Since 9/11, this Wahhabi intransigence has become more and more dangerous
for the average Bosnian citizen. The blind fanaticism that some adherents of the
Wahhabi sect have displayed has provided reason for alarm. In February 2006, a
young Muslim zealot in Sarajevo murdered his own mother because she would
not "convert" to Wahhabism from the traditional Bosnian Hanafi Islam, which
was handed down from the Ottoman Turks. After killing his mother, "the 23-
year-old man went to a Wahhabi mosque with blood on his hands and clothes,
telling his fellow believers that he had just made a 'sacrifice to God.'"[45] The
local media has carried shocking reports about the Wahhabis' roving "Sharia
militias" sent out in Bosnian cities, dispatched to harass couples for public displays of affection, in some cases even beating young women for wearing bathing
suits or short skirts.

Another major goal for the Wahhabis is to stoke interreligious hatred through
publishing anti-American and anti-Serbian diatribes and gruesome mujahedin
war photos on Islamic Web sites, as well as through more tangible means. On
Christmas Eve, 2002, as they prepared to go to midnight mass, three members
of a family of Croatian Catholics, former refugees, were murdered in their home
by a Wahhabi fanatic, 25-year-old Muamer Topalovic. He had been imprisoned
five years earlier for allegedly attempting to kill then-Yugoslav President Slobodan Milosevic. Muamer was quickly disowned by his father, who lamented that
he had once been "an excellent pupil. But he abandoned school when he met
one bearded vehabi [sic]. He came to me one day and said: 'I met a wonderful
man who preaches and teaches wonderfully.' Soon, he was completely theirs."[46]
Considering what the Wahhabis have proven capable of doing in the name of
religion, it is understandable that the average Bosnian might find it wiser to keep
quiet and avoid trouble. Yet even political leaders and mainstream Muslim clerics have been accused of showing excessive timidity. Vildana Selimbegovic, a
Sarajevo news editor, decried how in Bosnia "politicians do not want to or are
too afraid to talk. The majority of Muslims remain silent. It seems that they will
remain silent until the devil claims his due."[47]

However, some local experts, such as Anes Alic, think the danger of foreign Islamist influence may be overhyped. The executive director of Intelligence Sector Analysis at Bosnian private intelligence group ISA and senior Southeastern Europe analyst for ISN Security Watch, Alic believes that over the next two decades, the Wahhabi movement "will be rooted out." Pointing out that the majority of Bosnian Muslims "do not support violence or terrorist attacks on civilians," Alic maintains that "the Wahhabis do not have any power here, but have managed to sustain themselves riding largely on the unpopularity of the invasion and occupation of Iraq. But they do not have long-term sustainability or a coherent ideology."[48]

Nevertheless, some voices from within the movement itself see a greater lurking danger in the violent Wahhabi sect. Jasmin Merdan and Adnan Mesanovic, two former Bosnian Wahhabis, have caused a stir by openly speaking out against the cult, publishing a book about Wahhabism, and even creating a nongovernmental organization (NGO), ZAPRET, to inform the public about what they identify as the dangerous elements of Wahhabism for Bosnian society. In an August 2006 interview with a Croatian newspaper, the 26-year-old Merdan stated that the Wahhabis are "very active," with plenty of financial support, "extremely strong publishing, and a strong sales network in Bosnia-Hercegovina and abroad...the Islamic community underestimates the Wahhabis and their strength." Merdan blames the cult's ability to "brainwash" young minds on a poor educational standard in Bosnia and a larger post-Communist spiritual and identity crisis.[49]

The most dangerous of "legitimate" Islamist groups in Bosnia is Active Islamic Youth, a Muslim social organization dedicated to pushing Wahhabi doctrine and creating a Sharia state in Bosnia. It was created in 1995 by veterans of the El Mujahid militant brigade, and financed partially by Osama bin Laden's Al Haramain. It proved to be a haven for disaffected, radical young people like Muamer Topalovic, the murderer of the Croat refugee returnees. In 2002, AIO was involved in violent protests against the deportation of six Algerian terrorist suspects to the United States.[50] Although the group's Web site was shut down, it has started publishing a weekly magazine in Sarajevo called *SAFF*. According to a 2005 terrorism report from the U.S. State Department, AIO "advocates religious intolerance and openly labels Christianity and Judaism enemies of Islam," leading young Muslims into Wahhabism "under the guise of operating youth centers, summer camps, Internet cafes, and other outreach activities."[51] Nevertheless, despite the American allegations, Bosnian Islamic Community leaders have little appetite for taking on the radical AIO. In a 2005 interview for the group's magazine, Bosnian Islamic leader Reis Mustafa Ceric sought to avoid confrontation, demurring that there was room enough for all under Allah's big tent.[52]

However, behind the ecumenical façade, the simple truth remains that the Wahhabis, while making up only a small percentage of the population, are dangerous—and not only to those Muslim neighbors whom they would like to "convert." For the more fanatic of Wahhabis, terrorist attacks against American, European, Christian, or Jewish targets present limitless opportunities for honoring the faith. That said, their funders are inclined to make allowances should the aspiring terrorist's motivations be not primarily spiritual; substantial amounts of money have been offered to Wahhabi followers in Bosnia for carrying out terrorist attacks against Western interests. For example, $9,000 was offered for anyone who would blow up a Croatian Catholic cross on a hill near Mostar in southwestern Bosnia, and a similar amount for bombing the U.S. Embassy in Sarajevo.[53] Indeed, as Wahhabi whistle-blower Jasmin Merdan declared in his outline of today's growing terrorist threat from Bosnian Wahhabis:

> This is not about car thieves or marijuana dealers. This is a completely new phenomenon that the world has never encountered before. How to deal with a man who decided to die and who made himself into a time bomb? That person still does not have a police record and may have been an upstanding citizen. I therefore ask the following question: who has the right to consider Bosnia-Hercegovina immune to this kind of global threat? If any country has the prerequisites for this kind of activity it is Bosnia-Hercegovina.[54]

Political factors, some of which are discussed in subsequent chapters, indicate that though Bosnia may have now been peaceful for over a decade, a new internecine conflict—over religion—is bubbling up underneath. Parts of the country, most notably Sarajevo, are urbanizing and modernizing, whereas large rural areas are languishing, forgotten by outside investors—with the exception, of course, of the Islamists. However, both opposite conditions can create terrorists. Although fundamentalist Islam is often attractive for people with limited economic and educational opportunities, as Merdan points out, the next generation of jihadis will be led by middle-class, educated Muslims—as was seen with the London bombings of July 7, 2005. The future of terrorism will be shaped by middle-class, Internet-friendly youth, such as the would-be British Embassy bomber of Sarajevo, Mirsad Bektasevic, and his peers.

Bosnia's political, religious, and military leaders are today facing great pressure to do the impossible task of pleasing outside forces such as America, the European Union, and the Islamic world. Within the latter camp, numerous factions that have provided money and other support in the past all, rightly or wrongly, feel themselves entitled to exercise sociopolitical influence. When it comes to counterterrorism measures, the government's dilemma thus can, despite the occasional arrest or deportation, manifest primarily in sluggishness, inaction, and tacit tolerance of terrorist groups and supporters on Bosnian soil. The plot against the pope's funeral, after all, was only discovered thanks to Bosnian Serb intelligence services operating surreptitiously within the Muslim half of the Bosnian federation—an embarrassing indicator of the Sarajevo government's inability, or unwillingness, to clean up its own backyard.

Indeed, the continued resilience of terrorist-linked charities in Bosnia is indicative of this paralysis. In June 2006, the news broke that an al Qaeda-linked charity, the Kuwait-based Revival of Islamic Heritage Society (RIHS), was nevertheless flourishing in Bosnia. Although it had taken care to change its structure and address, this radical Wahhabi group was openly announcing its "humanitarian" projects and had received some 14 million euros into its accounts in two Bosnian banks, Volksbank and the Agricultural Bank of Sarajevo, between 2002 and 2005. The money came directly from its high-level sponsors in Kuwait.[55] The RIHS had been blacklisted by the Bush administration years earlier in Afghanistan and Pakistan, collaborated with Ayman Al-Zawahiri's Egyptian Islamic Jihad in Albania during the 1990s, stoked religious unrest in Azerbaijan, and was blamed for involvement in 500 simultaneous bombings carried out in Bangladesh on August 18, 2005.[56] That Bosnian officials still seem to be taking action only slowly and partially, despite these alarming affiliations, is indicative of the power of some internal forces within the Bosnian establishment that seek to further the Islamist cause. Nevertheless, argues Alic, by and large "the military and political classes in Bosnia are 'owned' first and foremost by Western nations, and particularly beholden to the US and the EU, [between] which they often times have a hard time balancing."

Nevertheless, the issue of Islam has clearly divided the Bosnian political establishment. In late November 2006, politician Dzevad Galijasevic of the New Democratic Party for Bosnia and Hercegovina claimed that a former close ally and major figure in Alija Izetbegovic's first independent Bosnian government, Haris Silajdzic, "was the organizer and sponsor of mujahedin coming into Bosnia."[57] Galijasevic revealed that the month before he had been attacked twice, prompting him to relocate his family to Croatia. Galijasevic had become hated by the Wahhabis back in 2000 when, as mayor of the Maglaj municipality, he ordered the removal of some 1,500 mujahedin who had occupied former Serbian Christian homes in Gornja Bocinja. The order was not carried out, and the mujahedin remained in the village that had been rewarded them by the Sarajevo government—their own private Afghanistan—as a spoil of war.

According to Galijasevic, his appearance in a televised panel discussion devoted to the future dangers of a Bosnian "white al Qaeda" on October 12, 2006, sparked renewed threats against him and robberies of his homes. What was most eye-opening about Galijasevic's testimony, however, was his contention that well-known figures associated with the political and security apparatus, such as Silajdzic and hard-liner Semsudin Mehmedovic, were nurturing the Wahhabis—and aiding foreign Islamic terrorist groups in Bosnia. In 1996, while police chief in Zenica, Mehmedovic was charged by the *New York Times* of "having sheltered foreign Islamic fundamentalist fighters, of crushing moderate Muslim political forces and of fostering hatred between Muslims and Croats."[58] According to Galijasevic, Mehmedovic remains "the chief of al Qaeda in Bosnia," while the "mentors" of the mujahedin were Silajdzic and another man, Irfan Ljevakovic, a former secret police chief and employee at the notorious Bosnian Embassy in Vienna during the war working closely with bin Laden's TWRA. All of the men were from the inner circle of the late Alija Izetbegovic.

In making his argument for the active participation of government officials in supporting terrorists, Galijasevic added that "Bosnia & Hercegovina is a part of the system of international organized crime," a country where "the recruitment of future mujahedin and terrorists is being carried out." Specifically accusing the police structures of radical ties, Galijasevic maintained that "in Maglaj municipality there are around 30 police officers who were trained by the mujahedin. In Zenica-Doboj municipality there are 280 [such] police officers." According to the politician, an Algerian who the United States had ordered to leave Gornja Bocinja and Bosnia in the spring of 1999 on terrorist suspicions, Abu El Mali, "was training all the members of Ministry of Internal from this canton. One of Abu El Mali's 'students' is Kasim Hasic, an assistant police commander."[59]

In mid-November 2006, the Bosnian religious establishment made its first concerted move against Wahhabism. An official resolution was proclaimed in mosques throughout the country, stating that Bosnia's Islamic Community "condemns and finds undesirable in Bosnia those who bring unrest into mosques under the excuse of implementing the 'real' faith." At the same time, Reis Ceric declared that "anyone who cannot accept and understand it [Bosnian moderate Islam], does not have to stay"—a blunt "love it or leave it" directive that, were it to be made in England or France, would probably result in street riots. The unprecedented nationwide action was apparently provoked by the realization that, as Sarajevo theological professor Adnan Silajdzic warned, the Wahhabi movement will not "diminish but would rather become stronger and more aggressive" in the absence of reforms.[60]

Indeed, Abu Hamza, leader of the protest movement against mujahedin deportation and figurehead for the Bosnian Wahhabi movement, continues to criticize the country's Muslims for living a "reduced version of Islam." Despite the Islamic Community's injunctions against Wahhabism, he still gets plenty of air time. And in a 2006 poll conducted by Sarajevo's Prism Research, over 3 percent of the population identified themselves as either members of the Wahhabi sect or favorable to it—a larger number than is usually attested. The poll results revealed that "though most people are against the Wahhabi interpretation of practicing Islam in Bosnia (69 per cent), still, every ninth citizen show[s] support for the presence of this kind of Islam (12.9 per cent)."[61]

And so, while recriminations continue to fly within Bosnia over who should be blamed for the growing "Wahhabi problem," fundamentalist groups continue to antagonize their fellow Muslims. In late February 2007, residents in the Bosnian village of Kalesija "were forbidden to play music, while their women were forced to cover themselves by the Wahhabis there, who called the local Muslims 'infidels.'" The leader of this group of approximately 200 extremists, Jusuf Barcic, also made a bizarre show of defiance against the local population, using their village slaughterhouse as a mosque. After performing obscure "religious services" at night, "the Wahhabis in the slaughterhouse played cassettes originating from military operations in the Bosnian war," according to a Bosnian news report of March 5, 2007.[62]

At the same time, the report quoted Bosnian Federation police director Zlatko Miletic, who disclosed that Wahhabi activity was a serious security threat on a national level. Radical leader Barcic had long been notorious for his altercations with fellow Muslims, and in early 2007 was banned by Reis Ceric from giving a lecture on so-called "original Islam" in Sarajevo's magisterial Careva (Imperial) Mosque; however, of greater concern was the news that Barcic was working closely with Karaj Kamel bin Ali, a Tunisian veteran of the Bosnian jihad and former member of the radical Egyptian group Jamaat al Islamiya. Believed to have had connections with the Hamburg Cell of 9/11 plotters, the Tunisian was jailed in Bosnia for killing an Arab, and remains wanted in Germany, Italy, and elsewhere.[63] Barcic, who did not respect symbols of secular authority such as traffic lights, ironically died when he plowed into a light pole on March 30, 2007. More than 3,000 Wahhabis from all over the Balkans came to Tuzla for his funeral; the formidable turnout shocked many who had underestimated the movement's popularity.[64]

The turbulence sparked by the Wahhabis, strengthened by Saudi funds and influence, raises further questions about the degree of control foreign Islamic states have over Bosnia, and the actual extent of the danger represented by the former mujahedin there. Although pressure from the United States and the European Union has reduced the political influence of countries like Saudi Arabia and Iran in Bosnia, this aspiring EU member has frequently contradicted Western foreign policy because of the Islamic factor. In June 2006, Bosnian President Sulejman Tihic assured a gathering of dignitaries in Qatar that his country considered the American occupation of Iraq illegal—despite the fact that Bosnia itself had committed troops to that very occupation. At the same time, the president raised eyebrows in the West with another statement that seemed to veer off from Bosnia's pro-Western course and back towards an old ally thought forgotten. "We consider Iran a friend of the Bosnians because of their support during the war," maintained President Tihic. "We cannot criticize it for enriching uranium."[65] These revealing statements indicated that, despite the heavy pressure placed on Bosnia to conform to Western policies, there are other political currents still at work. They also only alienated further Christian Serbs and Croats within the Bosnian Federation, who are not seeing their values and beliefs represented in a national foreign policy controlled by Muslim interests.

At the same time, Bosnian Muslim leaders have sought to capitalize on their country's image as a "moderate Muslim" state to argue for a leadership role, perhaps too ambitiously, in a European Islamic community that is very diverse, decentralized, and unlikely to accept any form of centralized control, especially not from a Balkan country. Nevertheless, in December 2005, Reis Ceric issued a document entitled "Declaration of European Muslims," which he wrote and "which mentioned for the first time the idea of institutional association of Muslims in Europe." It was no secret that Bosnia's Islamic leader fancied himself suitable for the "institutionalisation of Islam," according to him "the best way for Europe to free itself from the fear of 'political Islam.'"[66]

That there might be good reason for such an alleged fear manifested throughout 2006 in the form of several fairly strange statements from Bosnia's allegedly moderate Islamic leader, including a demand for an apology from Dan Brown, author of the bestselling thriller *The Da Vinci Code,* because his book was somehow "promoting atheism among Bosnian youths." Reis Ceric "also reproached local television for saying that the Bosnian 'Islamic community was turning Sarajevo into another Tehran.' He appealed to his followers to 'raise their voice against the fire of secular Kalashnikovs.'" The Muslim leader also accused his Catholic and Orthodox Christian counterparts of conspiring to destroy the Bosnian state.[67]

Nevertheless, despite such incidents some Bosnian experts, such as Anes Alic do not believe that the former sponsors from the Islamic world—Saudi Arabia, Iran, and Turkey—have real political control today. Iran, states Alic, "lost its influence in 1996 when the international community, led by NATO, closed down training camps and military units run by Iranian intelligence." Since 2001, when Bosnian authorities closed around a dozen Saudi charities, "Bosnia has had less than smooth relations with Saudi Arabia." For its part, Turkey, maintains the Bosnian expert, "has no real Islamic intentions for Bosnia, but continues to fund secular education, through the building of schools, colleges and institutions, and Turkish businessmen are increasingly prominent." As for the disgruntled former mujahedin, Alic believes that "those whose citizenships have been revoked are most likely not the most dangerous. Most of them were targeted not because of links to terrorism, but because of irregularities or minor fraud concerning their citizenship applications." He adds that "the mujahedin living in Bosnia are also under constant surveillance by Bosnian authorities and the potentially most dangerous of them left after the war, most likely to places like Chechnya and Afghanistan."[68]

British analysis firm Jane's has also downplayed the threat, arguing that by virtue of their highly visible, concentrated presence, the mujahedin are not capable of operating with the requisite secrecy needed for plotting terrorist attacks. One European military intelligence analyst cited by Jane's stated that "thanks to the publicity and attention surrounding [Bocinja village], it is quite possibly the worst place to be if you are an aspiring terrorist wishing to mount an attack." Where the real danger lies, according to Jane's, is from a new, younger, and less identifiable breed of terrorists, as symbolized in the October 2005 arrests. Within Bosnia, the physical threat is augmented by Sarajevo's plethora of "soft targets." With the exception of the U.S. Embassy, "nearly all diplomatic facilities in Sarajevo lack even the most rudimentary protection against attack...all the others remain vulnerable to truck bombs or determined individuals wearing suicide vests." NATO is also concerned with becoming a target itself. According to Claude Moniquet, a terrorism expert with the Brussels-based European Strategic Intelligence and Security Center (ESISC), the military alliance views the threat of terrorist attack on its troops as a "permanent problem." Today, the threat "is mainly focused on Bosnia, where terrorist cells have already been dismantled in the past." Even preliminary to outright attacks, NATO fears that the region could become "a logistical retreat for terrorists acting in Europe."[69]

Further, the easy availability of large amounts of military-grade explosives, due to the "hoarding" of military explosives by individuals since the 1992–1995 war, the proliferation of black-market explosives, and the presence of an explosives factory in the central Bosnian Croat-controlled town of Vitez mean that "the more compact, dense and deadly military grade explosive allegedly obtained by the Sarajevo suspects is much easier to procure in Bosnia than elsewhere in Europe." A Bosnian law enforcement official cited by Jane's attested that "while the terrorist threat is being exaggerated, the huge amount of explosives out there is not."[70] It is clear that black-market munitions, not only manufactured in Bosnia but also imported across porous borders from industrial locations in former Yugoslav republics like Croatia to the west and Serbia to the east, are easy to acquire and present a major security concern.

For Western Europe, however, the security situation does not depend on whether or not the former mujahedin are officially expelled; the mere threat of deportation to torture-prone home countries has already proven sufficiently scary to the veterans of the El Mujahid to prompt some of them to go underground and try to escape elsewhere in the Balkans, or to find shelter in the radical Muslim ghettoes of Western European cities. They fear sharing the fate of the unfortunate Abu Omar, kidnapped from a Milan street by the CIA in 2004 and sent home to Egypt for some good old-fashioned police brutality. Many of the mujahedin who made their way to Bosnia remain wanted in their home countries and, if deported, would face similar treatment. They are now becoming, in effect, the new desperados in the global war on terror. As will be discussed in more detail in subsequent chapters, ex-mujahedin fleeing Bosnia reach Western Europe or move from one Balkan safe haven or another; they remain on the run, cowboy outlaws of a new and borderless Wild West.

The fact that retired mujahedin accustomed to the pastoral life in Bosnian villages could become somewhat more dangerous when uprooted from their bucolic country existence is recognized. As an American military official in Kosovo observed, "When you go shaking up a hornet's nest, you got to be prepared for some stinging...the problem we have now is that [the mujahedin] have built up these big networks in Europe. They have places to run to, people who will shelter them, and the capability to be dangerous if boxed into a corner. It has become a total mess."[71]

In the face of the Bosnian government's crackdown on foreign fighters who were granted citizenship during the Izetbegovic years, the Islamists have developed new tactics. As is happening elsewhere in the region, they have begun to mimic the ideals of the West, invoking such sacrosanct concepts as human rights, freedom of worship, and so on in making their case for why the mujahedin should be allowed to stay. Indeed, the lawyer representing several of the naturalized mujahedin, Kadrija Kolic, declared that deporting the men would be a violation of their "human rights," ironically ignoring the complicity of the mujahedin in major wartime atrocities. Kolic promised to appeal the government's decision to "the international organisations and the EU," and called it a "crime" because the citizenships had been granted "by the wartime government of Bosnia's late president Alija Izetbegovic."[72]

In Bosnia and elsewhere in the Balkans, the strategic development of NGOs and other Islamic organizations that pretend to be devoted to Western values and democracy is a significant one; it shows the Islamists' awareness of the need to advance their goals surreptitiously, and by employing tactics that seem to "expose" alleged Western hypocrisy when it comes to treatment of Muslims and Islamic causes in general. In Bosnia and other Balkan countries in transition from Communism to Western capitalism, America and the European Union have long preached an idealistic sermon of multiethnic harmony, democracy building, religious tolerance, and freedom. In so doing, it has left itself defenseless, ideo-logically speaking, to challenges from Islamist fringe groups seeking to use the West's supposed universal values against it.

In other words, as Bosnia and other Balkan states move towards the "West," the Islamists are moving along with them, using subterfuge and rhetoric to dis-guise a very different goal: the creation of a country that is neither democratic nor tolerant, a social order that had been envisaged since the 1930s by Bosnia's modern founder and Islamic fundamentalist, Alija Izetbegovic. In the words of native Bosnian political analyst Nebojsa Malic, "Izetbegovic's vision of Bosnia was not a multi-ethnic democracy, but a multi-caste hierarchy of the kind that existed under the Ottoman Empire, the memories of which were still fresh at his birth in 1925."[73] This is the goal of everyone from the Izetbegovic loyalists in government structures to the radical young idealists such as Izetbegovic him-self once was.

In the end, as is true with the other Balkan countries, the question of Bosnia's future religious orientation is perhaps less important for Western security than is the degree to which Bosnian expatriates in Western Europe and America are allowed to develop existing radical networks. It is certain that Bosnia itself will see further fireworks, as the dramatic confrontation between moderates and the Wahhabi fringe plays itself out. Yet the real danger lies with extremist Bosnians now strengthening the networks established in the cities that had been selected by Western intelligence as the clandestine funding channels for the Bosnian Muslim government during the 1992–1995 war years, when supporting the Muslim side at all costs against the Serbs seemed a simple, consequence-free matter of policy. As Jason Miko, the American who worked on Bosnian and Croatian government lobbying contracts for Ruder-Finn in the early 1990s attests, "Back then, radical Islam was not on the radar screen for the American government or public...it just wasn't an issue. I don't think we anticipated the extent of just how radical Islam could be."[74]

Today, these old funding centers in Austria, Germany, and northern Italy are being bolstered, as the October 2006 Bosnia-related arrests showed, in Denmark, Sweden, Canada, and elsewhere. In the United States itself, Bosnian diaspora groups such as the Detroit-based Udruzenje Muslimana Sjeverne Amerike (UMSA, or Association of Muslims of North America) spread the radical message, allying with Wahhabi groups in Bosnia such as Active Islamic Youth. All liaise with one another and with other young European Muslim radicals of North African, Middle Eastern, Pakistani, and Iranian descent via Internet chat groups and Web sites. Bosnians in a Western world rich with targets, therefore, are more likely to pose a security threat than are those in Bosnia itself.

Indeed, in early December 2006, several Bosnians and Macedonian Muslims, alleged devotees of bin Laden and al Zarqawi, were arrested in and around the northern Italian cities of Trieste and Treviso. On November 29, the political crime unit DIGOS in Trieste had seized "more than 1,800 guns smuggled in from the Turkish city of Istanbul."[75] There were fears that the terrorists were considering reattempting a failed plot to poison Italy's water supply. It had involved one of bin Laden's "couriers," the 21-year-old Moroccan Madid Abdellah, arrested while entering Italy on July 28, 1995, en route from Zagreb to Milan. Abdellah's fake passport tipped off the police, and the floppy disk he had with him—containing information about explosives, weaponry, assassination techniques, and the reaction of the human body to various poisons—alarmed them. Although he was briefly imprisoned, the Moroccan was released and disappeared. It was likely that he had been connected with one of the radical Islamic charities existing in Zagreb to expedite the Bosnian jihad.[76]

With their focus of hatred transformed from the old Serbian enemy by the American wars in Afghanistan and Iraq, young Bosnian radicals and their Muslim peers from other states are, ironically, simply following the pattern of jihad metamorphosis witnessed 15 years ago, when Afghan-Arab veterans of the holy war against the Russians saw in Bosnia the logical continuation of their mission. Although the Western media usually presents Bosnia in the context of local hatreds and conflicts, the picture emerging by early 2007 was indicative of a far more global role for Bosnian Muslim extremists. In late January, Pakistani authorities arrested a 29-year-old Bosnian man whose terrorist ties led back to Germany and Bosnia, as he was circulating between al Qaeda's mountain training camps.[77] Soon after, in Australia, began the unprecedented trial of nine Muslim men (including a Bosnian refugee and handyman, Mirsad Mulahalilovic) who had been arrested in November 2005 while preparing homemade chemical weapons, with the final goal likely being an attack on a nuclear power plant near Sydney. The court heard the words that co-conspirator Mazen Touma had hoped would be his last: "Touma had told his mother he was about to enter paradise and that 'Allah's satisfaction is more important than yours.'"[78] Such developments remind one of the continuing relevance and appeal, for some extremists, of global jihad. The 1994 testimony of late Saudi mujahedin Abu Abdel Aziz is, indeed, revealing in this regard. "Only fifteen days lapsed (after the conquest of

Kabul)," the jihadi proclaimed, "and the crisis of Bosnia begun. This confirmed the saying of the Prophet (of Islam), peace and blessings be upon him, who said, 'Indeed Jihad will continue till the day of Judgment.'" Today, the same process is unfolding across Western Europe, where security forces have their hands full dealing with a terrorist network of Bosnian and other Balkan emigrants—a network that Western governments themselves helped to create. This, the proliferation of terrorism by an exquisitely shortsighted American and European leadership, is perhaps the most damning indictment of the Clinton administration's misadventures in Bosnia.

CHAPTER 2

Hotel Tirana and a Strange Enough Jihad

In 1991, on the Ides of March, the United States restored diplomatic relations with Albania after a 52-year hiatus. Although still recovering from its long experiment with extreme Communism, the mountainous country on the Adriatic coast was deemed so important for American strategic policy that the secretary of state himself, James Baker III, visited Tirana on June 21. A day earlier, the European Union had also renewed ties with Albania and invited it to join the Organization for Security and Cooperation in Europe (OSCE). By the end of October a new U.S. ambassador, William E. Ryerson, had taken up residence in a lovely colonial mansion that had hosted Italian diplomats during the Cold War. Thereafter, the American relationship with Albania would only grow stronger—as would the destructive power of imported Islamic fundamentalists. By decade's end, terrorism fears would force Defense Secretary William Cohen to abort a planned visit, and the mujahedin would almost succeed in their plot to destroy that lovely yellow mansion with facing pool.

The story of how foreign Islamic extremists became established in Albania, how their cause abetted the destruction to American interests half a world away, and finally how they contributed to the destabilization of the Balkans in times of war and peace alike is a complex tale and one rife with contradictions. Driven by a schizophrenic Balkan foreign policy under the Clinton administration, the United States both cracked down on extremists and allied itself with Islamic leaders in the Tirana government funding these radicals. The key ingredients that went into the toxic cocktail of Islamic extremism in Albania were political opportunism, widespread poverty, state corruption, and sporadic periods of anarchy after the fall of Communism in 1990. The late dictator, Enver Hoxha, had kept Albania sealed off from the outside world from 1944 until his death in 1985: political dissent and ownership of televisions and cars were all prohibited, and, in 1967, even religion was banned. Hundreds of bunkers, many still visible today, were built across the country, enduring symbols of Hoxha's paranoiac fears of foreign invasion. His experiment created a population hardened by poverty, neglect, and the authoritarian behavior of the Communist state.

Albania's sudden reintroduction to the light of day in 1990, when the Communist system finally sputtered out, presented great opportunity for numerous outside parties. The country's strategic geographic position, bordering Yugoslavia to the northeast and Greece to the south, with a long coast and deep-water port at Vlore made Albania enticing to Western governments and NATO. Further, its acute economic underdevelopment, rich deposits of minerals, metals, and perhaps oil, as well as its need for automobiles, food and drink, consumer goods, and telecommunications networks, all made Albania attractive to foreign investors, at least those with the requisite courage.

Religion presented another untapped source of wealth. Before Communist rule, 70 percent of Albanians had considered themselves Muslim. Around 55 percent of this subtotal was made up of Sunnis, while another 15 percent, mostly in the south, followed the Bektashi Sufi order popular during the long centuries when Albania was a part of the Ottoman Turkish Empire. In 1926, eight years after that empire's collapse, the new secularist leader of Turkey, Mustafa Kemal Ataturk, expelled 26,000 Bektashis from his country, thus making Albania the Bektashi capital of the world. Another 20 percent of the population, also primarily in the south near Greece, were Orthodox Christians. And around 10 percent were Catholics. The Islamicization of Albania had occurred during the Ottoman occupation, which ended only in 1912. In the Ottoman system, which considered Christians second-class citizens, converts to Islam enjoyed better career opportunities. Numerous Albanians had distinguished themselves as diplomats and military leaders in the service of the Ottoman Porte; indeed, there had been 26 Ottoman Grand Viziers (Prime Ministers) of Albanian background, as well as many military leaders. However, the reinstatement of religion after 1990 opened up the country to proselytizers from all of the major preexisting faiths, as well as various cults and American Evangelical groups.

The possibility to benefit from the combined factors of geostrategic location, economic potential, and religious appeal was not lost on Albania's first non-Communist leader, President Sali Berisha. More than anyone else, this cardiologist elected in 1992 embodied the spirit of enterprising opportunism that would see his country woo suitors as incongruous as the United States and Iran, NATO and the Organization of Islamic Countries, and regional rivals such as Greece and Turkey. Berisha's right-wing Democratic Party (DP), established in 1990, used its anti-Communist platform to become the largest Albanian opposition bloc. It was popular among many fed up with the Socialist Party and its lingering associations with the old guard. Berisha appealed especially to the previously neglected Albanians of Sunni Muslim background in his own power base, the rugged, underdeveloped northeast, near the borders with Kosovo and Macedonia. This clan-run area would later become notorious for its terrorist training camps and today is still not entirely under state control.

Candidate Berisha had also been supported heavily by the United States, visiting America in 1991. In fact, the future ambassador, William Ryerson, even appeared at his campaign rallies in the United States.[1] Following his election in March 1992, Berisha continued to develop strong ties with the United States and NATO, and an American military liaison unit arrived. However, Albania's interaction with Muslim countries and organizations, evident since 1990, increased dramatically as well. Disappointment with the West's perceived failure to make good on investment promises in Albania allegedly inspired Berisha to turn to the Islamic world.[2] However, there was another key factor. The second-most powerful official in Albania and Berisha's right-hand man, Bashkim Gazidede, was a "devout Moslem," and he used his extensive capabilities as head of Albania's national intelligence service, the State Information Service (Sherbini Informative Kombetare, SHIK), to expedite the local aspirations of foreign Islamic groups—some of which had intimate ties to international terrorist groups, as will be discussed later.

President Berisha opened the doors wide to wealthy foreign Islamic interests. In April 1992, at the same time the Soviet-backed regime was being toppled in Afghanistan, a Kuwaiti delegation to Tirana had presented an "ambitious" investment plan that would grant economic aid—if the Islamic state would be allowed to build mosques. Construction began almost immediately, even if most of the population had no idea what to do with the new mosques at first.[3] Later, in October 1992, a high-level delegation from the Islamic Development Bank (IDB), led by then-Chairman Ahmed Mohammad, offered substantial bank investment for agriculture, transport, Arabic-language training, and, of course, opportunities for young Albanians to study abroad in Islamic states.[4]

After making Albania the first European member of the Organization of the Islamic Conference (OIC) in 1992—a controversial decision that was never ratified by parliament—President Berisha sought to cash in on his new connections with oil-rich Arab suitors. Both he and his foreign minister, Alfred Serreqi, attended an OIC Summit in Jeddah, Saudi Arabia, causing the Socialists to complain that "Albanian membership of the OIC was a violation of the constitution and an attempt to divert Albania from its Euro-Atlantic orientation."[5] Nevertheless, a whole new Muslim educational and clerical infrastructure was swiftly being developed in Albania, thanks primarily to Saudi largesse. The charity Islamic Relief gloated that the Albanians "were like a dry sponge, ready to soak up anything given to them."[6]

Together with Gulf private sector investors, the IDB had set up a $100 million holding company for development projects. Berisha also signed significant bilateral agreements with Muslim countries like Malaysia, which opened a bank in Tirana and offered Islamic higher education opportunities to young Albanians. By 1994, Arab companies were investing millions in Albania, led by Saudi and

Kuwaiti interests. The Saudi Cable Company, for example, offered a $10 million line of IDB credit for the production of telecommunications equipment, and other Saudi firms invested in the transport servicing and textile sectors. Kuwait extended some $16.7 million in funding while Kuwaiti private investors created a local subsidiary, the Mak-Albania Company, to build a hotel.[7]

In 1994, President Berisha ensured a strong Islamic presence in Albania's nascent banking sector with the arrival of the Arab-Albanian Islamic Bank, ahead of other Western banks.[8] Osama bin Laden was reportedly the majority stockholder and founder of this bank.[9] The Arab-Albanian Islamic Bank oversaw the construction of hundreds of mosques, gave scholarships to Islamic universities abroad, and doled out cash to poor Albanians—on the condition that females of the family accepted wearing the *chador* (veiled outer garment).[10] As such, far more than a financial institution, it became an instrument of Saudi Wahhabist propaganda. Soon, the rapidly expanding Islamic infrastructure presented a problem—there were not enough trained imams for the former atheist country. Both the OIC and IDB made good on their stipulations, and by 1993, over 200 Albanian students were studying in madrasa, "mainly in Syria, Jordan, Saudi Arabia, Libya, Malaysia, Egypt, and Turkey. Islamic organizations helped to fund the expenses of those Albanians wishing to make the pilgrimage to Mecca; by 1993 more than a thousand Muslims went on the hajj."[11] While some Islamic charities did provide much needed aid to the desperately poor Albanians, the "true agenda" of the foreigners was to rebuild Albania as an Islamic state, a process "which would follow three steps: first economic, then propagation of the faith, and third, the establishing of Islamic government."[12]

The emerging special relationship with the Islamic world soon took on more sordid dimensions as the real goals of Berisha administration radicals became clear. While more secular-minded officials were waiting for the long-promised "economic miracle" to materialize, SHIK intelligence chief and chairman of the Islamic Intellectuals Association of Albania, Bashkim Gazidede was "working around the clock receiving official delegations from the Arab world, hence deviating from the official duties and even compromising national security."[13] Indeed, by 1994 the trickle of Islamic charities had become a flood, and Western security officials had become "deeply suspicious of Berisha's motives, fearing that Albania could become Islam's advance-post in Europe."[14]

Among the wealthy Arab benefactors invited to Albania was one Osama bin Laden. When the al Qaeda chief visited Albania in 1994, he presented himself as a wealthy Saudi businessman who wanted to help a fellow Muslim nation through humanitarian support.[15] However, his charities were merely fronts for proselytizing, for money laundering, and for hosting mujahedin and Arab extremists on the run from their governments. In Albania, Osama bin Laden funded Al Haramain,[16] while Kuwaiti sheikhs sponsored the lesser-known but equally dangerous Revival of Islamic Heritage Society (RIHS), which specialized in Islamic indoctrination of orphans. Despite later being banned by the Bush administration in several countries for terrorist activities, the activities of the

RIHS in the Balkans have inexplicably continued, as will be documented in sub-sequent chapters.

The umbrella group Islamic Charity Project International sheltered over a dozen Islamic charities, including the Muwafaq ("Blessed Relief") Foundation of Saudi tycoon Yassin al-Qadi and Iran's Ayatollah Khomeini Society. The International Islamic Relief Organization (IIRO), which had openly thanked the Berisha regime for helping it, employed individuals such as Mohammad al-Zawahiri, the younger brother of future al Qaeda mastermind Ayman al-Zawahiri. Mohammad had been tasked by bin Laden with finding "legitimate cover" for Egyptian Islamic Jihad members inside the network of charities, and overseeing terrorist activities in general. He entrusted the former task to Mohammed Hassan Tita, a carpenter, who arrived in Tirana in January 1993. Tita was also instructed to collect 26 percent of the salaries of each charity worker, to donate to the terrorist cause.[17]

In his new Tirana base, Mohammed al-Zawahiri plotted while observing American installations, supported by around 20 fugitive mujahedin. Some were veterans of the U.S. and Pakistani-supported Afghan jihad against the Soviets in the 1980s. Ironically, this clandestine support, which hastened the end of the Cold War and the USSR simultaneously, ensured that jihadis energized by the campaign would take the holy war home with them, violently challenging the leadership of various pro-Western Arab regimes.[18] This would present a major headache for the United States, even in Albania, where the CIA soon found its counterterrorism work to be essentially an extension of Egyptian state secu-rity. Failing to destroy their own governments, the would-be revolutionaries sought shelter in anarchic or conflict-ridden European countries like Albania and Bosnia. The Tirana call was assembled largely of such men. Shawki Salama Attiya, a forger and former trainer at Afghan al Qaeda camps, escaped to Albania from Sudan after the attempted assassination of Egypt President Hosni Mubarak in Addis Ababa on June 25, 1995, a plot reportedly organized by the Sudanese government. Sudan, then host to Osama bin Laden, was then also a major finan-cier of terrorism and the Bosnian jihad.

Another key figure from the Egyptian Islamic Jihad movement rushed to Alba-nia was the Afghan-Arab Mohamed Ahmed Salama Mabrouk, who had served seven years in prison over his role in the 1981 assassination of Egyptian President Anwar Sadat. He received a death sentence in absentia for conspiring to bomb Cairo's Khan Al-Khalili bazaar in 1995. Both men were sheltered within the Revival of Islamic Heritage Society and related charities.[19] A third, though apparently more mellow, "political dissident" was Hassan Mustafa Osama Nasr, or Abu Omar, who would later be kidnapped by the CIA in unceremonious fash-ion off of a Milan street in 2003. Abu Omar had been imprisoned in Egypt in the 1980s because he belonged to Jamaat al Islamiya, a radical group responsible for the 1981 Sadat assassination. After being released, Abu Omar reportedly went to a Pakistani mujahedin training camp for the Afghan jihad.[20] In Tirana, he was hired by the Human Relief and Construction Agency (HRCA). Other Jamaat members were given cover with this and other Islamic charities such as Al Haramain and the RIHS.[21]

Two months after the failed attempt on President Mubarak, the CIA urgently ordered the SHIK, which it had been mentoring, into action. The Egyptian foreign minister, Amr Moussa, was due to arrive, bringing with him investment promises and an anti-Serbian policy that harmonized perfectly with that of America and the Albanian government. The United States and Egypt were determined to eliminate any Egyptian radicals in Tirana. The chief of SHIK's First Intelligence Directorate, Flamur Gjymisha, was handed the "pick-up list" from his CIA liaison at the U.S. Embassy. Abu Omar's name was not there, but when it turned out that a suspect HRCA vehicle was registered to him, the SHIK was instructed to grab him too. On the night of August 27, 1995, Abu Omar was apprehended. After an uncooperative week in custody, he suddenly accepted the SHIK's offer to be an informant and to supply the agency (and by extension the CIA) with detailed lists of suspected terrorists and their affiliations. Of course, the CIA would hardly have needed this service had it chosen to rein in high officials such as Gazidede.

The covert work of Abu Omar provided solid leads and some interesting revelations. For the SHIK, above all, the recruitment of Abu Omar was a major coup and won them political points with the Americans. "We became a main player for the first time," senior SHIK official Astrit Nasufi told the *Chicago Tribune* a decade later. "We weren't just tools. We gave them a clear idea of who was monitoring the US embassy for [Jamaat], who was coming in and out of the country."[22] At the same time, this victory exposed a deeply embarrassing truth: Albania had acquired a reputation among jihadis. According to Abu Omar, they considered Albania a "safe hotel"—"a country where fundamentalist Muslims believed they could live without fear of political repression." The authorities did not need to fear any assassination attempt against the visiting Egyptian diplomat, he said, as this would have endangered the Islamists' tranquil existence.[23] Albania's membership in the Organization of Islamic Conferences had meant "the unilateral abolition of visas for citizens of Arab countries."[24] The country was open to all comers, whereas the West was all but off-limits to Albanian passport holders, who found more willing hosts in the Muslim world.

However, only days after he agreed to work for the SHIK, Abu Omar left Albania. SHIK officials later claimed that he went to Istanbul, while his Albanian wife, pregnant at the time, would later state that he went to Romania. Failing to get a visa for her, Abu Omar returned to Tirana. By the end of 1995, however, they were seeking asylum in Germany, encountering the same problem. While German authorities accepted Abu Omar's application, they did not allow his wife and now newborn child to remain, because she was an Albanian citizen. Mother and child returned home, but Abu Omar apparently stayed in Germany until May 1997, when he moved to Milan, remarried, and adopted the extremist persona that brought him to the attention of the Italian SISMI (Italy's military intelligence) and later, once again, the CIA.

In the bigger picture, the August 1995 Tirana crackdown actually represented a bold new counterterrorism policy devised by senior American officials to gather intelligence on the growing al Qaeda threat, which they had, of course, brought to Europe by expediting the Bosnian jihad. According to Michael Scheuer, the former CIA counterterrorism expert who helped establish the program, Egypt was the "obvious choice" for a collaborative partner. It was the second-largest recipient of U.S. foreign aid after Israel, a longtime ally with a famously brutal secret service, and also had serious issues with various dissidents and former mujahedin. The fact that several senior al Qaeda suspects were Egyptian was another argument in favor, said Scheuer, who ensured the Mubarak government that the United States "had the resources to track, capture, and transport terrorist suspects globally—including access to a small fleet of aircraft."[25]

Almost simultaneously with the Tirana arrests, on September 13, another enemy of the Egyptian state "disappeared," this time from Croatia. Talaat Fouad Qassim, wanted in the 1981 Sadat assassination, was en route to Bosnia when Croatian police arrested him. Qassim was handed over and interrogated by the CIA on a Navy vessel in international waters before being extradited to Egypt, where he was tortured and presumably killed.[26] Although the Bush administration has been frequently attacked for its policy of extraordinary renditions, partisan critics do not say—or choose not to say—that the ethically dubious kidnapping program was actually created and carried out with gusto during former President Clinton's first term in office. By 1998, many prominent jihadis in Tirana would suffer Qassim's fate, ending up seized, rendered, and sent to a gruesome end in Egypt.

The August 1995 counterterrorist operations that netted Abu Omar's services, if temporarily, did not, however, affect Islamic penetration of Albania or its continued use as a "safe hotel" by foreign terrorists. Both renegade political dissidents and aspiring jihadis for Bosnia continued to show up. In January 1996, Ayman Al-Zawahiri sent money and another Egyptian Islamic Jihad member, Ahmed Ibrahim, to Tirana to join key Islamists who had survived the SHIK raids, like Mohammad Hassan Tita, Mohamed Ahmed Salama Mabrouk, and Shawki Salama Attiya. Ibrahim was promptly employed by the shadowy Al Haramain. Although a few charities had been closed in 1994 and 1995, the funding spigot remained open.

Indeed, despite its efforts to crack down on suspected terrorists in Albania, the U.S. government had many things going against it—chief of all, itself. The outright favoritism and support it had provided to the Bosnian Muslims in a complex civil war had the disastrous effect of transubstantiating the holy war from Southeast Asia to the heart of Europe. Indeed, with Islamist funding channels and cells having been set up in every major Western European city, the Bosnian jihad had essentially created a global empire for terror. To fulfill its extreme pro-Muslim Balkan policy, the United States was actually cooperating, as has been detailed, with state sponsors of terrorism such as Saudi Arabia, Sudan, Iran, and Pakistan. With European allies like Germany and Austria, the United States aided and abetted their secret services, their banks, and their charities and thus created the terror network in both Balkan and Western European countries that would later provide the logistical support and some of the manpower for the 9/11 attacks. Further, the United States actively sought out political support from its Islamic allies for the NATO bombings of Serbs in Bosnia and, soon after, in Kosovo. However, the Americans did not show sufficient foresight about what this co-operation would ultimately entail. While Bill Clinton, Madeleine Albright, Richard Holbrooke, and Wesley Clark were ostensibly out to stop genocides and show America's benevolent, humanitarian motivations, the Islamic countries were using the opportunities presented by war, poverty, and social dislocation to try and rebuild the Balkans in their own image.

On the official level, America and Albania found the political backing of Islamic countries for their war policy in the Balkans useful. Critics have argued that the American policy of supporting Bosnian and Kosovar Muslims amounted to a cynical attempt to show that, despite its hostilities against Muslims in Somalia, Iraq, and Afghanistan, the United States deserved praise for aiding the "good Muslims" of the Balkans. Albania's tolerance of foreign Islamist encroachment also meant that it could count on unanimous support in terms of securing floor votes at the United Nations from OIC countries when resolutions on Kosovo came up.[27] While President Berisha was no religious fundamentalist (rather, he was an entrepreneurial politician who wasted no opportunity to capitalize from whomever he could at whatever the price), some of his closest collaborators were. Bashkim Gazidede, the SHIK chief, played a double game, assisting the CIA while aiding terrorist leaders such as Al-Zawahiri and bin Laden. This situation would not start to change until mid-1997, when the Berisha government was ousted and the SHIK was reformed. But by then it was too late.

Organized crime also aided the entrenchment of Islamic terrorists in Albania. Money laundering, drug smuggling, the weapons trade, and human trafficking were just a few of the illegal industries that flourished in post-Communist Albania. A sudden rise of organized crime came after the UN sanctions regimes placed on wartime Yugoslavia and the 1994 Greek economic blockade of Macedonia over the disputed name issue forced regional commercial activity to go underground.[28] Given the weakness of state structures and endemic poverty, it was not difficult for sophisticated mafia clans to corrupt border guards and government officials into opening the logistical networks of the state.

The massive increase in heroin production and trafficking that the United States and Pakistan created in 1980s Afghanistan had flooded Europe with cheap heroin.[29] The established drug smuggling route, through Afghanistan, Iran, Turkey, and the Balkans into Western Europe, was both reinforced and augmented in the early 1990s. Turkey lost tens of billions of dollars when the 1991 Gulf War cut off business with neighboring Iraq and during its scorched-earth campaign against Kurdish insurrectionists. However, with the assistance of corrupt secret services, it was able to recoup its losses through increasing heroin trafficking—in 1995, this amounted to $25 billion and grew to $37.5 billion the next year.[30] The sudden proliferation of heroin, combined with regional embargoes and sanctions, also changed the mafia structures and augmented the trafficking routes. A nascent Albanian mafia grew in prominence, with new routes through Albania and Albanian-controlled western Macedonia and Kosovo flourishing. At first the Albanians had merely been the link between the Turks and Italians, but, because of their tight clan structure, violent tactics, and indecipherable language that no one else spoke, they soon took a leading role. By 1994, the Albanian mafia was responsible for $2 billion worth of heroin imported into Europe.[31] Switzerland's jails were overflowing with more than 2,000 émigré Albanians arrested for trafficking.[32] Ominously, the drug money was being invested into weapons destined for Albania and the looming war with the Serbs in Kosovo.[33] And, while the drug lords could hardly have been mistaken for men of religion, a secondary motive for selling heroin to Europeans was, as one Albanian trafficker in Milan put it, "to submerge Christian infidels in drugs."[34]

Far from stopping drugs and arms smuggling, disenchanted Albanian intelligence officials would later allege, the Berisha government indulged in it. Cabinet members, SHIK personnel, and others were accused of profiting from the illicit business, while funding violent secessionist movements in neighboring Macedonia and Kosovo. Then-Defense Minister Safet Zhulali allegedly used his ministry to move weapons, oil, and contraband cigarettes.[35] Corrupt officials and Italian mafia partners laundered this money creatively, through the pyramid schemes that offered unbelievable rates of return (up to 300 percent). Thousands of credulous Albanians committed their life savings, even selling their homes, to participate in these funds run by companies connected with the regime. Between $1.5 billion and 2 billion disappeared into ten or so pyramid schemes between 1994 and 1996. The biggest one, VEFA Holding, was heavily connected with the Calabrian 'Ndrangheta mafia—as well as Albania's official representative to NATO, Democratic Party fundraiser, and Berisha relative, Vehbi Alimucaj. In the DP's May 1996 campaign, their amusing slogan was "with us, everybody wins!" That the pyramids stood strong even after the elections owed to the amount of laundered mafia money being put into it, which concealed the logical impossibility of a payout.[36]

When the pyramids swiftly collapsed starting in January 1997, thousands of ordinary Albanians went bankrupt, leading to street protests and total anarchy. Armed militias roamed the streets, businesses were looted, the state arsenals were emptied, and Berisha even begged for a NATO intervention. As the violence worsened in March, government notables helped their families escape to Italy or Greece. Order was restored only with the creation of a "national unity" government and an Italian humanitarian mission that arrived in April. Berisha soon stepped down, returning to his mountain redoubt in the north. VEFA chairman Alimucaj would later be sentenced to five years in jail for stealing some $325 million of investors' money in the pyramid schemes, as well as for arms trafficking.[37]

Albania's collapse into anarchy was a windfall for nationalist militants preparing for war in neighboring Kosovo, as well as for al Qaeda, which captured hundreds of blank passports. The ransacking of the state arsenals meant free weapons for the Kosovo Liberation Army (KLA or UCK, "Ushtria Clirimtare e Kosove" in Albanian), a paramilitary organization seeking to overthrow the Yugoslav government of then-President Slobodan Milosevic. Although Kosovo was historically and legally a Serbian province, the ethnic balance had shifted dramatically since the Second World War; it is estimated that from 1945 until the NATO intervention of 1999, 140,000 Orthodox Christian Serbs departed, both voluntarily and by force, from a culturally and socially incompatible land dominated by clan-based Muslim Albanians.

Despite the significant participation of Albanians in Kosovar state institutions, military power remained in federal Yugoslav hands. Rough treatment from the police and perceived discrimination fueled Albanian resentment, but dissatisfaction with the economic situation (Kosovo had always been the least developed region in Yugoslavia) also led to ethnic scapegoating and created a generation of unemployed young men with too much time on their hands—anywhere in the world, perfect ingredients for armed conflict.[38] Kosovar Albanians developed parallel institutions and armed themselves in order to forcibly claim their independence. Sali Berisha had, early in his reign, called for NATO intervention in Kosovo, and his military and intelligence staff cultivated close ties with Kosovar and diaspora Albanian nationalist elements as the Clinton administration moved to address the "Albanian Question" in Kosovo.

The CIA and other Western intelligence services, especially the British and German, had long taken a keen interest in goings-on in Albania and Kosovo. Each had operations in Tirana and, through international organizations like the OSCE, a smaller presence in Kosovo. Germany hosted a significant Kosovar Albanian immigrant population and, in the city of Ulm, the nonrecognized Kosovo "government-in-exile" of Bujar Bukoshi, which raised funds to equip, train, and deploy the Kosovo Albanian rebels. Another fundraising group, Fatherland Calls, was based in Germany and active throughout Europe. Both raised substantial funds from drug money, as well as from an obligatory "war tax" from the wages of diaspora Albanians. In 1996, Germany's BND established a major station in Tirana under new director Hansjörg Geiger and another in Rome to select and train future KLA fighters. According to Le Monde Diplomatique, "special forces in Berlin provided the operational training and supplied arms and transmission equipment from ex-East German Stasi stocks as well as black uniforms."[39] The Italian headquarters recruited Albanian immigrants passing through ports such as Brindisi and Trieste, while German military intelligence, the Militäramschirmdienst, and the Kommandos Specialkräfte Special Forces (KSK), offered military training and provisions to the KLA in the remote Mirdita Mountains of northern Albania controlled by the deposed president, Sali Berisha.[40]

In 1996, BND Chief Geiger's deputy, Rainer Kesselring, the son of the Nazi Luftwaffe general responsible for the bombing of Belgrade in 1941 that left 17,000 dead, oversaw KSK training of Albanian recruits at a Turkish military base near Izmir.[41] This Aegean port city was also the headquarters of an Albanian expatriate separatist group set up by the Turkish intelligence service, the MIT (Milli Istihbarat Teskilati, National Intelligence Organization) as early as 1982, which in 1993 was reborn as the Kosovo People's Movement (Levizja Popullore e Kosoves, or LPK).[42] The LPK was a leftist group that created the KLA from its power centers in Germany and Switzerland. Turkey had significant intelligence operations in Albania and was an obvious choice as military liaison with the KLA. Alleviating the alleged oppression of Muslims resonated more among the Turkish population than among European publics who disapproved of the Albanian mafia's exploits in their own cities. With some 5 million citizens of Albanian descent, Turkey also had old historical and religious links with Albania. As early as 1990, it had begun renovating Ottoman mosques and planning strategic economic investments. Backed by Islamic banks, Turkish investment was aggressive, as was the case with a fertilizer company that "pushed aside" its American competition by offering "extremely advantageous conditions to Albanian importers and exporters."[43] Albania also lay directly northwest of Turkish rival Greece. By partnering with Tirana, Turkey could exert pressure from two fronts on Athens. It suited the Albanians as well to have a powerful ally on the other side of its sometimes prickly neighbor to the south. With the collapse of the Cold War world order, Greece and Turkey became increasingly estranged; indeed, during the 1990s the two countries almost went to war over disputed islets in the Aegean and violations of airspace by each other's (U.S.-supplied) fighter planes.

The first major military cooperation agreement was signed in July 1992 by then-Turkish Minister of Defense Nevzeta Ayaza and his Albanian counterpart, Safet Zhulali. A month later, a Turkish naval vessel entered the port of Drac (Durres) for the first time since the Ottoman days. Albania's strategic value to the United States, Germany, and Turkey explains why it received very privileged NATO treatment even long before joining the alliance's "Partnership for Peace" program. Defense Minister Zhulali visited Turkey soon after, touring top-secret NATO military installations—something that "would not have been possible unless it was sanctioned by NATO members at the highest coordinating and decision making bodies within the Alliance." However, despite the increasing Turkish cooperation, America was the single largest source of military aid to the Albanians.[44]

By late 1997, with a showdown between the West and Milosevic dividing NATO allies, there were ominous signs that the fundamentalists—that is, Islamists not under the control of NATO or Turkey—were preparing to join the party. The State Department and CIA were alarmed. Islamic involvement would not only pose a threat to U.S. troops; it would also be exquisitely bad public relations for the Clinton administration and the Albanian-American lobby to be perceived as sponsoring a jihad, especially after the Bosnian debacle. The dismantlement of the Berisha regime provided a new opportunity, therefore, for the CIA to try and eliminate the Tirana Islamist cell before it could channel foreign fighters to Kosovo.

Following the restoration of order after the collapse of the pyramid schemes, caretaker Prime Minister Bashkim Faso had on April 1, 1997, suspended the SHIK and blocked its funding. Bashkim Gazidede, who along with Berisha had been blamed for the government's heavy-handed crackdown on protesters in the south, resigned along with his deputy, Bujar Rama.[45] As expected, the Socialists won the June 1997 parliamentary elections, and Fatos Nano, an Orthodox Christian previously jailed by Berisha, became prime minister. He reinstated the SHIK, appointing Fatos Klosi as its new director. Two days after the election, Bashkim Gazidede fled Albania for the Middle East, fearing reprisal from his now empowered political enemies.

The new Socialist government had to contend with insurmountable social and economic challenges. Bravely, considering the state of economic collapse, the government turned its back on Berisha's old Islamic sponsors. As part of a tacit plan "to leave as inconspicuously as possible [from] the Islamic Conference," Albania sent no delegation to the Tehran Summit of the OIC in 1998, nor to a subsequent foreign minister's meeting in Qatar. A contemporary analysis stated that "Tirana's absence did not pass unnoticed and has caused some problems in relations with Islamic countries."[46] The government's relative coolness with the Islamic world, while meant to show fidelity with the West, aroused the ire of OIC states that had been heavily subsidizing Albania since 1991.

In October 1997, the reengaged CIA sent an expert team to overhaul and retrain the SHIK through a three-month training course.[47] The agency also became more proactive against Tirana-based terrorists. For U.S. officials, Osama bin Laden and his cohorts were increasingly being seen as representing the main terrorist threat. Bin Laden had gone off the radar since Sudan had expelled him— due to U.S. pressure—and disappeared into the wilds of Afghanistan where, protected by the Taliban, he would strengthen the al Qaeda base and plot for the day he would hit the American homeland. In Albania, foreign Islamist elements became more cautious following the new government's purge of the security services. Pro-Islamic SHIK officers appointed by Bashkim Gazidede since 1992 were replaced, while the government restaffed the Albanian Islamic Community's leadership with younger and less radical officials.[48] The CIA began to request more cooperation, which the reformed SHIK was eager to give.

With Germany and interventionists in the Clinton administration gaining influence, a showdown with Milosevic seemed inevitable. In February 1998, the U.S. State Department officially removed the KLA from its list of terror organizations. At the same time, on February 23, Osama bin Laden issued his first fatwa, or religious decree, that urged Muslims to kill Americans and Jews anywhere in the world, causing alarm in Washington. The CIA thus paid attention when their SHIK protégés, who had been using U.S.-donated wiretapping equipment to eavesdrop on Islamists in Tirana, started picking up heavy chatter between local Islamists and leaders abroad. The man on the other end of the line was often Ayman Al-Zawahiri, who had recently merged his Egyptian Islamic Jihad (EIJ) with al Qaeda. SHIK head Fatos Klosi was brought to CIA headquarters in Langley, Virginia, in the spring of 1998 to plan a joint operation. The CIA now considered the merged EIJ-al Qaeda cell in Albania as "among the most dangerous terror outfits in Europe."[49] Egypt was asked to issue an international arrest warrant for one of the leading suspects, Shawki Salama Attiya, and did so on June 25. His immediate arrest led police to computer equipment and a false document production lab.

In the following weeks, the SHIK would perfect what it had pioneered in the summer of 1995—secret kidnappings for the CIA. The July 1998 operation got slightly messy, however, with one of the suspects being killed and another two escaping. Other veterans on the Tirana jihadi scene such as Ahmed Ibrahim, Mohammad Hassan Tita, and Mohamed Ahmed Salama Mabrouk were taken alive, however, and like Attiya were flown to Egypt. They, and some of their family members, would face torture in the weeks ahead; by 2000, all were dead or faced lengthy prison sentences.

Disastrously, however, some "euphoric" SHIK agents had proudly leaked news of the American involvement in the raids to the media, with the result that "any hope of keeping Washington's fingerprints away from the operation had died."[50] With no doubt about U.S. involvement, al Qaeda issued a swift and stark reply. On August 5, 1998, an Arab-language newspaper in London published a letter signed by the International Islamic Front for Jihad, an umbrella group created by bin Laden and encompassing al Qaeda and several other terrorist organizations. In the letter, the Islamists vowed to respond to the Americans for the Tirana operation in a "language they will understand." Two days later, al Qaeda terrorists carried out massive attacks against two U.S. embassies in East Africa. A car bombing in Nairobi, Kenya, killed 213 people and injured more than 4,000. The second attack, in Dar es Salaam, Tanzania, killed 11 and injured 85. At a loss, the Clinton administration responded lamely on August 20 with "Operation Infinite Reach"—the bombing of an al Qaeda training camp in Afghanistan and a Sudanese pharmaceutical plant erroneously connected with terrorists. These largely symbolic strikes were undertaken three days after Clinton had admitted to a relationship with intern Monica Lewinsky. They had no impact on the al Qaeda network, though they did embolden the terrorists and inspire virulent anti-American rhetoric from Islamic extremists around the world.

Although the embassy bombings had been planned well in advance, it was telling that al Qaeda made a point of weaving the violent kidnappings in Tirana into the greater causal narrative of events justifying their East Africa attacks. Al Qaeda had always put great importance on symbolism, and, thus, in their minds at least, there was a clear and immediate relationship between the street justice their people got in Tirana and the street justice they handed out in Tanzania and Kenya.

If the U.S. administration had been unaware of the full ramifications of their complacency during the seminal years of Islamic infiltration in Albania, they were certainly aware of it now, though the government would not regard terrorism as a vital national security issue until 9/11. They therefore pressed on with plans for a Kosovo intervention, one that was aggressively supported by all of the Islamic states, against a country, Yugoslavia, which had never threatened or invaded any NATO country and which had sided with the United States in two world wars. Incredibly, despite all the warning signs, the United States prepared to embark on yet another "humanitarian intervention" that would inevitably spread the radical Islamic cancer to yet another Balkan country, for the second time in less than a decade.

Despite the careful balancing act of the United States, the situation was already out of control. American officials professed to be alarmed when foreign mujahedin turned up in the KLA ranks. American diplomat Robert Gelbard stated openly, two months before the embassy bombings, that Iranian and Chechen mujahedin were already in Albania.[51] Afghans, Algerians, and Egyptians were also offering their services.[52] Gelbard did not elaborate on how the mujahedin might have infiltrated Albania. However, the previous activities in and around Bosnia had allowed the SAVAMA, Iran's state intelligence service, to establish a wider Balkan network. Then-Director of the U.S. Congressional Task Force on Terrorism and Unconventional Warfare Jossef Bodansky claimed that by very early 1998, SAVAMA was moving heavy weapons from stockpiles in Albania to Kosovo, including grenades, machine guns, assault rifles, night vision equipment, and communications gear under conditions of "absolute secrecy."[53] The Iranian Central Bank's order to Iranian companies to invest in Albania regardless of risk or profit provided cover for SAVAMA to launder money for purchasing weapons and training terrorists. Forming a "strategic axis" with Bosnia, Albania was envisioned as an entry point for Iranian intelligence activities in Greece, Italy, and Austria.[54]

As skirmishes between KLA irregulars and the Yugoslav Army intensified in spring 1998, material evidence of mujahedin, in the form of dead bodies, began to pile up. One KLA volunteer killed in western Kosovo in May was a Sudanese citizen. Several Bosnian Muslims were also killed. In July 1998, Yugoslav border guards shot a KLA member trying to cross over from Albania; documents found on the man, Alija Rabic, "indicated he was guiding a 50-man group from Albania into Kosovo. The group included one Yemeni and 16 Saudis, six of whom bore passports with Macedonian Albanian names."[55] A KLA volunteer interviewed in Albania by a Dutch journalist testified that Kosovo would be his "eighth jihad," while another eyewitness in the central Kosovo village of Malisevo would later note the embarrassment on the local KLA commander's face as a contingent of Arab fighters drove past.[56] An obituary for a Turkish holy warrior later killed in Chechnya indicated that he was one of the many Turks who had volunteered for the Kosovo jihad.[57]

At the same time, KLA leaders like Hashim Thaci and Ramush Haradinaj were fervently claiming that theirs was a strictly nationalist, ethnic-based revolt. The claim was accurate but at the same time deceptive. It was true that most Albanians were not fighting under the green banner of Islam; however, if they won, Christian Serbs would almost certainly face expulsion and a highly effective Yugoslav border security structure would be destroyed. These predictions, which came true as soon as NATO stepped foot in Kosovo the following summer, would result in a practically "clean" Muslim statelet with very porous borders —a smuggler's and terrorist's paradise. Although this inevitability should have set off alarm bells in advance for American officials, Islamic terrorism for them was insignificant compared to finishing off the Cold War, by keeping NATO robust during a crisis period in which its historic self-defensive mandate had become irrelevant. And so unfolded the spring 1999 intervention.

The bombing was meant to be a quick operation demonstrating NATO's unquestioned strength, while stopping an oppressive dictator and sending a clear message to Russia and China. Yet any perceived Islamist involvement could endanger an already opaque military adventure deeply opposed by many U.S. Republicans. For this reason, the CIA and British secret services took over the clandestine training of KLA fighters in Albania, running it through U.S. military contractor Military Professional Resources Incorporated (MPRI), similar British firms, and Britain's MI6 and its elite Special Air Service (SAS). By early 1999, the SAS was operating secret training camps near Tirana and on the front lines in the mountains of northern Albania.[58]

These security agencies knew about another stream of volunteers, however, which were somewhat less docile than Albanian nationalists. These were the British-born Muslims of Middle Eastern and South Asian background whose interest in the Kosovo jihad was at best tolerated and at worst possibly manipulated by British intelligence. Nevertheless, it was not until a major terrorist attack took place in Britain, in July 2005, for that government's long-standing Muslim appeasement policy to be criticized. As long as they did not attack within Britain, known radicals were allowed to carry out recruitment and funding activities for jihads everywhere from Kashmir to Kosovo. This reality also reaffirmed an endemic arrogance of British society, which saw itself as a more welcoming and multicultural society than continental European countries. The result of this spirit of "tolerance"—more accurately, widespread English disinterest in its minorities—was seen on July 7, when homegrown but foreign-trained Islamic radicals, some veterans of Kosovo, carried out multiple bombings on the London Underground.[59]

In 1998, however, there seemed no reason for Londoners to fear those odd chaps with the bushy beards and funny clothes. Even the one with a hook for a hand, Sheikh Omar Bakri Muhammad, was just an amusing eccentric despite his stated desires to kill the infidels and make England an Islamic state. However, this fundamentalist sheikh from North London's Finsbury Park Mosque was also promoting al-Muhajiroun, a group that recruited aspiring mujahedin for jihad against the Serbs. A rally in London for the Kosovo jihad, held on Friday the 13th of March 1998, was backed by over 50 indigenous Islamic groups, ranging from "mainstream" ones to devoted backers of the Taliban and Hamas. At the same time, the Albanian Islamic Society of London, headed by Kosovar Sheikh Muhammad Stubla, was lobbying and raising money for the KLA's campaign. According to Sheikh Stubla, Serbia's goal was "to wipe out the Islamic roots of the [Albanian-populated] region." In contradiction to the KLA leadership's claims about secularism, the Kosovar sheikh specifically defined the militant group as "an Albanian Islamic organisation which is determined to defend itself, its people, its homeland, and its religion with all its capabilities and by all means."[60] The Society was based near Finsbury Park Mosque, at the 233 Seven Sisters Road complex of offices, which also houses the headquarters of the UK's main Islamic organization, the Muslim Association of Britain (MAB).[61] The chief bank account for fundraising was in the London branch of terrorist-linked Habibsons Bank of Pakistan.[62]

In a last-ditch effort to allegedly prevent war, an international conference was held in Rambouillet, France, in February 1999. However, under U.S. pressure it placed terms on the Yugoslav leadership that were impossible to accept, for example, that NATO would have free and unrestricted access across the entire country. Of course, Yugoslav President Slobodan Milosevic refused and was misleadingly blackballed in the Western media as an obdurate nationalist unwilling to seek a peaceful settlement. Since Russia and China were certain to veto any potential UN Security Council resolution, NATO lumbered ahead with its own unilateral deployment, contrary to international law, against a state that posed a threat neither to the United States nor to any NATO ally. An alleged Serbian "massacre" at the Kosovo village of Racak, later proved by a UN forensics team to have been a place of legitimate battle, provided the necessary justification for Clinton to start the bombing. Perversely, the large-scale population displacement NATO was ostensibly acting to prevent began only after the bombs started falling.

After 78 days and an estimated $13 billion of military expenditure, NATO forced Yugoslav President Milosevic to the bargaining table. However, the Alliance's high-altitude bombing campaign did negligible damage to the Yugoslav army, which lost only 13 tanks and managed to shoot down an American fighter plane. NATO had "won" only after causing unbearable civilian misery, by bombing hospitals, schools, bridges, factories, and oil refineries in Serbia proper, far away from the alleged theater of operations in Kosovo. NATO also used two highly controversial weapons, cluster bombs, and depleted uranium. Ironically, however, the highest percentage of depleted uranium was dropped over the ethnic Albanian stronghold of western Kosovo, ensuring that the people NATO had come to "liberate" would suffer cancer and birth defects for years to come. Indeed, Italian NATO soldiers deployed in the region soon suffered the telltale signs of depleted uranium exposure that had been known about since at least the first Gulf War, when American soldiers returning from Iraq were afflicted by what became known as the "Gulf War Syndrome."

Following the cessation of hostilities in Kosovo and the arrival there of a NATO peacekeeping mission, large-scale "reverse" ethnic cleansing began. The vulnerable Serbian minority, which made up only 10 percent of a population of 2 million, was targeted for reprisals and attacks by vengeful Albanians. After NATO arrived in 1999, over 200,000 Kosovo Serbs were forced to flee to Serbia. Scores of Serbian Orthodox churches, some 700 years old, were destroyed by the KLA. For the United States, however, this was hardly a concern, since the strategic imperative—the construction of an enormous new military base, Camp Bondsteel—had been forcibly enabled.

However, with NATO's victory in Kosovo, Albania itself waned in importance. It was no longer needed as a staging post for secret military trainers, and Albanian nationalist elements there—just months before, the West's most valuable local allies—could now actually become a headache for the UN administration in Kosovo (UNMIK), tasked with keeping a shaky peace and preventing irredentist forces from attempting to continue the war into southern Serbia or Macedonia. And so, while the U.S.-led victory over Milosevic gave the Clinton regime something to thump its chest over, the Islamist presence in Albania quietly continued to grow, and al Qaeda continued exploiting its new Balkan networks to prepare for "the big one"—the strike on the American mainland that would materialize only 26 months later.

To be sure, the United States did not neglect the extremist threat in Albania to the same extent that it had ignored the Afghan jihadis after the Soviet withdrawal from Kabul. However, with the Kosovo war completed, Albania had served its purpose and the administration could move on to other priorities. These included the $2.9 billion Baku-Tbilisi-Ceyhan oil pipeline in the Caucaus, strategizing for the upcoming presidential election of November 2000, and returning to the perennial future enemy, China. Relations with the Asian giant had sunk to their lowest level in history following NATO's bombing of the Chinese Embassy in Belgrade—allegedly, a mistake, though many suspected that this astonishingly reckless act had been a deliberate tacit warning to tell the Chinese to stop supporting the Yugoslav military.

Although the war was over for Western policymakers, for the Islamists it had hardly begun. American Defense Secretary William Cohen was forced to suddenly cancel a celebratory visit to Albania in mid-July 1999, fearing a lethal sting from the "hornets' nest" of al Qaeda operatives said to be operating from Tirana.[63] Following this embarrassing abandonment, Albania deported two Syrians and an Iraqi who had been charged in February with falsifying official documents but who "were released after serving a prison sentence."[64] Earlier that year a Saudi-trained Albanian, Maksim Ciciku, had been arrested for allegedly spying on the U.S. Embassy. Ciciku claimed that he had been detained because of his Saudi connection and because his company provided bodyguards for visiting Arabs. The emergency closure of American offices in Tirana after the East Africa embassy bombings had left a lingering air of paranoia, and a year later, Americans were still being warned to avoid Albania.

A new chapter in the story of Islamic fundamentalism in Albania was set to begin. In its typical practice of using whole peoples and foreign government agencies as pawns on the grand global chessboard, the United States had ignored the social factors leading to the next phase in al Qaeda's long-term strategy: the creation of a homegrown Islamic-political movement in Albania. Although both then and now the vast majority of Muslim Albanians are neither radical nor pro-Arab, as in Bosnia, a small but stubborn Wahhabi movement was being established. This, the unsurprising result of a decade of Islamist infiltration of the economic and religious spheres of society, would eventually become powerful enough to challenge the mainstream Islamic leadership—a trend that has been noted in every single Balkan country that has been penetrated by foreign Islamist interests.

However, it was only after 9/11 that the United States would again focus its attention on the threat from Albania. Although the Arab proselytizers and donors had not succeeded in winning over the masses, they had strengthened their position considerably, spreading their economic tentacles and developing an "opposition party" of young and energetic Wahhabi Muslims, many trained in the Arab world and determined to spread "true Islam" back home. They could also offer substantial funds to those who converted and who were willing to spread the fundamentalist doctrine. Further, despite the dramatic CIA-sponsored kidnappings of 1995 and 1998, the essential structure of terror-linked charities and money laundering safe havens in Albania remained unaffected. As everywhere else, charities shut down by the authorities could simply rename or relocate, and a vast stock of stolen and counterfeit Albanian passports allowed terrorists to create multiple identities for both local and foreign-born operatives. Crime and corruption had hardly been eliminated during the Nano government, and the lucrative trade in people smuggling on small craft crossing the Adriatic from Vlore to Brindisi in Italy was flourishing, to the extent that the smugglers overpowered police. This industry continued to allow terrorists, Islamic fundamentalists, and asylum seekers easy passage into Western Europe.[65]

It would not be until after 9/11 that Albania's links with international terrorism would be scrutinized more carefully. Although almost forgotten now, in the immediate aftermath of the attacks, tight-lipped U.S. government sources disclosed an explosive fact: that there was a definite connection between the 9/11 plotters and Albania-based Islamic terrorists.[66] Further, these officials attested that KLA members had indeed been trained at al Qaeda camps in Afghanistan, but did not discuss details. Ironically, the adjoining 15-story business centers that would be seized by the Albanian government in 2002 were known as Tirana's "Twin Towers." They were being built by the Karavan Construction Company of Yassin al-Qadi, the founder and chief investor in the Muwafaq Foundation. Alleged to have laundered $10 million for bin Laden through his business interests and charities, al-Qadi was blacklisted by the U.S. Treasury in October 2001. This prompted the Albanians to expel Abdul Latif Saleh, a 45-year-old Jordanian extremist who ran al-Qadi's sugar importing firm, medical center, and construction company. In April 2007, Albanian media revealed that Saleh was part of the "first wave" of al Qaeda-connected individuals to penetrate Albania; by special decree of President Berisha, Saleh and 40 other foreign extremists received Albanian citizenships on October 21, 1992.[67] Saleh funded the Egyptian terrorist cells in Albania through al Qadi's Muwafaq and al Haramain. Osama bin Laden, U.S. officials claim, gave Saleh $600,000 for this purpose.[68]

Curiously, however, Saleh had already been arrested once before, "following a tip-off from US security services" on November 12, 1999. A Tirana newspaper claimed that the arrest was related to President Clinton's upcoming visit to Kosovo. The Jordanian was mysteriously flown by the United States "to an unknown country."[69] Where he went, and how he returned, remain unknown, but it is likely that he was released because of his affiliation with Yassin al-Qadi. The Saudi businessman, who continues to vehemently contest the U.S. government's charges, is a powerful mogul with substantial investments around the world; his clients have included the U.S. military.[70] (A source with close ties to the U.S. intelligence establishment would not confirm the scenario for this author, but conceded that "this possibility cannot be denied.") According to the U.S. Treasury, Saleh's last known address was in the United Arab Emirates.

In October 2002, the U.S. government demanded Albania shut down Al Haramain, Al-Furkan, SHRC, and the local branch of the militant Bosnian Wahhabi group, Active Islamic Youth. Another U.S. Treasury report would later attest that, despite the arrest and deportation to Egypt of Al Haramain financial officer Ahmed Ibrahim al-Naggar in 1998, two years later "a close associate of a UBL operative moved to Albania and was running an unnamed AHF subsidiary."[71] Despite these efforts, the fundamentalists had already begun to muscle in on the leadership of Albania's Islamic Community—with deadly effect. Al Haramain was reportedly behind the January 2002 murder of Sali Tivari, a senior official. Just before his murder, Tivari had told a local radical and Al Haramain Foundation (AHF) collaborator, Ermir Gjinishi, that he was determined to reduce "foreign Islamic influence" in the Albanian Muslim community. This was not what AHF wanted to hear. Since Tivari "controlled finances, personnel decisions, and donations within the Albanian Muslim community," stated a U.S. Treasury report, he wielded "significant power, enabling him to survive several attempts by extremists trained overseas to replace him or usurp his power." Although the circumstantial evidence in Tivari's murder clearly pointed to the involvement of the extremists, there was not enough evidence to prosecute Gjinishi (who was also linked with Abdul Latif Saleh) and he was released. Nevertheless, Al Haramain would not be closed until early 2003, a year after the shocking murder.[72]

In the general elections of July 3, 2005, the Nano government was defeated, and Sali Berisha was swept back into power. Albanian voters had become disillusioned with the perceived arrogance of the Socialists and once again embraced a man who had been cast as a corrupt, authoritarian villain just eight years before. Berisha promised good behavior, cooperation with the West, and amusingly, considering the character of his first administration, pledged to stamp out corruption and crime. Time will tell whether he can achieve these goals; so far, however, an element of concern for the West, preoccupied with finding a final status solution for Kosovo, has been some unusually strong nationalistic statements by Berisha cabinet members, some of whom have said Kosovo should be annexed to the motherland—thus providing more ammunition for Serbs and others who have long pointed out the ulterior motive of a "Greater Albania" behind the Kosovo independence project.

A more tangible concern has to do with the return of former SHIK chief and Islamist supporter, Bashkim Gazidede. Two reports based on European intelligence sources and published in *Defense & Foreign Affairs* reiterated claims that Gazidede was cooperating with al Qaeda—as well as with the Turkish MIT intelligence agency—while in exile. According to the intelligence sources, the MIT had hosted Gazidede in Turkey since he fled Albania in 1997, only "returning" him in December 2005 after old patron Sali Berisha had once again seized power. This report also claims that Gazidede had cooperated closely with two men, Kosovar Albanian intelligence chief and KLA man Xhavit Haliti and Abdul Latif Saleh, the Jordanian who disappeared from Albania in 2002. According to the intelligence sources cited, Saleh had "accompanied Osama bin Laden during his visits to Albania and Kosovo, via Turkey, from and to the airport of Adana and afterwards from Istanbul," and had later gone to Kosovo to develop a terrorist base there. The report also claims Haliti was involved in the January 2002 assassination of the moderate Albanian Islamic Community leader, Sali Tivari.[73]

In May 2006, a report from the Prague-based *Transitions Online* (TOL) claimed that radicals have made headway in Albania, citing a foreign-influenced Muslim group's efforts to change the statute of the Islamic Community, "to make it closer to their way of worship." Although they lost that battle, the war was still on; soon after the decision, both the head of the Albanian Islamic Community, Selim Muka, and the chairman of the government committee for religions, Ilir Kula, received death threats.[74] TOL further asserted that the fundamentalists have established "parallel structures," using nongovernmental organizations such as the Muslim Forum of Albania to further their cause.

The growth of Wahhabism in Albania was also attested in a second *Defense & Foreign Affairs* report, which claimed that the Wahhabis have illegally built 140 mosques, mostly in northern Albania and financed largely by the King Fahd Foundation of Saudi Arabia. According to the report, the "spiritual leader" of the radicals in Albania is Ulema Abul Sakir Aslam, a Pakistani who was granted asylum by the Albanian government in 1997 and who had sent 400 children to study in Saudi Arabia and Pakistan in 2005 alone. The article further points to a televised interview in which Sheikh Aslam appeared with leaders of the "Chameria" irredentist group, which seeks to annex the northwestern Greek province of

Epiros to Albania.[75] According to the report, the Sheikh raised the call to "fight against the Greek minority in Albania under the name of Islam."[76]

The ultimate goal of the Wahhabi movement, al Qaeda, and other radicals is the proliferation of Islamic governance globally. This is to be done in stages, and the specific methods differ according to the country in question. In heavily Muslim countries like Pakistan or Egypt, assassinations or coup attempts are possible and well-attested options, whereas the authority of countries with only immigrant Muslim populations, such as Britain, are being challenged by protests, nonassimilation, and attempts to convert non-Muslims. However, as is the case in Bosnia and other nominally secular, pro-Western Balkan "transition" countries with an endemic Muslim population, different methods are sometimes required.

Indeed, in Albania the Islamists have proven clever in adapting their rhetoric to the discursive norms of society, while never losing sight of the bottom line. Thus, a group like the Muslim Forum of Albania (MFA), singled out in the *Transitions Online* article, describes itself as a simple nongovernmental organization, a member of "civil society" dedicated to protecting human rights and opposing discrimination. Behind these ostensibly laudable goals, however, is a trend of gradually escalating political activity disguised as simple advocacy. Ironically, in this respect the MFA has just mimicked the behavior of the myriad of opportunistic NGOs in transition countries that seek to gain political and media influence (and inevitably, more and more money) through their apparently altruistic aims. Despite its alleged openness, however, the MFA is not open to interviews, nor does it readily reveal its sources of funding.[77]

The cleverness of such a strategy is that such "human rights" groups cannot be criticized on principle by Westerners without incurring charges of hypocrisy. However, their hidden agendas are more radical. A sense of where this is heading can be seen in the kinds of positions the MFA has taken: attacking the pope for his comments on violence in Islam, criticizing Christian groups and church building, denouncing the Danish cartoons of the Prophet Mohammad, and, most interesting of all, demanding more rights for foreign Islamists in Albania. The wealthy foreign backers of Wahhabism are well aware of the need to disguise substance with style; the declarations of the MFA are written in English as spotless as the group's stated charter. In the years ahead, it is likely that groups such as the MFA will make increasingly radical demands. As in Western Europe, liberal democracy is being regarded as a stepping-stone to something else.

Perhaps the most significant emerging trend in the case of Albania is the rise of internecine strife based on religious difference. Rallying a decade ago under the nationalist banner of "one nation, three religions," the paramilitary KLA claimed support from Muslim, Catholic, and Orthodox Albanians during its war in Kosovo. Today, while most Albanians still do feel their ethnicity strongly, religious tensions have nevertheless been growing. In October 2003, police arrested author Kastriot Myftari, charging him with inciting religious hatred against Muslims for writing that Albanian Muslims should convert to Catholicism. While the prosecutor wanted to imprison Myftari for six months for this thought crime, he was acquitted in June 2004—as a result of pressure from Western embassies in Tirana, Muslims alleged. Later, in November 2005, Muslims were further enraged when Albanian President Alfred Moisiu, speaking in England before the Oxford Union, stated that only a "shallow" sort of Islam could be found in Albania, a country whose Christian roots were much stronger.[78] The MFA and other Islamic groups in Albania heatedly accused the president of "insulting Islam."

Other, more large-scale incidents are also now occurring. In the northern, Catholic majority city of Shkodra, which borders on Montenegro, mutual provocations between Catholics and Muslims are suddenly emerging. A cross was put up in the city, and then mysteriously vandalized in January 2006. And when civic leaders decided to honor national hero Mother Teresa with a statue, three Muslim groups—the Association of Islamic Intellectuals, the Albanian Muslim Forum, and the Association of Islamic Charities—publicly protested. The MFA, which allegedly supports interfaith relations, declared that a statue of one of the world's most renowned humanitarian figures would be a "provocation" to Muslims, and that the religious situation in Shkodra was "not so calm."[79] Considering that the Association of Islamic Intellectuals was formerly headed by extremist Bashkim Gazidede and that the charities' organization is influenced strongly by foreign Islamic forces, it seems that there might have been something else behind the Muslim Forum's stated goal of safeguarding interfaith relations.

In any case, it seems that the West is finally starting to come to terms with the next generation terrorist threat in Albania. A former British MI6 agent who carried out a comprehensive computer tracking operation on Albania-based radical groups and noted their heavy usage of cryptography stated that in the summer of 2006, "MI6 doubled its presence in Tirana, as part of a general increase in their Balkan operations."[80] At the same time, Albania—usually, an exporter of immigrants—became the final destination for several prisoners released from the U.S. military base at Guantánamo Bay in Cuba. After "more than two dozen countries declined requests to take them in," Albania accepted five Chinese Uighur detainees in May 2006.[81] In November, another three Guantánamo prisoners—an Algerian, an Uzbek, and an Egyptian—also were granted freedom, of a sort, in Albania. The government's decision to provide shelter to these unfortunate Muslim captives represents a strange sort of closure for the country that was used as an experimental ground for the CIA's "extraordinary rendition" program of kidnappings back in 1995. In stating why he should not be sent home, the unnamed Egyptian detainee said that he "feared being tortured because he had been held at Guantánamo."[82]

CHAPTER 3

A Plain of Black Beards?

On November 28, 2006, angry Albanian protesters in Kosovo's capital, Pristina, clashed with police and hurled red paint at the buildings housing the UN Mission in Kosovo (UNMIK) offices. Led by an activist group called Vetevendosje ("Self-Determination"), the protest was the most serious of several that had been held periodically for over a year against the UN interim government by Albanians demanding immediate independence and no negotiations with Serbia. Police had to use tear gas to disperse the 3,000-strong mob, which breached concrete barricades leading to the building.[1] A day earlier, UN authorities had disclosed that "credible threats" against the leaders of the UN mission had been made by unknown parties.[2] The international administration that had been greeted with cheers when it took the place of the Yugoslav government of Slobodan Milosevic in July 1999 had, predictably enough, worn out its welcome with the locals.

Tensions over Kosovo's unresolved final status continued to build over the coming months, with UN-mediated negotiations between the Belgrade government and Kosovo Albanian leadership having failed, predictably enough, to bring the rival sides any closer to an agreement. The Self-Determination protesters came out in force again in the streets of Pristina, on February 10, 2007, forcing a flurry of official resignations after two protesters died at the hands of police. The "compromise package" devised by UN Special Negotiator Martti Ahtisaari, stipulating Kosovo's independence in everything but name, was unsatisfactory to both Serbs and Albanians. As winter turned into spring, ominous reports of black-uniformed Albanian paramilitaries returning to action in rural

Kosovo set the stage for what might be a renewed battle for control of the province—with NATO peace-keepers and UN officials directly in the line of fire.

Ever since NATO's 1999 intervention, the issue of Kosovo has been presented mainly along ethnic and national lines. This bitterly contested land, a historical province of Serbia but over 90 percent settled by Albanians, is claimed by both peoples, who have long argued for their inherent rights to ownership. The Western media, for its part, has tended to support the conventional wisdom of Western governments—that NATO's intervention to dislodge government forces under Slobodan Milosevic was justified in order to stop human rights violations. Yet ironically, during the UNMIK and NATO occupation which followed that bombing, some of the worst human rights violations in modern European history have been carried out, as Albanian extremists continue to ethnically cleanse the province's minority Serb, Roma, Croat, and Slavic Muslim populations. To date, they have almost succeeded: over 200,000 Serbs alone have been driven from Kosovo since 1999. According to the estimates of an experienced high official from the International Organization for Migration (IOM) in Kosovo, the remaining 150,000 Serbs "will all be gone after ten years."[3]

While most would agree that this is a tragic situation, the connections that nationalist-motivated ethnic cleansing have with Islamic terrorism, by intent and by default, are somewhat less clear. They have been obscured further by the Serbian lobby's tendency to sensationalize and distort the relationship between Kosovo Albanians and Islamic extremism, thereby damaging their own case. Yet amidst all the acrimony, one simple and fundamental fact seems to have been forgotten: that is, that the end of the national question in Kosovo is the beginning of the religious one.

Kosovo Albanians trace their struggle for independence back to the "League of Prizren," a collection of irredentist intellectuals and provocateurs gathered in the eponymous southwestern Kosovo town in 1878. Despite the opportunism they have shown in siding at various times with the Turks, the Austro-Hungarian Empire, Mussolini, Hitler, and, most recently, NATO, the national narrative has it that hostile outside powers have always been to blame for the Kosovo Albanians' chronic failure to achieve independence. Yet with the practical liquidation of the Serbs and the imminent replacement of the post-Yugoslav UNMIK regime with some sort of independence, Kosovo's Albanians are for the first time being stripped of that external threat which has historically caused them to rally around their national identity. Without any threats, real or perceived, to their ethnic cohesion and nationhood, Kosovo Albanians will soon suffer two forms of internal conflict: one, the struggle for political and economic control between the various clans and mafia groups; and two, challenges for spiritual and social control from religious groups (most Kosovo Albanians are Muslims, though there is a notable Catholic population as well). Given the present rise of religion and especially Islam around the world, this phenomenon is inevitable; in fact, it is already being witnessed.

The story of how foreign Islamic extremists were able to fill in the cracks of Kosovar society starts with the 1999 war which, as was discussed in Chapter 2, involved the participation of mujahedin in the Kosovo Liberation Army. However, it was only after the war that the Islamists began to really make inroads. The methods were the same as in Bosnia: through charities, banks, nongovernmental organizations, and religious societies. Saudi Arabia, Kuwait, the Emirates, and other states began major construction of mosques, staffing them with radical preachers. At the same time, hundreds of young Albanians were sent to universities in the Islamic world, creating a new generation of trained and educated imams to spread the Wahhabi doctrine back in Kosovo.

No matter how new and strange radical Islam might have seemed to the Albanians, their country hardly seemed new or strange for the foreign Islamist proselytizers. For them, Kosovo simply represented the spot on the map to be filled in between Albania and Bosnia—both of which had been successfully penetrated almost a decade earlier. The massive social dislocation beginning in June 1999, when the Serbs were pushed out and a wave of Albanian immigrants from northern Albania flooded into Kosovo, created a chaotic and fluid situation that the new international administration could not fully comprehend or control. Strangers in a strange land, the UNMIK authorities quickly came to an understanding with the KLA leadership. According to international police sources, after the bombing U.S. Military Police removed the old Yugoslav police dossiers compiled on Albanian criminals and paramilitaries, and handed them over to the KLA's leaders. Evidence about the most dangerous men in Kosovo was thus destroyed, but not before the KLA could assassinate Albanian police informers and other "Yugoslav loyalists" named in the files. The KLA, and its criminal partners, it was tacitly understood, would not be touched, and in exchange the "internationals" (as the UN and NATO officials came to be called) could enjoy the spoils of peace—everything from mafia-supplied prostitutes to multimillion dollar embezzlement on privatization deals and budget "discrepancies."

Caught up in the pleasures of what became known as a "paradise mission," the internationals paid little attention when "a few funny-looking foreign Muslims," as one European official wryly notes, busily set up shop. From the beginning, Islamic charities and cultural associations worked to develop Wahhabi influence in Kosovo. These organizations were also used by states such as Iran, Saudi Arabia, and Turkey to provide covers for their intelligence operatives. At the same time, military intelligence agents from Pakistan, Egypt, the United Arab Emirates, and others were embedded within military detachments pledged to the NATO-led Kosovo Force (KFOR) mission that was supposed to guarantee stability. Yet contingents from Islamic states in KFOR did other things besides keeping the peace in Kosovo.

Important details on Islamist subversion in Kosovo have emerged from the testimony of a former security officer for the Organization for Security and Co-operation in Europe (OSCE), Thomas Gambill, a former Marine and one of the few willing to speak openly about the issue. He had worked for four years in Saudi Arabia, and thereafter in Kosovo, overseeing security for OSCE personnel in the southeastern region of Gnjilane, where the American military's enormous Camp Bondsteel was built. Gambill worked in Kosovo from October 1999 until May 2004; his contract with the OSCE was not renewed, he suspects, because he "would not shut up" about the growing threat from radical Islam. Indeed, sympathetic colleagues had warned Gambill that the OSCE and UNMIK authorities would get rid of him if he kept speaking out about the Islamists, because of their overriding desire to sweep everything under the rug.

The former security officer recalls specific incidents that revealed the efforts of Islamic governments and charities to penetrate Kosovo. His testimony complements stories from numerous other sources, both open and covert, which cumulatively tell a story of how a population with no history of Islamic fundamentalism could be seriously affected by foreign Muslim powers in only a few years—while the Western-installed UN government chronically looked the other way. Initially, however, complacency seemed tolerable. "The [Albanian] mafia leaders had scared the hell out of the imams, warning them that they would be killed if they called for any attacks against the international forces, or for any general radicalization of the Muslim population," Gambill attests. While this unwritten law applied to local Albanian religious extremists—of which there were not yet many, in any case—the mafia had less influence over the foreign Islamists, who had their own funding sources and powerful backers. As early as fall 1999, says Gambill, reliable Albanian sources were providing solid information that "the Saudis were increasing in strength, through new NGOs. They were playing on nationalism, urging the poorer people to 'run out the KFOR like you did the Serbs!' They also handed out leaflets with anti-American slogans, which the pro-American Albanians ignored...the main actor, we were told, was the Saudi Red Crescent Society, which handed out food, clothing, supplies and—religion—the same pattern as in Bosnia."[4]

At the same time, money for jihad continued to flow into Kosovo, courtesy of the KLA's previous Islamic sponsor in Britain, Sheikh Omar Bakri Mohammad, the head of bin Laden's International Islamic Front and founder of the Al-Muhajiroun brigade whose participation had been, at the very least, tolerated by British intelligence during the 1998–1999 war. Yet while NATO had given the KLA orders to pack it up and put down their weapons, someone had forgotten to tell Sheikh Mohammad that the war was over. In April 2000, London's *Sunday Telegraph* reported that the KLA's "divinely inspired" struggle against the Serbs was being extended through "fundraising events...being held by mosques and internet groups" in Britain, subsidized partially by a wave of prescription fraud among poor British Muslims exploiting the National Health Service.[5] Britain's socialized health care allowed them to obtain expensive drugs for next to nothing, and then sell them "on the black market to raise funds for Jihad struggles including the one in Kosovo." Further, according to the newspaper, "many of the drugs are shipped direct to frontline fighting units." Sheikh Mohammad stated that "we are continuing to support the fighters in Kosovo...because we believe the KLA should rearm." Clearly, the Islamists had a different vision for Kosovo than the West when it launched a NATO intervention ostensibly for humanitarian reasons.

Meanwhile, Arab-directed Muslim extremists were launching small terrorist attacks against Kosovo's few Albanian Protestant Christians. A Protestant church was attacked by "masked Islamic militants" on April 29, 2000; according to a contemporary report, the thugs "bound several members, stole equipment and money, and daubed slogans on the door and walls, while also threatening a fourteen-year-old boy to convert to Islam at gunpoint." It was the third such attack against the church within a year. Fanatics loyal to Osama bin Laden were responsible, according to the pastor, who said he had received numerous anonymous phone calls threatening "to kill us all and burn this church down." He added that an Islamist publication had begun printing hate-filled articles about Christianity.[6]

Indeed, from early on in the Kosovo occupation, foreign Islamists were seeking control of propaganda channels, something that left local Albanians suspicious. "In May 2000 I conducted a short interview with the [Albanian] announcer on a local radio station," attests Tom Gambill. "On or around May 12, four KFOR soldiers from the United Arab Emirates came seeking a spot on the KFOR radio hour to talk about religion and stated that it would be good if the announcer would cooperate. The announcer did not accept, however. The four soldiers stated that Osama bin Laden was a good man and a man of God. And so an official NATO-led Arab military detachment was thus trying to broadcast al Qaeda viewpoints to Muslims in Kosovo."

First and foremost, however, the Arab missionaries utilized more tangible forms of propagandizing. The Saudi Joint Relief Committee for the People of Kosovo and Chechnya (SJRCKC), the primary sponsor of Wahhabism in Kosovo, took the lead in not only handing out humanitarian aid but in building mosques. There was certainly work to be done, as many mosques had been destroyed during the 1999 war by Serb paramilitaries. Yet the SJRCKC's unique methods raised suspicions. According to a former German soldier deployed to western Kosovo at the time, "In summer 2000, I witnessed Saudi charities build a huge mosque in the village of Landovica on the Prizren-Djakovica road. It also had two subterranean levels—and they weren't for parking." The soldier added that ironically, "while the villagers desperately needed a new water supply system from the 'humanitarian' organization, instead they got this mosque."

Indeed, observers noted that the Wahhabis' aid always came with conditions. Tom Gambill recalls how an Islamic charity visited another Kosovo village, Dugagjini, offering to pay for the reconstruction of homes, hospitals, and schools, "but only if a mosque was built in advance in each village." The same story was repeated innumerable times elsewhere in Kosovo, prompting both local Albanians and international officials to suspect that "humanitarian" donors had other ambitions. In Dugagjini, says Gambill, "the Albanians grumbled, 'how could UNMIK allow this to happen?' It was clear that their real needs were not being met by the Saudis, and this irritated them."

However, with the mosque-building project itself, the Wahhabis not only irritated but actually outraged their Albanian coreligionists. In August 2000, the Saudis sent construction workers armed with official permits to the western Kosovo town of Djakovica, where they bulldozed parts of an Ottoman library and Koranic school dating back to the sixteenth century. The Wahhabis had little tolerance for the traditional aesthetics of Ottoman Islam. To be "authentic" places of worship, as a contemporary article put it, mosques should be "white, boxy structures devoid of detail." Predictably, NATO troops in the area kept out of it, allowing the Saudis to destroy the centuries-old Ottoman structures.[7]

Arab charities also engaged in the wanton destruction of gravestones, mausoleums, and, especially, shrines devoted to Kosovo's storied Sufi order of Islam. For Sunni Wahhabi purists, this Shiite group is blasphemous and such objects are idolatrous—symbolizing violations of the prophet's injunction against graven images. Almost a year earlier, in October 1999, visiting Harvard University Fine Arts librarian Andras Riedlmayer had observed charity workers from the United Arab Emirates ordering local Albanians in the village of Vushtrri "to sledgehammer the graves of their ancestors, completely clearing two historic graveyards next to the Gazi Ali Beg and Karamanli mosques of more than 100 gravestones dating back to the 15th century. Only the grave marker of Gazi Ali Beg himself remained, as the locals refused to allow that one to be smashed." According to Riedlmayer, the United Arab Emirates (UAE) charity pledged to rebuild the village's damaged mosques "twice as big and twice as Islamic," but only if they were allowed to remove the allegedly idolatrous gravestones. He added that "the agency, the largest aid organization in the town, also made an implicit threat to withhold humanitarian aid if the donors' request was ignored."[8]

The danger of radical Islam taking root in Kosovo schools was noted early on by other international experts. In September 2000, an advisor on religious affairs with the OSCE, Andreas Szolgyemy, noted the "tremendous interest among the young" in Islam. The Hungarian expert showed a prescient awareness of the motives of Kosovo Muslim leaders: "If they want to teach the Wahhabi ideas, which is what I'm afraid they want to do, I don't think it will be so good," said Szolgyemy. "The Wahhabis are not so tolerant...They forbid, for example, mixed marriages. They treat women as second-rank citizens. They don't like dancing, the cinema, or television."[9]

Unsurprisingly, with such methods and tastes the Wahhabis won themselves few friends among the local Albanian Muslim population. It was clear from early on that, as was happening at around the same time in Bosnia, the radical Islamists' real targets were not Christians, but Muslims. Less than a year after NATO had saved the Albanians from the Serbs, a new aggressor was appearing. The chauvinistic and patronizing behavior of the Saudis even provoked the leader of the Kosovo Islamic Community, Rexhep Boja, to heatedly proclaim, "Albanians have been Muslims for more than 500 years and they do not need outsiders

[Arabs] to tell them what is the proper way to practice Islam."[10] However, within a few years, as it became clear the Arabs were not planning to go away, Boja would become much more open to Arab participation.

Yet even despite such early Wahhabi antagonisms, local Albanian Muslim leaders were by no means despondent over the sudden arrival of so much money for the development of religion. As in Bosnia, the Arabs began to buy influence. In January 2000 the Imam of Mitrovica, Rexhep Lushta, thanked Morocco's royal family for their assistance, and "called on the Muslim world to build more mosques in Kosovo to consolidate Islam in the Balkans." Like other Arab governments, the Moroccans had funded Kosovo Albanian pilgrims visiting Saudi holy sites, through a special program called the Moroccan National Committee of Support to Kosovo and headed by Princess Lalla Meriem, sister of Moroccan King Mohammad VI.[11]

At the same time that the Wahhabis started building hundreds of mosques, existing mujahedin networks in Albania and Bosnia also sought to capitalize on the new opportunity in Kosovo, where the international authorities were proving both lenient and unaccountable. The mixed nationalities of the UNMIK civil administration created a confused chain of command, with officials of wildly differing levels of education and experience, while some from countries like Nigeria, Pakistan, Sudan, and other Muslim states actively assisted the Islamists. Further, on all fronts, the Kosovo border was not just a sieve—it was a ripped sieve. The unwillingness or inability of the UN administration to police Kosovo's borders soon allowed ex-KLA elements to wage war in neighboring Macedonia, beginning in late January 2001. By that time charities linked with al Qaeda in Kosovo were already in touch with others in Albania, Bosnia, and beyond. The result of the porous borders and the new logistical infrastructure meant that Kosovo became an ideal terrorist transfer zone. After all, the local mafia had only ordered the Islamists to not ruin their "business" by attacking internationals. They had not outlawed sanctuary.

Kosovar Albanians were thankful to the United States for saving them from Milosevic. Yet this was not of interest to the foreign Islamists. In any case, the terrorists and their sponsors required not a sea of adulating masses, but merely channels of support from a few like-minded fanatics willing to provide lines of communication, safe houses, space to operate unimpeded, as well as access to weapons, money, and "legitimate cover" as employees of aid agencies. And this was eminently possible in Kosovo. The war-ravaged province was poor, had always been severely underdeveloped, and was thus soon infested with wealthy Arab charities. Pristina became the second most important hub for moving Arab money to charities and extremist groups in Kosovo, Macedonia, and the Sandzak border region of Serbia to the north. Meanwhile the dysfunctional UN mission was concerned only with safeguarding its interests. So, at precisely the moment when the Bosnian and Albanian governments were increasingly pressuring known Islamic radicals to leave their country, Kosovo materialized as a useful escape hatch.

However, Kosovo's international overseers would soon be distracted by events unfolding in Macedonia to the south, where Albanian paramilitaries organized and supplied from inside Kosovo were waging war against the government. Emboldened by their victory over the Serbs in Kosovo, irredentists sought to take the next step towards realizing the dreams of the 1878 Prizren League—for an "ethnic Albania," comprising Albanian-populated portions of six Balkan countries. Indeed, as Ali Ahmeti, the chief of the Albanians' so-called National Liberation Army (NLA), told a Western journalist in March 2001, "our aim is solely to remove [Macedonian] Slav forces from territory which is historically Albanian."[12] Long after the conflict, one of Ahmeti's former commanders would state, "like all wars, ours was for territory—not because of some 'human rights' problem!"[13] Nevertheless, skilled Albanian propagandists were able to portray the war as a Kosovo redux—another struggle for human rights waged by an oppressed people—though its ultimate causes remain murky.[14]

The war could not have happened to a less deserving country. During the 1999 NATO bombing campaign, little Macedonia had taken in some 400,000 Kosovo Albanian refugees—roughly a quarter of the country's population of 2 million. Around the same number of ethnic Albanians already lived in Macedonia, chiefly concentrated in the northern and western areas of the country, in the regions of Kumanovo, Tetovo, Gostivar, Debar, and Struga. Further, Albanian political parties had enjoyed major roles in every government since Macedonia's independence from Yugoslavia in late 1991. Nevertheless, mutual provocations and mistrust continued to fester between the majority Macedonian and minority Albanian populations, though on a much lower level than in Kosovo. Still, there was no special urgency for Albanians to go to war in early 2001, when Macedonia was coming off a year of unprecedented economic growth and when candidacy for European Union membership was foreseeable in the not too distant future.

The NLA's leadership included KLA veterans from Kosovo, Macedonia, and the Albanian diaspora. Ali Ahmeti and his uncle, Fazli Veliu, originally from the western Macedonia village of Zajas, were both longtime agitators and among the original founders of the KLA in Kosovo. As with that organization, the NLA enjoyed significant material support from the Albanian diaspora and, according to numerous media reports, from mafia drug profits. An alleged "tax" placed on Albanian families in Macedonia by the rebel group—demanding either a son for the paramilitaries or a large sum of money instead—served to press-gang individuals into a war of "national liberation" for which there was no real and urgent justification. Despite the façade of a struggle being mounted by and for Macedonia's Albanians, many commanders and foot soldiers were actually KLA veterans from Kosovo.

At the beginning of the conflict, the West seemed to be firmly behind the Macedonian government. In March 2001, the *Washington Post* reported that "U.S. Army soldiers and a U.S. Special Forces unit in Kosovo forced the [Albanian] fighters from the village, shooting and wounding one guerrilla who refused to lay down his weapon."[15] In early May, then-NATO Secretary-General George Robertson even called the NLA "a bunch of murderous thugs whose objective is to destroy a democratic Macedonia and who are using civilians as human shields [to provoke] another Balkan bloodbath."[16] However, this tough line quickly softened. The NLA became more adept at public relations, utilizing Albanian-American lobby groups, and the Macedonian army failed to quickly put down the uprising. Under increasing pressure, a badly divided Macedonian government was forced to begin peace negotiations, not with the rebels themselves, but with the representatives of the major Macedonian and Albanian parties and the international community. A treaty was signed on August 13, 2001, named the "Ohrid Agreement" after the placid lakeside tourist town where the talks were held.[17] In exchange for more Albanian language rights and a national decentralization-of-power package, the NLA stopped fighting. The Macedonian army, meanwhile, was instructed to pull out of strategic areas, and yet another NATO peacekeeping force moved into yet another beleaguered Balkan country.

While they were minor participants in an overwhelmingly nationalistic struggle, foreign mujahedin did, indeed, assist the Albanian rebels. However, as had the KLA in Kosovo, the NLA leadership tried—at least officially—to keep foreign fighters out. Yet news of oppressed Muslims naturally aroused the interest of freelance jihadis, while Arab charity organizations saw in civil chaos and bloodshed the opportunity to penetrate a new "market." At the time, already existing charities assisted the NLA from Kosovo to the north. On August 9, 2001, CNN disclosed that three Iranians had been arrested for "running arms to rebels fighting in Macedonia." Ostensibly employees of an Islamic charity in Kosovo, the Iranians had been apprehended near the Macedonian border by British KFOR soldiers almost three weeks before. However, an unnamed U.S. official told CNN that the terrorists were "expected to be released shortly." Iranian diplomats at the UN would claim credit for smoothing over the situation.[18]

While the NLA sought to keep the fundamentalists out, this did not stop them from soliciting the Islamic world for donations. One unpublished videotape created by the NLA in May 2001 was, according to Macedonian intelligence sources, created to appeal to al Qaeda and other Islamist donors. The video, shot in the Kumanovo-area villages under NLA control, shows NLA bunkers, uniformed rebels in procession, scenes of Macedonian army shelling, and emotive images of Albanian women wailing over a fallen soldier, as well as NLA medics (somehow equipped with the latest Western medical supplies) performing surgery on a wounded fighter's bloodied leg. Aside from the propaganda value of such images, analysts pointed to a curious segment near the end in which armed NLA fighters accompany a mock charge with shouts of "Allah Akbar!" Obviously, the religious zeal was staged, but "they needed to show Osama, or whoever, that they were waging jihad in order to keep the money coming."[19] According to the *Washington Times,* al Qaeda had earmarked over $6 million to the NLA's cause.[20] *The Scotsman* added later that fighters "from a number of Arab states" had fought for the Albanian rebels.[21]

Some of these fighters were, according to the Macedonian government, organized into a special brigade especially active in the Kumanovo area, the scene of some of the fiercest fighting of the war. Remote and insular Albanian-populated villages such as Lipkovo, Matejce, and Slupcane became flash points by early May, when a so-called "Free Zone" was briefly established by the NLA. The terrified Macedonian and Serbian residents of these villages, mostly elderly people, were forced to flee south to the city of Kumanovo. Some stated afterwards that long-bearded, non-Albanian foreign fighters had tortured them. War veterans such as the former chief of the government's Rapid Reaction Force, Goran Stojkov, claim that NATO was aware of mujahedin training camps nearby, in the Lipkovo wilderness.[22]

Throughout the fighting, jihadis were also penetrating Macedonia from the other, western front in Tetovo and reportedly had connections with Kosovo Albanian officials such as Daut Haradinaj, chief of general staff of the Kosovo Protection Corps (KPC) and brother of ex-KLA leader Ramush Haradinaj, according to other Macedonian military sources. On April 28, 2001, a Macedonian Army patrol of nine soldiers was ambushed and massacred near the Tetovo-area village of Vejce. The only survivor attested that mujahedin "with long beards and knives ...conducted the massacre to its gruesome end, killing only one person by shooting, and cut to pieces or burned alive the rest."[23] An NLA commander confirmed this to Canadian war reporter Scott Taylor, stating that Vejce could "only have been committed by the foreigners...because Albanians do not cut up bodies." This commander and other NLA fighters had fought in Chechnya and Bosnia, and attested the presence of mujahedin in Macedonia.[24]

Tasked with raising war funds from Muslims in Europe was a well-traveled, 50-year-old Albanian imam, Jakup Asipi, who hailed from the capital of the so-called "free zone," muddy Slupcane. Beloved by Albanians as a fatherly moral authority, and feared by Macedonians who considered him a radical Islamist, Asipi had received clerical training in Egypt and developed strong contacts with Albanian Islamic communities in Europe, especially in Switzerland and in German cities such as Leverkusen. While the Macedonian media soon linked Asipi with the mujahedin, his friends and family would later deny that he had anything to do with Islamic fundamentalism, but was rather a nationalist who also happened to be a very devout Muslim. On January 7, 2006, Asipi, then head of the Kumanovo Islamic Community and candidate for the national leadership, died in a tragic car accident. Some 15,000 Albanians from around Europe, among them both NLA/KLA leaders and Islamic clerics, attended the funeral, held at a new NLA war memorial center above Slupcane.

Out of nowhere, the terrorist attacks of 9/11 had an immediate and sobering impact on Macedonia's volatile peace. There was little talk of "liberation armies," at least not for the moment. The NLA had been incredibly lucky to get its window of opportunity during the spring and summer of 2001; after the attacks on America, Western support for another Balkan guerrilla uprising would have been nonexistent. While most Kosovo Albanians were saddened at

America's tragedy, an eye-opening incident soon occurred, one which showed the true colors of their Islamic benefactors: At a candlelight vigil in the western town of Pec, a group of young, bearded Islamists rushed in, blew out the candles, and told the mourners to go home; this led to a fight "in which the men with beards beat up the people who were expressing sympathy for the victims of the New York attacks."[25]

Everywhere in Kosovo, and especially in Pristina, the change of atmosphere could be felt, especially between the Muslim and non-Muslim UNMIK and KFOR contingents. One murky event, still unreported, is perhaps most surprising: the arrival of six Albanian-American fundamentalists in Skenderaj in the weeks before 9/11. According to Tom Gambill, who recounts a joint security meeting in the town on September 21, the men had "spread anti-American slogans and stated, one week before 9/11, that the US would soon be attacked." Claiming to instruct the youth about Islam, the Albanian-Americans slept in mosques—until their anti-American vitriol finally caused a local imam to expel them. According to Gambill, the radicals were "linked to a wealthy Mafioso in Mitrovica"—a shock admission linking Islamic radicals and the Albanian mafia. More shocking, however, was the utter disinterest with which UN authorities greeted this apparent "smoking gun" case. While investigators elsewhere were racing furiously to track down anyone and everyone with foreknowledge of the 9/11 attacks, the CivPol officer who identified the agitators, according to Gambill, "was frustrated that no one above him [in rank] was interested, and no one above him really pushed [for this investigation]...there was little said about it—and no follow-up."

However, in the days after 9/11, says Gambill, nine suspected fundamentalists associated with radical Islamic movements were arrested and questioned by CivPol (UN Civil Police). As everywhere else, charities in Kosovo were raided, documents seized, and suspicious elements rounded up. On December 15, 2001, the BBC reported that one of those raided, the Chicago-based Global Relief Foundation, was "suspected of supporting worldwide terrorist activities and is allegedly involved in planning attacks against targets in the US and Europe." The police raids, on offices in Pristina and the western Kosovo town of Djakovica, came after international authorities received "credible intelligence information." The GRF would later be prosecuted by the U.S. Government. Curiously, however, the biggest and most dangerous charities were left untouched. The former OSCE security officer learned from Italian military intelligence and other security sources that terror-linked charities operating under the Saudi charity umbrella group, the SJRCKC, continued to move millions of dollars openly through Kosovo's banks. "The Al Waqf Al Islami charity was receiving approximately $100,000 per month in its account at MEB bank in Pristina," he states. "The outfit was led by a Saudi director Madgi Osmand, and representatives Majdi Gabbab and Agala Alghamdi, as well as a Sudanese cashier named Abel Azim Khider."

The intelligence information suggested that Al Waqf Al Islami had developed a banking network with the Western-funded Micro Enterprise Bank branch in Sarajevo, Fefad Bank in Albania, and Nova Ljubljanska Bank in Slovenia, "to launder money and link with the other Saudi organizations in those locations." According to Gambill, this and other SJRCKC-affiliated charities liaised with a local Albanian one, the Mother Teresa Society, which regularly sent lists of Albanian Muslim families prepared to become "stricter Muslims" in exchange for receiving $300–500 per month—a windfall in a province crippled by an unemployment rate of over 60 percent.[26]

Other charities under control of the Saudi Committee included the Saudi Red Crescent Society (SRCS) and known terrorist affiliates from the Bosnian war, such as the Islamic Youth Organization, the IIRO, and Al Haramain. In overall control of the committee's operations in Kosovo was one Wael H. Jelaidan. According to Gambill's security sources at the time, Jelaidan "had ties with Bin Laden." However, in the summer of 2006, the Turkish government would exonerate both Jelaidan and the noted sponsor of radical Islam in Albania, Yassin al-Qadi. Political factors were behind the Turkish decision, and al-Qadi remained on the U.S. blacklist.

After 9/11, the Saudi charity organizations not only became more secretive: they also became more hostile, at times showing classic signs of organized intelligence activity. According to Gambill, who a year earlier had personally witnessed soldiers from the United Arab Emirates filming the U.S. military base, Camp Bondsteel, by the fall of 2001 the SJRCKC had begun conducting "aggressive surveillance of US personnel and property...[SRCS] ambulances were thought to be transporting weapons and explosives—they had never been seen transporting sick or injured locals."

However, despite these abundant reasons for concern, UNMIK signed a memorandum of understanding on February 5, 2002, with the Al Haramain Foundation, which was allegedly supporting refugees from Macedonia in the southeastern Kosovo municipality of Kacanik. Yet again the behavior displayed by Al Haramain officials struck Gambill and other international officials as odd. "The [Al Haramain] regional Director, a Mr. Abdul Aziz Al-Said, was very uncooperative with the local Head of the UNHCR," he states. "Due to the nature of the MOU, Al Said should have been working closely with him, I was told."

Less than a month after the agreement was signed, on March 11, 2002, the U.S. Treasury officially blocked the accounts of Al Haramain's Somalia and Bosnia and Hercegovina branches. Yet the Kosovo branch was left untouched. Al Haramain had, back in 1999, run something called the Kosovo Relief Fund out of its Ashland, Oregon, headquarters, back in the days when NATO and the Islamists were fighting for the same goal—expulsion of the Serbs from Kosovo. At that time, the known terrorist and al-Qadi's "business partner," Abdul Latif Saleh, who was later mysteriously removed from Albania, questioned, and released by the CIA, was serving as charge de affaires at the Saudi embassy in Tirana. Saleh headed the Kosovo "relief" efforts through Al Haramain, not only helping the mujahedin volunteers but ensuring that Saudi groups "got to" incoming Albanian refugees before the rival Jewish and Christian organizations. Several months later, these refugees returning to Kosovo brought back stories of religious indoctrination at Saudi refugee camps.

One month before UNMIK had signed on the dotted line with Al Haramain, a Russian KFOR military patrol had detained 30 Albanians near the southwestern Kosovo town of Prizren, suspected to be members of Islamic Jihad, according to a Russian military spokesman.[27] Meanwhile, continuing tensions in Macedonia sparked concerns that Pakistani, Jordanian, Bosnian, and other Muslim NLA veterans were intent on causing more trouble. In March, *The Scotsman* quoted a European security official who revealed that "these fighters are those who have been least amenable to the idea of disarming...they want to keep on fighting, whether it's the Macedonian government or western embassies who may be the target."[28] Nonetheless, attention soon turned from the mujahedin to the crisis within Macedonia's Albanian political parties, which engaged in internecine fighting during the inevitable postwar struggle for power.

The charged atmosphere and renewed antiterrorist activities during 2002 temporarily impeded the Islamists in Kosovo. However, by November 2002—when the U.S. war plan for Iraq was becoming more definite—both local Albanians and UN officials had noticed that the stubborn Wahhabi proselytizers were making a comeback. It was also feared that they might retaliate unpredictably should the Bush administration invade Iraq. In March 2003, when the U.S. invasion to topple Saddam Hussein unfolded, UNMIK and NATO thus went on heightened alert. All regional UNMIK police commanders, as well as the mostly Albanian Kosovo Police Service, were warned about potential retaliatory suicide bombings in Kosovo. According to the Serbian news agency Tanjug, "the information on suicide-bombers was obtained from the US office in Pristina, a fax sent to regional commanders said, and pointed out that the persons involved in these possible attacks were members of a certain Islamic non-government organization."[29]

The Saudis were, indeed, bringing more than humanitarian aid to such impoverished Kosovo backwaters. According to Tom Gambill, by March 20, 2003, a stream of police reports were attesting to Wahhabi unrest in the villages of Malisevo, Dobercane, Urosevac, Mogila, and Velekince; some of these remain major centers of radical Islam. Attests Gambill, "The group in Malisevo was reportedly recruiting for fighters in Iraq about four weeks before [the U.S. invasion began]." At the same time, however, the UNMIK authorities were not catching everything; according to Gambill, some 12 Chechens arrived via a Turkish Airlines flight into Pristina Airport, "allowed to pass through, unchecked or unimpeded. The report was investigated after the event was learned by a professional military unit." Nevertheless, UNMIK's failure to develop an effective border control mechanism left Kosovo open to all comers.

Steadily losing popularity amongst the Albanians, who viewed it as an occupier rather than a liberator, UNMIK in 2003 was challenged by the so-called

"Albanian National Army" (ANA or AKSH in Albanian), which conducted terrorist attacks against Serbian enclaves and internationals in Kosovo. The shadowy group, composed of ex-KLA malcontents, was reportedly led from Tirana by two nationalists, Gafur Adili and Idajet Beqiri, who claimed to enjoy the support of generals within the Albanian military, though this could not be confirmed. At that time, the Kosovo Protection Corps (KPC, also known as the TMK for its Albanian name, Trupat Mbrojtëse të Kosovës), a civil defense unit created out of the remnants of the KLA, was headed by the Albanian Agim Ceku, a former general in the Croat army and suspected war criminal who later became Kosovo prime minister in 2006. Embarrassingly for Ceku, two of his KPC men were involved in an ANA bridge bombing attempt on April 12, 2003, near the northern Kosovo town of Zvecin. For the stated goal of making Kosovo a multiethnic society based on rule of law, having members of the civil police moonlighting as terrorists was not auspicious.

Five days after the failed bridge bombing, then-UNMIK chief Michael Steiner branded the ANA a terrorist organization, irritating hardcore nationalists who had increasingly begun to see the UN/NATO occupying government as a new oppressor, rather than as the liberating force it initially was depicted as being. This sentiment of estrangement was not felt just by a few hotheads, however. Along with the minority Serbs, who blasted the UN for failing to protect them from continuing Albanian attacks, the majority Albanian population was losing patience with UNMIK. The Western-led government was perceived as arrogant, unaccountable, and ostentatious in its conspicuous displays of wealth—almost a provocation in a country stricken by poverty and unemployment. Seeing wealthy internationals wining and dining their womenfolk, while they themselves had no jobs and no prospects, understandably made young Albanian men resentful.

A further reason for local disgruntlement was UNMIK's inability to deal with important issues such as property ownership, due to the unresolved question of who owned Kosovo. UN Resolution 1244, which was negotiated to end the 1999 NATO bombing, had decreed that Kosovo was still a part of Yugoslavia, though everyone knew Belgrade would never control it again. Nevertheless, the legal limbo over Kosovo's status prevented UNMIK from enacting key reforms and certainly contributed to the province's economic torpor. The Albanians thus had good reason to dislike the UN presence; however, their political leaders also knew that keeping UNMIK rule was essential for propping up the service industries. The UN also represented that symbolic scapegoat to replace the Serbs in Albanian politicians' endless laments over statehood withheld. It was clear that tensions were rising fast and that a violent reaction was looming against both the internationals and the minority Serbs, whose determination to remain and share power in Kosovo was regarded by Albanians as an anchor dragging down their own ambitions and futures.

As 2003 lurched into 2004, UN officials received heightened intelligence indicating that a major incident was on the way. Steiner's weak successor, Harri Holkeri, had infuriated Agim Ceku on December 3 by ordering the suspension of two

KPC generals, the former KLA leaders Nuredin Lushtaku and Rrahman Rama over the April bridge bombing debacle. Ceku darkly intoned that "this decision is unacceptable for us."[30] While the UNMIK top brass continued to put on a brave face and describe attacks against Serbs and other minorities as "isolated incidents" some, such as Tom Gambill, sought to preempt organized violence from disgruntled Albanian militants. "Other internationals laughed at Tom when he decided to put up concrete barriers in front of OSCE buildings," recalls a former colleague, UNMIK Field Coordinator for Protection of Minorities Michael Stephen Harrison. "They thought he was crazy. But the March riots proved that he was right."[31]

Indeed, from March 17–19, 2004, some 50,000 Albanians rioted throughout Kosovo, pillaging and burning Serbian enclaves as well as international offices and vehicles. The riots occurred in the aftermath of two fatal events. First, on March 15, a Serbian teenager was shot in cold blood by an Albanian drive-by shooter, leading to road blocks by protesting Serbs. Soon after, three Albanian boys drowned in northern Kosovo's River Ibar. Although the international authorities urged for a thorough investigation, the deaths were immediately blamed on Serbs. The news spread like wildfire, and soon the torching, looting, and gunfire began. All in all, over 1,000 people would be injured, and another 3,500 people displaced. Hundreds of Serbian homes were destroyed, and 30 churches torched or vandalized. An "agreed" number of 19 individuals died, including Albanians, Serbs, and internationals; however, the number was more likely over 30 dead.[32]

While some in the Western media tried to explain the riots as a spontaneous show of indignation and pent-up fury, UN officials privately described them as the "Kristallnacht" of the Kosovo Serbs.[33] "Let's be realistic," said then-UNMIK regional media officer in Mitrovica Tracy Becker, "it's impossible to have Kosovo-wide riots without organization." An unnamed senior UN police official told *The Scotsman* that the riots were "planned, coordinated, one-way violence from the Albanians against the Serbs...nothing happens spontaneously in Kosovo."[34] Oliver Ivanovic, a Kosovo Serb political leader, stated that the riots were "very well organized. Simultaneous attacks on 15 different places can only be done if you have strong logistics and coordination. It was all in accordance with a plan."[35] Even UNMIK chief Holkeri admitted that extremist groups, perhaps the ones he had angered just four months before with the KPC suspensions, had masterminded the riots.[36]

Nevertheless, UNMIK immediately looked to control the damage—even as they "controlled" the situation by locking down staff and failing to give the command to use lethal force to save Serbs from ethnic cleansing. Derek Chappell, a UN police spokesman, was "internally relocated" after stating that there was no evidence of Serbian involvement in the Albanian boys' drowning deaths. This had a sobering effect; when asked to comment on the controversy, another spokesman in Pristina asked not to be named, lest "they shut me up like they shut up Derek." And other international officials claimed that UNMIK had deliberately deflated the casualty count, hushing up that six KFOR soldiers had been killed by the Albanian rioters. Most embarrassing for the UNMIK authorities, Agim Ceku's KPC officers actively aided the mobs. The suspicious complicity of leading Kosovo Albanian politicians and KPC commanders was attested to by other internationals, such as the Greek policeman who pondered, "Why did [Hasim] Thaci and [Agim] Ceku not say 'stop' until three days into the riots?...And why, once they did say 'stop,' did everything suddenly stop?"[37]

The thesis that the March riots had been carefully planned well in advance as part of an organized policy of expelling the last of Kosovo's beleaguered Serbs would take a dramatic twist in November 2004, when Germany's National Public Television (Zweites Deutsches Fernsehen, ZDF) aired a documentary proving that the German BND intelligence service had possessed information, through wiretaps of KLA and Islamist provocateurs, indicating a pogrom was imminent, some three weeks before it went down. The documentary also reaffirmed that German soldiers based in Prizren stood and watched as the rioters ethnically cleansed Serbs and torched centuries-old churches. A former German soldier in Kosovo explains that the military's inability to stop the rioters owed partially to a failure of nerve from the brigade's commander—who was later fired due to this inaction—as he waited for an order that never came from UN higher-ups. "In the confusion, lacking leadership, the individual soldiers panicked and looked to save themselves," attests the former soldier. "It also didn't help that the Albanians put women and children in front of our barracks as 'human shields' so that our vehicles couldn't get out."[38]

Some UNMIK and KFOR detachments did, however, work bravely to save Serbian civilians, though they often had to transgress the orders of UN superiors to do so. What the riots showed was that Kosovo's international administration, divided between its numerous nationalities, organizations, and a dysfunctional chain of command was, for all its firepower, helpless in the face of large-scale organized violence. The organizers thus succeeded in their tacit goal of showing the UN who was really in charge in Kosovo. The riot set a precedent that has been invoked ever since by Western supporters of Kosovo independence, warning that it could happen again should Albanian demands not be satisfied—a twisted interpretation of the adage that violence pays.

While the March 2004 riots were seemingly fueled only by ethnic hatred and general frustrations, evidence indicated an Islamist dimension to the violence. The Albanian Muslim rioters did everything from slashing the throats of Serbian farmers' pigs (animals banned under Islamic law) to the dynamiting, burning, or vandalizing of 35 churches. The symbolic, not merely destructive, dimension of these attacks was irrefutably proven by graphic photos that show Albanian rioters taking the trouble to scale ladders onto church domes and actually rip out their crosses by hand. Priceless medieval frescoes were also defaced by rioters. While UNESCO pleaded for action to save Kosovo's Christian heritage, videotapes glorifying the destruction of such Christian monuments were soon being circulated throughout radical Islamic mosques in Western Europe, for the purpose of jihad fundraising.[39] These facts contradict statements from Islamist luminaries such as Pristina University's Qemajl Morina, who at a September 2006 Islamic conference stated that for Albanians the Kosovo conflict "has only a natural and ethnical character," while for "the Serbs it has a religious character." However, the destruction and devastation since 1999 of over 150 Serbian churches, not to mention several dozen attacked during the decades preceding it, indicates a very different reality. Whether or not the riots were motivated primarily by ethnic or religious hatreds, the destruction of so many of Kosovo's remaining churches can hardly be considered a great victory for Christendom.

Some of the Islamist radicals accused of having participated in the riots, such as Mitrovica native Ekrem Avdiu, allegedly had old connections with al Qaeda. Educated in Saudi Arabia and a veteran of the Bosnian jihad, Avdiu collaborated with Abdullah Duhajman, the manager of a Zenica-based charity [the Islamic Balkan Center (IBC)] that had been created by the radical Kuwaiti charity, the Revival of Islamic Heritage Society. In 1994, a British journalist quoted one 15-year-old participant there who described the IBC's activities thus: "We are shown films about the Islamic jihad. The films are different, some in Bosnian, some in Arabic, but they are all about jihad. The war was started to destroy the Muslim people, so now it must be a jihad."[40] Avdiu also had close ties with the radical Bosnian group Active Islamic Youth, a strong advocate for Wahhabism whose members have been linked to several terrorist and civilian attacks. In January 1998, Avdiu established the "Bureau for Islamic Calling in the Balkans" in South Mitrovica. In May 1998, Avdiu took part in a short-lived mujahedin unit to fight the Serbs, Abu Bekir Sidik, consisting of 100 Kosovo Albanians. According to Shpendu Kopriva, the man in charge of the unit's "discipline and faith," the Albanian jihadis were trained by foreign mujahedin, including some European converts to Islam, and "was a branch of the KLA."[41]

On August 5, 1998, Avdiu and Kopriva were arrested at the Kosovo-Macedonia border crossing by Yugoslav police, who recovered large amounts of military equipment and propaganda tapes calling for jihad. While the mujahedin were subsequently jailed in Serbia, the new UNMIK authorities, incredibly enough, pressured for their amnesty in 2001. Today, Avdiu is considered by regional intelligence services to be one of the major players in the nascent jihad movement in Kosovo today. Part of a tight network of radical Islamists from Bosnia, Montenegro, Albania, and Macedonia, intelligence sources attest, Avdiu continues to actively push Wahhabi views and literature with the financial backing of Arabic states and charities such as Islamic Relief.

Another Kosovo jihadi, and the one accused of being a major leader in the March 2004 riots was the Prizren-based Samedin Xhezairi, also known as Commander Hoxha. The November 2004 ZDF documentary claimed that Xhezairi had worked for the CIA, Austrian intelligence, and the BND—while also being "an intermediary between Albanian extremists and al Qaida." Citing "transcripts of conversations from the intelligence services as well as confidential NATO documents" the authenticity of which were later confirmed by BND officials, the documentary claimed that through wiretaps of Xhezairi's phone calls, the spy agency knew about the imminent riots at least three weeks prior to March 17—and failed to pass on this information to the German military KFOR detachment in Prizren.[42]

The confidential NATO report, written on May 17, 2002, by the BND and the German military intelligence (Zentrum für Nachrichtenwesen der Bundeswehr), stated that Xhezairi had been "tasked with forming a branch of Allah's Army—Hezbollah, and his telephone number has been found in confiscated documents from identified members of al-Q'aida." In Prizren itself, the NATO report stated, Xhezairi was a key part of a network with its own "paramilitary units, intelligence service and logistical, financial and propaganda network," centering around a radical cleric in the town, Hoxha Mazlumi. The NATO analysis of the Xhezairi/Mazlumi syndicate's capacities is remarkably prescient, in light of the turbulence of March 2004: both "quick mobilization of the masses for demonstrations" and the "initiation of unrest to demonstrate the failure of the international community" were listed as central goals of the Prizren Islamist cell. The wiretapped conversations between the jihadi leaders had eerie similarities with those captured by the FBI before 9/11:

> It was said, for example, that "in two or three weeks the party will begin" and that "in Prizren everything is prepared for a hot party;" then it was asked whether the interlocutor "can guarantee it will be a blast in Urosevac?" Some of Xhezairi's interlocutors also complained that they still had not organized enough buses to transport the activists. According to transcripts in the possession of ZDF journalists, Samedin Xhezairi commanded the March operations in Prizren and Urosevac, and probably in Orahovac, too. The BND knew, but they were not alone.[43]

Like Avdiu, "Commander Hoxha" and his colleagues remain of intense interest to regional and Western intelligence agencies, which have traced their links to Afghanistan, the Bosnian jihad, and contemporary Albanian Wahhabi extremists in Kosovo, Macedonia, and Montenegro. Slowly but surely, the proselytizing of Arab fundamentalists in Kosovo, especially successful in its poorer and more insular western villages, has added a new dimension to the age-old Albanian-Serb conflict. A Serbian academic originally from Kosovo and specializing in Islamic studies, Sladjana Djuric, believes that Wahhabism has become more prevalent since 2004 because "Albanians are disappointed with the poor economy and impatient with the UN, which has not granted them independence yet, after seven years of occupation...because of this desperation, they have started to accept more Arab money."[44]

The Wahhabis' radical and exploitative aspirations have been noted not just by Serbs, but by Albanians as well. Academic Isa Blumi contends that "by blindly deferring the care of the educational, housing, and nutritional needs of much of rural Kosovo's population to organizations that promote a rigid and intolerant teaching of Islam-Wahhabism, UNMIK and the OSCE may be threatening the future stability of the region." Nevertheless, whether through ignorance or, more likely, political interest, Kosovo's UN administration has not only tolerated the Saudi charities—it has actually praised their efforts. Just a couple months after the March 2004 riots, for example, an UNMIK official stated that the SJRCKC had "played a significant part in efforts to relieve the humanitarian crises in Kosovo and Albania."[45]

According to Blumi, the Wahhabi fundamentalism imported by Saudi Arabia is endangering the liberal, syncretistic Sufi form of Islam that had traditionally been central to Kosovo's religious life. In the immediate postwar period, he discloses, the Saudi Joint Committee for the Relief of Kosovo and Chechnya (SJCRKC) spent 4 million Saudi Riyals (about $500,000) to bring 388 Wahhabi missionaries to indoctrinate Kosovars. Afterwards, one of the Committee's subsidiaries, the Islamic Endowment Foundation, supported "more than 30 specialized Koranic schools in Kosovo's rural areas, all built after 1999." In the first three years of the UN occupation, the powerful charity umbrella group managed to build almost 100 primary and secondary schools in rural Kosovo. These efforts have created whole rural communities that are "more or less dependent on the SJCRKC for their basic needs," creating a new generation of young Albanians who "are increasingly vulnerable to specific worldviews that are inherently hostile to Europe and the West as a whole."[46]

Another Albanian commentator, Genc Morina, makes a similar case. Although he makes a rather improbable claim (though one widespread among Albanians) that the Serbian secret services are behind the Wahhabi movement, Morina notes correctly that the SJCRKC "are profiting from poverty in the suburbs of Kosovo cities but also to a large degree in the surrounding villages." He adds that "the *modus operandi* of the Wahhabi movement in Kosovo is religious indoctrination of the poverty-stricken Albanian, Bosnian Muslim population, as well as Egyptians and Ashkalis. Such examples are most apparent in Shipol (Sipolje), a settlement in the suburbs of Mitrovica; in the settlement of Kodra Timave, formerly Vranjevac, i.e. in the suburbs of Pristina; in Prizren, Pec, in Radevac near Pec, in Junik Voksi, Urosevac, Kacanik, and so on and so forth."[47]

In his critique, Morina condemned the "lack of courage and will to intervene" on the part of UNMIK and the Kosovo Albanian government, charging that "all media without exception" were advancing the "orientalization" of Kosovo, by increasing coverage of Islamic rituals, fasting, Muslim education, and the Wahhabis' political demands. He questioned why the Norwegian Pakistani and al Qaeda terrorist suspect Arfan Qadeer Bhatti had liaised with local Albanian Wahhabis in the western Kosovo town of Pec, voicing concern that with the Saudi schooling and propagandizing, "work is being done to create a new generation of loyal Muslims—not (loyal) to Kosovo but to the Islamic internationale."

Citing information published by the SJCRKC's Islamic Education Foundation, the commentator decried that the Saudis are "offering Kosovo children 'an education' in over 30 Koranic schools throughout Kosovo. The children are being offered 50 euros to learn certain ayats and suras from the Koran by heart." Further, "widows, people fired from their jobs, peasants, unemployed youth [and] some 'intellectuals' are receiving financial means (150 euros and other kinds of assistance) to lead a completely Islamic manner of life in its most radical form."[48]

In Kosovo, the Wahhabis have cleverly concentrated on those areas historically most susceptible to radicalization and rugged individualism, areas such as Drenica, Skenderaj, Djakovica, and Decani, all strongholds of the former KLA. By concentrating on these centers of Albanian nationalism, the foreign Islamists are banking on the idea that any sort of extremism is just extremism and can simply be redirected, like a stream, as and when needed. Indeed, as one active global charity, the Birmingham, UK-based Islamic Relief makes a point of noting, Skenderaj is "a place with a long history of Albanian defiance of Serbian authority." Eventually, hopes the foreign Islamic movement, that defiance can be redirected towards the West.

Media and policymakers in the West, however, have always blindly assumed that since the KLA and its supporters were once "pro-American" any Albanian extremists remaining among them will always remain eminently controllable nationalists. However, as has been noted, the end of the national question in Kosovo is the beginning of the religious one, as new challenges to the social and clerical order arise from radical Islam. At the same time, the next generation of Kosovo youth is now growing up with no direct and formative experience of Serbian repression; their only contact with this, the historic shaping force of Albanian nationalism, will only exist for them in the war stories of older relatives. While in any culture such accounts of past injustices do, indeed, have a powerful affect on shaping the prejudices and opinions of youth, they cannot substitute for direct individual experience. In Kosovo, the ideological vacuum left after the banishment of the Serbs is already being filled by the Islamic question.

Since extremism often stems from poverty, a lack of opportunities, and a closed society, it is no wonder that fundamentalist Islamists have looked to areas that are among the poorest in Kosovo. The hostile reaction Arab charities provoked in 1999 and 2000 prompted them to rethink policy. For the past few years, Islamic groups have sought more subtle ways to buy their way into the hearts of Kosovar Albanians. Since 2003, for example, Islamic Relief has disguised its proselytizing purpose through projects such as infrastructure repair and water supply construction, health clinics, and orphan care. The current focus of their efforts is the 65,000-strong, nationalist and poor municipality of Skenderaj in north-central Kosovo where, it should be remembered, a half-dozen Albanian-Americans arrived in early September 2001, gleefully predicting that America would soon be attacked. In April 2003, Islamic Relief began subsidizing orphans, along with a microcredit program for farmers and small businessmen. By September 2004, it had disbursed over 500 loans, all "based on Islamic principles." Aware that Kosovo's Western backers have, as scholar Blumi says, "less and less money to offer," the Islamist donor states are moving to integrate Kosovo tightly within their own spheres of influence. As in Bosnia, Kosovo will come under increased pressure to purchase products from certain Muslim countries, to prohibit the sale of non-Islamic goods, and to invest and do business within the Arab banking system.

In this light, as the Albanians of Kosovo move closer to their dream of independence and as the helpless Serbian minority is driven out, the previously unifying force of nationalism will slowly start to dissolve amidst the dissonance of religious challenges. Kosovo society, traditionally split between rural and urban communities as well as between familial clans, will further fragment along religious lines. As is happening in Albania too, signs of a confrontation are emerging not only between Catholics and Muslims, but, microcosmically, within Islam, between Wahhabis, Bektashi Shiites, and "traditional" Ottoman-style Hanafis. Behind these groups are the foreign powers—especially the Gulf states, Iran, and Turkey. In addition, there is the significant population of Albanians who want nothing to do with religion at all. The potential for disruptive civil strife under such a scenario will have far more unpredictable results than anything that the traditional Serb-Albanian antagonism of the past could cause.

Another major development directly attributable to the foreign Islamists' strategic planning is the stocking of the Kosovo Albanian government with diehard Islamists, some with ties to terrorism and organized crime. Numerous interviews with UNMIK police from the United States and Western European countries indicate that Kosovo's current civil service, police service, and judicial service have been compromised by the systematic appointments of unqualified and sometimes dangerous Islamists to important decision-making positions. "This trend is already having an effect," said one UNMIK special police investigator, adding:

> Still, not too many are aware this process is going on, it's so quiet. The truth is, Islamist-sympathizing officials are increasingly being inserted into the bureaucracy, and they are the ones deciding who gets to own what, who will go free in court cases, who gets permission to build things, who gets various licenses, and so on... But none of the international big shots seem to care when they are warned about it. Considering we are supposed to be fighting this so-called "war on terror" right now, their disinterested attitude—man, it's beyond belief.[49]

In October 2006, this investigator pointed to a case from a couple of years earlier, in which UNMIK police arrested several Islamic extremists plotting terror in a village near Mitrovica, home of the famous "Osama bin Laden" mosque. "They were all Albanians, and all of them had British passports," said the investigator. "Some were related to leading officials in the Kosovo government. It was all hushed up and never reported in the media." Other intelligence sources have drawn a connection between this group, civil administration appointees, and arrests made by the British government in the July 2005 bomb plots in London.

Today, many still doubt that Kosovo could become a recruiting base for white-skinned European jihadis. Such critics have been given ammunition by the Serbian lobby's tendency to sensationalize and even provide false information incriminating the Albanians, something that ironically damages their own cause.

However, the cynics' assurances are based on an outdated interpretative model: they attempt to predict future trends based on Albanian belief structures pertinent to the last wars, in Kosovo and in Macedonia, where the prevailing thesis of a pro-American, strictly nationalist Albanian struggle for human rights and self-determination captured the hearts of gullible (and sometimes not so gullible) Western journalists and diplomats.

Nevertheless, both wars ended before 9/11, and both were fought by people who had suffered real or imagined persecution at the hand of "evil Slavs," whether Macedonian or Serbian. The young and numerous generations growing up today in Kosovo and in Albanian-populated parts of Macedonia, by contrast, have and will have no such repressive experience. What they will have, however, is the experience, either positive or negative, of radical Islam. While most Kosovars are resolutely against Wahhabism, a dedicated minority continues to defend it and seeks to aggressively expand it throughout Kosovo and the Balkans in general. With Western donors now funding more needy parts of the world, the Saudi strategy of becoming Kosovo's largest funder is becoming a distinct possibility.

As with all cults that preach the inherent superiority of their adherents, and thus the need to either convert or to shun individuals outside the group, Wahhabism nurtures dogmatism and extremism; perversely, it can even become more dangerous the fewer devotees it has; the presence of a chosen few, in any cult, creates a toxic cocktail of perceived oppression, self-exclusion, and righteous superiority that often manifests in a need to take revenge on society at large. As was seen on September 11, 2001, it does not take many extremists to cause widespread destruction.

Albanians, whether from Albania, Kosovo, or Macedonia, have scoffed at the idea of a major religious fundamentalist incursion in their midst. So have their Western yes-men. The West heavily backed the Kosovo Liberation Army during the NATO bombing, despite the presence of mujahedin in its ranks, and for Western publics to suspect that this cause has been muddled up with an Islamist one would amount to a public relations disaster for both Clinton-era political veterans and for the Albanians themselves. Indeed, it would call into question the entire rationale for Western intervention in Kosovo.

Nevertheless, in 2007, Albanians in the Balkans identify themselves by ethnicity over religion and indulge in loosely Western tastes and fashions. Yet as in Bosnia what the local Muslim population in Kosovo wants or believes is not important to persistent and well-funded Arab proselytizers. The challenges of specific local realities merely force them to tailor their methods to best influence the particular society in question. What works in Brazil or China or Belgium might not work in Kosovo. But where there is a Wahhabi, there is a way.

And so, while it is true that Kosovo's Albanians are mostly not interested in radical Islam, this fact alone cannot magically exempt them from the possibility that a small minority might be drawn to Islamic extremism and related activities. For wherever there are certain root causes—poverty, poor levels of education, social dislocation, corruption, and crime—radicalism of whatever kind is not far behind. Kosovo, which the West has chosen as a test subject for many strange experiments in nation-building, cannot claim to be any more immune to the threat of homegrown terrorism than can any other nation where these root causes of extremism also exist. However, for largely political reasons—specifically, preserving the happy, self-serving myths surrounding NATO's "humanitarian" intervention during the Clinton years—this fact continues, at the West's own peril, to be ignored and suppressed.

CHAPTER 4

The Macedonian Enigma

In June 2005, just weeks before the deadly 7/7 terrorist attacks on the London Underground, a group of five Pakistani nationals and British-born Pakistanis landed at Skopje International Airport. They were greeted by local Islamic leaders and soon disappeared into the wilds of southern Macedonia. However, the Interior Ministry's secret service, the DBK (Direkcija za Bezbednost i Kontrarazuznavanje, or Directorate for Security and Counterintelligence), was alerted to their presence.

There was little they could do, however, but watch. The Pakistanis, who ranged in ages from 22 to 49, did not come up on any terrorist watch list. And the government could ill afford another "Islamic scandal," considering the furor over its alleged complicity with a CIA rendition in early 2004, an affair that had caused a sensation in world media and that worsened relations with the European Union just as Macedonia was making its case for future membership. Further, the West had just criticized the government over the very recent acquittal, in late April, of four police officials accused of allegedly murdering seven Pakistani migrant workers in 2002, in order to "impress" Western countries of Macedonia's devotion to the war on terror. Clearly, the authorities had to tread cautiously.

While Macedonian investigators did not know it yet, their Pakistani visitors were representatives of the world's biggest fundamentalist Islamic missionary organization, Tablighi Jamaat. The group had made strong ties with fundamentalist Muslims from the local Macedonian Muslim community, which was also connected with Bosnian radicals in Italy and Austria; two of these local leaders had, according to a DBK agent involved in the investigation, stayed for some time at Tablighi Jamaat's European headquarters in Dewsbury, England.[1] This claim was later substantiated privately by a leading member of the sect in Macedonia.

Created in 1926, Tablighi Jamaat arose as a reaction to Hindu missionary activity among Muslims in India. However, today its ambitions are somewhat greater. Tablighi Jamaat's missionary work has succeeded to such an extent that its annual conference in Raiwind, Pakistan, is second only to the Hajj as an Islamic event, with more than 1 million followers turning out from all over the world to celebrate a fundamentalist vision of Islam that shares some of the fundamentalist views of Saudi Wahhabism. While the group claims to eschew violence and anything political, its nonrecognition of state authority and its goal of spreading Islam worldwide are revealing, as conservative critics have pointed out: "they may not become actively involved in internal politics or disputes over local issues, but, from a philosophical and transnational perspective, the Tablighi Jamaat's millenarian philosophy is very political indeed."[2] A onetime Tablighi Jamaat member, UCLA Islamic law professor Khaled Abou El Fadl, gave the *New York Times* a frank appraisal of the danger presented by the group's sovereign ideology: "you teach people to exclude themselves, that they don't fit in, that the modern world is an aberration, an offense, some form of blasphemy... By preparing people in this fashion, you are preparing them to be in a state of warfare against this world."[3]

Indeed, Tablighi Jamaat has been connected with terrorist activities in the United States and elsewhere. In 2003, deputy chief of the FBI's international terrorism section Michael J. Heimbach stated that "we have a significant presence of Tablighi Jamaat in the United States, and we have found that Al Qaeda used them for recruiting, now and in the past." At the same time, another senior security official added that the group was being used "to evaluate individuals with particular zealousness and interest in going beyond what's offered."[4] One of the most famous such acolytes interested in "going beyond what's offered" was "American Taliban" John Walker Lindh, who wound up in a Pakistani madrasa, and then mujahedin training camp, because of Tablighi Jamaat missionaries. Would-be shoe bomber Richard Reid frequented a Tablighi mosque. The so-called "20th hijacker" in the 9/11 plot, Zacarias Moussaoui was a "regular worshipper" at a Parisian Tablighi Jamaat mosque. Further, according to the *Sunday Times,* "investigators believe that all four of the July 7 London bombers worshipped at the British headquarters of Tablighi Jamaat in Dewsbury, West Yorkshire. Mohammad Sidique Khan, ringleader of the bombers, lived near the mosque."[5]

Such connections could hardly have shocked U.S. officials. After all, they knew from prior adventures in Afghanistan that the organization provided mujahedin wherever and whenever needed. With its intimate ties to high officials in Pakistan's Inter-Services Intelligence (ISI), Tablighi Jamaat was an invaluable tool for the Americans in the anti-Soviet Afghan jihad of the 1980s. The group's role in the Islamic war effort was a "well guarded secret," attested veteran journalist John K. Cooley, who gives the remarkable example of Tunisian prison inmates "converted" by Tablighi missionaries and shipped to Pakistan, where they were trained by the ISI in mujahedin camps.[6]

In Pakistan, Tablighi Jamaat was closely affiliated with the Harkat-ul-Mujahideen (HUM), a militant group formed in the 1980s to aid the jihads in Afghanistan and Kashmir. Like Tablighi, the HUM was also based in Raiwind. Blacklisted by the U.S. government in 1997, the HUM had previously supplied approximately 5,000 fighters, mainly Tablighi Jamaat recruits, to fight the Soviets. Later, HUM jihadis fought in Bosnia, Chechnya, Tajikistan, Burma, Kashmir, and the Philippines. They have also threatened the governments of pro-Western Muslim states. In fact, a plot to overthrow the government of then-Pakistani Prime Minister Benazir Bhutto and replace it with an Islamic state was narrowly averted in October 1995. Some 40 Pakistani army and ISI officers were arrested; many were found to be devotees of Tablighi Jamaat.[7]

Back in Macedonia, the DBK surveillance operation followed the five Tablighi Jamaat missionaries to a small group of villages near Lake Ohrid in the southwest of the country, Podgorci, Oktisi, and Labunista, populated by the Torbeshi—a Slavic, Macedonian-speaking Muslim minority that had converted to Islam during the long centuries of Ottoman rule. Usually neglected by the majority Orthodox Christian Macedonian population, and intimidated by Albanians who suggest that they are "really" Albanian on account of their religion, the Torbeshi have always been a hardworking, tight-knit community seeking merely to avoid trouble with its neighbors. Like most rural populations in Macedonia, the Torbeshi have a long tradition of sending husbands, fathers, and brothers off to work as laborers in Western Europe, especially in Italy and Austria, to subsidize their families back home in the villages.

It was in Europe that some of these villagers came into contact for the first time with radical Islam, at mosques visited by other Balkan Muslims and immigrant extremists from across the Muslim world. Some embraced the strict Wahhabi doctrine and began to grow long beards, while wearing the typical short baggy pants and cloaking their wives and daughters, due to several years of proselytizing by Islamic missionaries from the Gulf states, Pakistan, Malaysia, and elsewhere. Some studied in Saudi Arabia or Egypt, others in Bosnia. While another Macedonian intelligence source in Tetovo recalls Tablighi Jamaat members as having passed through some ten years ago en route to Greece, without stopping, there did not seem to be much activity from the group until a couple of years ago. Every year, villagers now attest, small groups of Torbeshi men spend 3–4 months in Afghanistan and Pakistan, while their families live comfortably back home without needing employment.[8] These accounts are very similar to openly stated plans of Tablighi Jamaat leaders elsewhere. The Guardian, for example, quoted a Tablighi leader addressing the masses in England, as saying, "We shall go to India and Pakistan for four months to follow these [Islamic] ways."[9]

However, the attraction to a movement demeaned as a sect (the word used locally, "Sektashi," is a pun on the English word and the name of a local dervish order, the Bektashi) is by no means universal. The great majority of Macedonian Muslims are not Wahhabis, though they do identify themselves first and foremost as Muslims, owing to their unusual ethnic-religious identity. (Indeed, in parliamentary elections of July 2006, the leader of a new Torbeshi political party handed out copies of the Koran at campaign rallies.) Today, life in the typical Torbeshi village remains conservative, meaning alcohol and nightlife are scarce, and taking photographs, especially of females, is frowned upon.

Nevertheless, while the bearded Wahhabis still stick out conspicuously in these dusty villages animated mostly by chickens and cows, both local residents and security officials speak of a noticeable increase in their numbers over the past five years. This seems to be due partially to the fact that if one man becomes a "believer," as they are also referred to locally, his family must also convert. In addition to missionary work and foreign study, the slow rise of fundamentalism also has to do with a ramp-up in youth group activities and the publishing of Islamic literature, both made possible by funding from Saudi Arabia, Kuwait, and the United Arab Emirates. Further, converts can receive over 200 euros per month—equivalent to the average Macedonian's monthly salary—just to dress and act according to Wahhabi mores. One young, Sarajevo-trained imam from the Torbeshi-majority village of Labunista was offered much more to preach in the village's large, Saudi-style mosque by a mysteriously affluent youth group. He declined, in favor of the clerical life in Switzerland.[10]

The arrival of secretive, foreign-connected Islamic fundamentalists on the scene in villages such as Labunista, Podgorci, and Oktisi over the past six or seven years has attracted significant, if muted, attention from the intelligence agencies of various Western countries, though the media has taken no notice whatsoever. According to the DBK agent, intelligence operations have been conducted in the area by the Italian, French, and American secret services, among others. "The Italians were especially concerned," stated the agent. "They presented us with a list of Macedonian Muslims from these villages who were working in Italy, who had some potentially suspicious connections...we were able to give them good background information about those people. The Italians were very satisfied."[11]

Several months before the June 2005 visit of the Tablighi Jamaat missionaries to Macedonia, a second European intelligence agency was receiving startling data that attested to the presence of up to 100 local and foreign Islamists, who were allegedly moving between these mountainside villages and summer houses and camps in the heavily forested Jablanica mountain range to the west, which forms the natural border with Albania. According to a former officer with PROXIMA, the European Union policing mission that took over for NATO peacekeepers in 2002, nationals from Saudi Arabia, Yemen, Jordan, Egypt, Morocco, and other Muslim countries were among them. Substantial material evidence had been collected regarding the foreigners, including photographs and copies of passports, and passed on to the second European intelligence agency. Local villagers themselves had voluntarily provided information on these unusual outsiders; "but being villagers, they were not really aware of the significance of these funny-looking people in their midst," the officer said.[12]

Almost simultaneously with this private revelation, a very public one had caused a media sensation in Macedonia. In December 2004, French terrorism expert Claude Moniquet stated in an interview with local media that "between 10 and 100 people who are dangerous and linked to terrorist organizations currently reside in Macedonia." Moniquet did not specify the sources for his information regarding the alleged terrorists in Macedonia, but did note that his group, the European Strategic Intelligence and Security Center (ESISC), works closely with the French, Belgian, and other special services and police services.[13] Stopping short of saying that the Islamists were seeking to pull off attacks in Macedonia—indeed, a fairly low-value target for al Qaeda—Moniquet repeated local intelligence experts' prevailing analysis, which remains that the biggest current threat here is the ongoing use of the country as a terrorist safe haven.[14]

In a new interview, Moniquet sheds light on the controversial report. He recalls that his team was initially drawn to Macedonia because in early 2004, "some 'usual contacts' in three European military intelligence services told us that a new concern had developed recently with Macedonia," he attests. "This confirmed other information we had previously from Balkan sources and that's why we decided to take a look in the situation." According to him, "approximately 10 to 20 [local Muslims] were considered as potentially dangerous, from a terrorist point of view, by some European intel agencies." However, the politicized and sensationalistic treatment his comments received dismayed the French expert, who subsequently "discontinued" work on Macedonia. He believes that there was "a clear misunderstanding" on the part of local journalists who were "confusing Islamism and terrorism. We are concerned by both, as we think that, on the long term, Islamism is more dangerous than terrorism. The terrorists cannot win, [but] the Islamists can, by playing the communities and by dividing the developed world into Muslims and non-Muslims, which is a clear and obvious goal of the Muslim Brothers." Nevertheless, Moniquet considered the threat in Macedonia to be of a "limited" nature.[15]

However, a wealth of data gleaned from additional sources painted a more disturbing picture. In September 2005, two high-ranking Macedonian law-enforcement and intelligence officials stated that Malaysian nationals, in groups of 10–20 at a time, had for the past two years made regular visits to the Torbeshi villages, as well as to larger Muslim-populated Albanian areas in Skopje, Tetovo, and Gostivar. As other experts had concluded about proselytizers such as the Tablighi Jamaat contingent, the Malaysians' visits to Macedonia were considered part of a well-worn "route" through the Balkan and other European countries. "When they stop here, they bring money and instructions" from foreign fundraisers, one law enforcement official stated. Further, stated this official, Macedonia was also hosting extremists traveling on EU passports; some of them had either been expelled or feared being expelled from Western European countries due to their political or extremist activities.[16] Another expert, former counterterrorism chief and deputy director of intelligence Zoran Mitevski, claims that Macedonia is, indeed, part of the Balkan "transit zone" for foreign Islamists, both proselytizers and men desperate to escape the clutches of Western security services. Former mujahedin escaping Bosnia for Albania in some cases have arrived there through western Macedonia, coming first from Kosovo.[17]

One-and-a-half years after the revelation over training camps in the Jablanica Mountains, the Macedonian authorities were growing alarmed over the ongoing construction of "summer homes" by known Islamist leaders in this densely forested mountain range. By September 2006, at least three such structures had been built, in the almost inaccessible triangle between Oktisi, Labunista, Podgorci, and the village of Gorna Belica near the Albanian border. What was going on there? In interviews with several sources from the DBK, Macedonian border police and local residents, the same story emerged: the hidden camps were—for now—simply being used for educating young people about "real" Islam. However, at least one facility was said to have outdoor physical training courses such as those depicted in videos of mujahedin training in Bosnia and Chechnya, videos that are readily available from transient vendors on the streets of Skopje and in some mosques. There are fears that if the fundamentalist movement continues to pick up adherents, especially young ones, such remote facilities can be used in the future for more advanced training.[18]

Such fears have already been confirmed elsewhere in the country. In September 2005, hikers on another mountain range, the Karadzica-Golesnica massif that dominates north-central Macedonia, reported having seen bearded, black-clad men training with weapons on Mt. Kitka. While the local park ranger denied the allegations, other, similar reports began trickling in days after the story appeared. It is hard to confirm the story, but there are definitely precedents: in the very beginning of the 2001 war, an elderly Macedonian writer, 77-year-old Josif Ilkovski, was murdered by Albanian militants on Kitka as he sat at his desk in the mountain lodge. "We are waiting for you in the forest" was the sinister message left by the radicals.[19] The proximity of these even more remote mountains, which run from 1527 to 2538 meters high, to isolated Albanian Muslim villages known to receive funding from Saudi Arabia indicates their tactical value to potential jihadist trainers. This operational zone is perhaps even more ideal than the Jablanica range, because of its sparse and dispersed population, as well as its lack of strategic targets or international borders to be guarded. These factors make it perfect for terrorists to train under the radar.

Despite the very real potential threat coming from such mountainous rural areas as Jablanica and Karadzica, international experts and the local media alike have paid more attention to the rise of Islamic extremism in Macedonia's capital, Skopje, where most Muslims are by ethnicity Albanian. Even though Muslims make up a concentrated minority of the population, the feuds between them have been much more voluble and explosive than in the villages. Several years of turbulence in the Macedonian Islamic Community (Islamska Verska Zajednica, or IVZ) have been blamed on the aggressive pretensions of foreign-funded

Wahhabis who have taken over or built several mosques in and around the capital, while challenging the IVZ's legitimate leadership for political and economic gain—sometimes violently.

According to both police sources and Muslim residents of Skopje, the troubles ultimately go back to the mid-1990s, when Saudi Arabia and other foreign sponsors were able to exploit the internal divisions in the IVZ, which came along with a general crisis of confidence regarding the capability of the older, Communist-trained clerics, in order to gain a foothold in Muslim society (then, around 25 percent of the national population). The radicals were also enabled, above all else, by the existential dangers in which the new state soon found itself. Macedonia was unique among the former Yugoslav republics not only in that it broke away peacefully, but also in that its very right to exist was challenged repeatedly. This fact is important for understanding how radical Islam could take root in this small Balkan nation of only 2 million inhabitants.

The saga of Macedonia is far too complex to be explained in brief, but essentially the problem boiled down to a case of contested identities. Greece was furious that a new country calling itself Macedonia should exist, and that its residents —whom they demeaned as "Slavs"—would accentuate historical and visual links with the ancient Macedonian empire of Alexander the Great, the remains of which largely came from below the border, in Greek Macedonia. For the Greeks, this amounted to nothing less than theft of history. In 1994, they slapped a trade embargo on the Skopje government, a move that directly expedited the growth of organized crime and the new state's reliance on its old Yugoslav big brother, Serbia. Greek lobbying in the West also left Macedonia officially branded with a ridiculous "interim solution" of an official name—the Former Yugoslav Republic of Macedonia. Today, over a decade later, it remains a testament to the power of Greek lobbying that the United Nations and the European Union still must use this interim name (though a great many countries, including the United States, recognize Macedonia by its constitutional name, Republic of Macedonia).

The Greeks were not the only problem, however. To the east, Bulgaria was also suspected of harboring certain aspirations based on its own historical opinions. Three times in less than a century, in the Balkan Wars of 1912–1913, World War I, and World War II, Bulgaria had taken military action to recover its "lost province" in Macedonia, which had been the seat of a proto-Bulgar kingdom over 1,000 years before. While Bulgaria was the first country to recognize an independent Macedonia, it did not acknowledge the Macedonian ethnicity or language, claiming that both were "really" Bulgarian. For these reasons as well as historical ones, Macedonian right-wing parties were dogged with the accusation, rightly and wrongly, as Sofia's secret advance guard. At the same time, the left-wing, former Communist SDSM (Socijal Demokratski Sojuz na Makedonjia, Social Democratic Union of Macedonia) was associated with the Serbian regime. Finally, although Greece, Macedonia, Bulgaria, and Serbia were all majority Orthodox Christian countries, the others did not accept the independence of the

Macedonian Orthodox Church. All of this intrigue tremendously weakened the new Macedonian state, its economy, and its social outlook, creating the conditions for opportunist action that materialized violently during the ethnic Albanian uprising of 2001.

The weaknesses of the Macedonian state and church did not, however, mean that conditions were exactly perfect for Islamic institutions or Muslim minorities. A half-century of Communist neglect had left the IVZ with an old guard more interested in bureaucracy and ownership than in religion. As awareness of Islam in the outside world grew among the younger generations of Muslims, they became increasingly dissatisfied with their leaders' offerings and began to look elsewhere for answers. The Saudis were just the most prominent of those who tried to win their souls. For Muslims, the feeling of being ignored and alienated from a majority population that was preoccupied with greater concerns also fed frustrations that augured ill for the future.

Macedonia's major Muslim minority, the Albanians (around 25 percent of the population) live primarily in the northwest of the country, with the city of Tetovo their traditional power base. More socially conservative than their ethnic kin in neighboring Kosovo and Albania, Macedonia's Albanians are also more likely to attend mosque, follow religious customs, and cloak women. Although conditions differed in urban areas, this conservatism has increased after the end of Yugoslavia, with heavily walled familial compounds in villages, built to ensure that outsiders cannot see the family's women—and, presumably, vice versa. In many villages, customs dating from the Ottoman period are preserved, such as "living rooms" with no furniture, filled only with males seated on Oriental carpets against the walls. Such compounds have become more and more widespread and lavish—testimony to the earning power of sons and brothers who have worked in countries like Switzerland, Germany, and Italy for decades. While many former Yugoslav nationals traditionally worked throughout Europe, in the postindependence period, Albanians especially became foreign-oriented, claiming to have been frozen out and excluded from state employment and structures.

Since independence in 1991, Macedonian governments have always included Albanian political parties, which have grown increasingly important as king-makers in parliamentary and presidential elections. At first, they were thought to be mere objects for manipulation, and some schools of thought even state that the first Albanian paramilitary groups were secretly created by the state in the case of any Serbian invasion, at a time when radical leaders in Serbia and Greece were considering the option. In any case, demographic trends (a high birthrate, plus illegal immigration from Kosovo and Albania) soon indicated that the Albanian parties would become more than objects of manipulation. Along with their Macedonian colleagues, leading Albanian politicians and businessmen amassed small fortunes in ill-begotten wealth, benefiting from the opportunities provided by regional instability and organized crime, as well as various patronage schemes that helped cement their rule.

All this meant that, while the country's leadership and those lucky enough to be associated with it prospered, the majority of urban and rural poor, of whatever nationality or religion, were left to their own devices. It was the same story as everywhere else in the post-Communist Balkans. In the absence of a strong and unchallenged sense of national unity, Macedonia became a tangled web of intrigue, where the representatives of different causes, parties, and countries clashed and cooperated. Among these were Islamic charities and relief offices that came along with the conflicts in nearby Bosnia and Kosovo. Wahhabi pros-elytizers began to move aggressively, offering scholarships for young Muslims to study theology in the Arab world and paying local acolytes a monthly stipend to grow beards and veil their wives and daughters. However, because people had other options and because America was so popular among Albanians for NATO's 1999 Kosovo intervention, the fundamentalists never enjoyed mass conversion.

Interestingly, regional crackdowns resulted in an attempt to shift the balance of foreign influence in 1996. The CIA-ordered mass arrests and deportations for August 1995 in Tirana, which briefly netted the services of the Egyptian Abu Omar, had put the Egyptian Islamic Jihad cell under Mohammad al-Zawahiri, and all of bin Laden's Albania operations, under threat. In 1996, when Macedonian intelligence veteran Zoran Mitevski was the chief of a special group on counterterrorism in the interior ministry's DBK (it would later be reorganized under the aegis of the Agency for Intelligence, which answers to the president), a plethora of Tirana-based Islamic charities like the IIRO, the Saudi High Commission, and Islamic Relief all came seeking permission to set up shop in Macedonia. However, officials there were less welcoming than had been Sali Berisha and SHIK chief Bashkim Gazidede in Albania. "Because we knew what they were up to, we tried to keep making obstacles for these groups' registration," says Mitevski. "And American officials called us 'undemocratic' for doing this. I met the then-US Embassy License Officer...he denounced me as a very bad Communist!"[20]

Even the Helsinki Human Rights Committee was attacking the government for denying bin Laden's charity arms a new sanctuary in Skopje. Despite the pressure, Mitevski says he would not sign off: "I told them I would quit the service if they forced me to sign...we knew what they were up to because we had a lot of information about such groups, even from Yugoslav times, when Belgrade kept very good relations with the non-aligned Muslim world...So Yugoslavia had a good agent network there, but also there were many foreign Muslim students in Yugoslavia, some spies." In 1997, when the charities realized they would not be allowed to register, they returned to Tirana. However, they found ways to make inroads, says the former counterterrorism chief, "through funding the IVZ through the Tetovo mufti, as well as the madrassah in Kondovo...in return, they asked for the best of their students to be sent to their universities, in Egypt, Saudi Arabia, Kuwait, Qatar, Yemen, and more. When it started, this meant only seven or eight a year, but the number increased. These young people, trained in foreign styles of Islam, returned to Macedonia and began to spread that influence here."

The Wahhabis were more successful in latching onto existing feuds and internal intrigue within the IVZ for the purpose of winning political influence. The man most often blamed for abetting this movement, former Skopje Mufti Zenun Berisha, would seem an unlikely candidate for a radical cause. Yet this clean-shaven, suit-wearing Albanian has been blamed by local and foreign experts, such as Claude Moniquet, for maintaining unusually close ties to radicals. According to Islamic officials in Skopje, however, Berisha's racket largely involved renting the IVZ's numerous properties in Skopje's old town, the Čar-šija, to his friends for a pittance and then re-renting them for an extortionate price—and pocketing the difference. For this purpose, loyalists were put in charge of the paperwork covering deeds and rentals.

Berisha's flirtation with the Wahhabis, locals say, began in the late 1990s. The IVZ had already been torn by factional strife for almost a decade, and the perceived illegitimacy of the elder generation of leaders made foreign Islam an attractive alternative. More and more young Muslims began heading abroad, from Saudi Arabia and Malaysia to Egypt and Iran. When they returned, the young scholars were able to prove their elders' embarrassing ignorance of the "true" Islam. After taking power, Mufti Berisha began surrounding himself with the pro-Wahhabi faction, primarily because in and around them were ill-educated and impressionable young men with a penchant for violence. This would become more and more useful for Berisha to maintain a grip on power, though in the end the radicals would alarm the IVZ and general Macedonian public by a number of violent acts that showed they were not actually under anyone's control.

The Wahhabi challenge began with small provocations, strategically leading to the virtual takeover of one of Skopje's oldest and most beautiful mosques, Yahya Pasha Mosque. Berisha's faction compelled the highest Muslim cleric in the land, Reis Arif Emini, to do its bidding after one symbolic and humiliating incident. The current Skopje Mufti and Berisha's successor, the moderate Taxhe-din Bislimi, recalled how the trouble began. In a service at Yahya Pasha in the year 2000, a deputy of Berisha's, Hamza Hasani, greeted Reis Emini "not as Reis, but merely as a 'citizen.' Ever since that time, [Reis Emini] was always treated like that."[21] The IVZ's internal problems simmered as the Wahhabis increased their influence, through foreign-supported charities and the redirection of official funds. The distraction of ethnic war in 2001 meant that the Islamic communal tensions did not explode until 2003, when Zenun Berisha was up for another five-year term as mufti. Opponents claimed that Berisha used force to falsify the vote in his favor, and that his reelection was thus invalid.

Soon thereafter, an armed group with ties to Berisha and the Wahhabis stormed the office of Reis Emini, ordering him to install their members in the IVZ. Shocked by the attack, the majority of IVZ members created a Coordinative Body of Imams to try and bring order to the volatile solution. The battle for control worsened in 2004. In October, some 150 imams from the IVZ signed a petition to get Mufti Berisha replaced. "Amid the turmoil, for the first time in history, the Reis was not allowed to greet the believers for Ramadan."[22] Although Taxhedin Bislimi was appointed by the emergency council, Berisha refused to go, rather through his armed detail continuing to pressure a timid Reis Emini who wanted to keep as low a profile as possible. The anarchy, which lasted for over a year, only came to an end with Berisha's ouster in the formal mufti elections of February 2006.

However, several violent incidents from the Wahhabis during that period represent a worrying precedent for how radical Islamists, once empowered, can wreak havoc within mainstream Muslim communities as a whole. Several such events occurred in June 2005, at the time of a planned mufti election at the Skopje-area madrasa of Kondovo. In one incident, armed Wahhabis started shooting in the air to disperse the gathered imams. Several days later, the Assembly of Skopje Muftis' president, Metin Izeti, resigned; he would be followed soon after by Reis Emini, who cited "health reasons" in his decision to quit. Soon thereafter, the leadership of the Coordinative Body, including outspoken Berisha critics like Muhamer Veselj and Taxhedin Bislimi, were intercepted and attacked while driving near Kondovo by the same gang that had threatened the former Reis at gunpoint and violently dispersed the imams at the madrasa. Some of those attacked had to be hospitalized.

Multiple witnesses confirmed the Wahhabi orientation of the gang. The thugs blamed the Coordinative Body members for denouncing "Islamic fundamentalism" on television, according to one of those attacked. Another imam, Saban Ahmeti, stated that "the people who attacked us...were definitely representatives of radical Islam, or as we call them Wahhabis, proponents of Zenun Berisha, who for more than a year have been trying to take over the Islamic Community."[23]

This group, which had also been involved in various armed intimidations against then-Reis Emini, was led by a self-professed Islamic cleric named Sukri Aliu, who was once allegedly arrested entering the country from Albania with large quantities of dynamite. Although Aliu apparently studied in the Arabic world, stated Bislimi, "no one knows exactly where, or exactly what he studied." Another gang member, Ramadan Ramadani, was arrested by U.S. forces in Kosovo later in 2005. Sulejman Suri was also stopped at Kosovo's Pristina Airport after having been sprung from jail in Skopje by crooked prison guards. Several Muslim sources in Skopje claim that this gang was employed as a sort of private security detail by Berisha. While the partial breakup of the gang certainly helped to limit Berisha's armed options, IVZ officials posit another explanation for why the violence stopped after June: Berisha, essentially driven from power, could not afford to pay them any longer.

Months after Zenun Berisha's disappearance, however, the system he had crafted was still continuing to work in the interest of the Wahhabis. The situation was most surreal in the IVZ headquarters itself, where estranged officials from the rival camps ignored one another as they had for years. In one office, Berisha and the Wahhabis were scorned, while in another, bearded men who refused to give their names furtively sifted through scores of lease agreements. In each mosque in Skopje, at least one imam or administrative worker was connected with the Wahhabis, meaning that everything from the style of prayer to salary payment could be controlled. Some clerics, like the young Imam Abdurahim Yashari of the historic Mustafa Pasha Mosque, claimed to have not received a salary for two years, because he was not "loyal to Zenun Berisha." Even in late December 2005, the situation afflicted not only this imam, "but many others, too. For the past seven years, nothing has been paid for pensions, for example... only the administrative workers and clerics on the side of the Wahhabis and Berisha were taken care of."[24]

Even with Berisha sidelined, the recent history of turbulence caused the IVZ to take numerous precautions. On January 10, 2006, the opening service of the annual Kurban Bajram celebrations had to be changed from its usual place, Yahya Pasha Mosque, to another one, Sultan Murat Mosque. At the same time a Berisha deputy, Osman Mehmeti, had been appointed as Skopje representative for the annual Hajj delegation, although IVZ officials stated that he was not even employed in the institution—no surprise, considering which interests Saudi Arabia was supporting in Macedonia. The French terror expert, Claude Moniquet, had voiced fears over a year earlier that then-Mufti Berisha was "playing the game of the Saudis, [of] fundamental Islam in the Balkans...to promote very radical Islam in Macedonia." Berisha, of course, denied the charge at the time, and he, indeed, allowed the February 2006 mufti elections, which brought Bislimi officially to power, to pass without incident. This paved the way for a new Reis, Rexhep Sulejmani, to also be elected later in the year. For the time being, therefore, the political turbulence within Macedonia's Islamic Community has been suppressed.

However, this does not mean that the Wahhabis have simply given up or moved away. Confirming the widespread suspicion that their former enabler had been interested in them only to help him cement his grip on power and profit, Bislimi notes, "We can imagine Zenun Berisha as anything—a communist, a criminal, a businessman—but a jihadi? Hardly!" Indeed, with Berisha out of power, the Wahhabis have continued to develop "parallel structures" of religious worship and fund-raising. At the same time, a strong testament to the Berisha legacy is how difficult it has proven to dislodge them from the IVZ infrastructure. For example, the infamous Yahya Pasha Mosque, where radical jihadi DVDs can be freely purchased, still remains under their control and was the organizational nerve center for the February 10, 2006, protests against the Danish cartoons of Mohammad, in which some 5,000 angry young Muslims targeted the Danish Consulate and the office of a newspaper, *Vreme* (*Time*), that had printed some of the cartoons.

These protests were fascinatingly opaque, with both major ethnic Albanian parties accusing each other of being behind them, in an effort to tar the other with the "Islamic radical" association (the IVZ itself did not support the protests). The event reached spectacle proportions when a vehicle containing notable persons from the then-opposition Democratic Party of Albanians (DPA) pulled in front of the mob, blocking its path. DPA leaders Ernat Fejzulahu and Daut Rexhepi-Leka and Kondovo branch leader Agim Krasniqi pleaded with the demonstrators to go home, as they were damaging the image of the Albanian people in the eyes of the world.[25] DPA Secretary-General Ruzhdi Matoshi, who also tried to dissuade the protesters, later stated that "we worked for 30 years to build a partnership with the West...and [the protesters] would like to destroy that in 5 minutes. What if it had been broadcast on CNN, with images of Albanians in Macedonia looking like something out of Beirut or Pakistan—it would have been a [public relations] disaster!"[26]

DPA's rival, the then-government coalition member Democratic Union for Integration (DUI) of former NLA leader Ali Ahmeti reacted with cynicism, charging that the DPA had stage-managed the protest in order to herald itself as the moderating force capable of stopping it. In the end both agreed on the fail-safe solution—that the Russians and Serbs were secretly behind everything. More realistically, from witness testimony and other evidence, it seems more likely that Skopje's protests were shaped by foreign forces channeling money from groups in Western Europe, especially Austria, through to Bosnia and other Wahhabi outposts in the Balkans. Well before the protests, officials like Taxhedin Bislimi maintained that the extremists' goal "is to put [the IVZ] under Sarajevo, and more radical Bosnian control."

The expulsion of Zenun Berisha from the IVZ leadership, and gradual normalization of the Community's control over its property and affairs, has led the radicals to explore different means of controlling their territory. In 2006, two mutual processes in Skopje converged: one, the construction of an all-new mosque in a part of Skopje with very few Muslims, and two, the creation of a private security firm employing Wahhabis, to cover the old part of the city, the Čaršija, and Cair neighborhood where the IVZ headquarters is located and where most of Skopje's Muslims live. Both had strong connections with the DUI party of the former 2001 war guerrilla commander, Ali Ahmeti, who has frequently denied any involvement with Islamist interests, radical or otherwise. The company had been approved by a municipal mayor from his party, and quickly caused a sensation in the local media by attempting to racketeer shop owners into paying for "security"—in one case ruining thousands of dollars' worth of a Macedonian shopkeeper's wedding dresses by spraying ink over them.

The story of the new mosque attests to the ongoing attempts of radical Islamic forces to entrench themselves as widely as possible. In the Skopje neighborhood of Taftalidze (95 percent non-Muslim), unknown builders got to work in 2005, stating that no one could deter them from building a new house of worship. They reportedly almost fired on Macedonian journalists who stopped by to ask about the curious new structure.

Unrestrained mosque-building has been, in Macedonia as everywhere else in the Balkans, a prime mechanism for Islamists to "mark" their territory. The extent to which an area has been Islamified usually goes together with the number of mosques it possesses. Indeed, it can hardly have been the need to handle capacity that has led the Albanian residents of several small villages in northern Macedonian to construct three or more mosques, when at the same time they have no functioning economy, let alone good roads or proper plumbing. Mosque-building is even more central to the pan-Islamist ideology in areas of religiously mixed populations. By creating imposing structures that are physically and audibly intrusive for non-Muslims, over time the latter simply leave. In a small and weak country like Macedonia, where illegal building cannot be stopped and no one, neither the authorities nor the general public, wants to risk the wrath of Muslims by resisting, the reaction all too often has been to meekly submit to "progress."

According to one Macedonian resident living near the new Skopje mosque, this is precisely what non-Muslims feel forced to do. "At first [the Islamic representatives] said they would not use the sound in the minaret, which was considerate," the woman said. "Of course, now that the mosque is built, they have forgotten about that promise. Tell me, what young person with another option would want to live next to something like that?" Although it is not terribly politically correct, the term "sonic cleansing" is an apt one to describe the process by which aggressively visible and audible Islam gradually grinds away at non-Muslims, who gradually move out of what become, essentially, ghettoes by choice. This story, long attested across large parts of Kosovo and northwestern Macedonia, is now playing out in the West, especially in Europe's cities and industrialized towns.

Another fascinating case of what is happening now can be seen in Macedonia's southwestern town of Struga, an ethnically mixed tourist destination on Lake Ohrid whose civil administration changed from Macedonian to ethnic Albanian control following the 2004 territorial decentralization, which introduced several heavily Albanian villages into the Struga municipality. This politically manipulated demographic change has caused a rapid transfer of political power—and with it, religious power—that has at the same time introduced new actors into the picture, the Saudis, who on historical grounds should have no say in the matter.

Macedonia's decentralization paved the way for Struga's first Albanian mayor, in March 2005, and soon after permission was given to remove a small Ottoman mosque, which had been built over a Byzantine church, replacing it with a huge, Saudi-style mosque. Like all other such structures in the Balkans, the mosque is entirely out of keeping with the traditional architecture and ethos of the town. Built very close to a hotel on Struga's placid lakeshore, the new mosque's well-amplified minaret blasts out the call to prayers five times a day, something that has irritated local non-Muslims and, significantly, foreign hotel guests. As a manager at one hotel on the shore opposite the mosque sadly conceded, "the European tourists coming for a quiet vacation get jolted out of bed by the noise coming from the mosque...and don't return." When asked whether such a policy was fair to non-Muslims, an imam at the Islamic Community of Struga demurred that the volume issue "was something for the city to decide." Startlingly, he suggested that music wafting from cafés in the evenings was equally offensive to Muslims.[27]

That the real goal of the mosque-building project is to fundamentalize and Islamicize a majority Christian society was driven home more powerfully when, in July 2006, a Wahhabi fundamentalist group from a nearby village converged on a beach close to the Struga hotel. The unprecedented sight of 100 bearded, fully dressed Islamists gathered on a Macedonian beach seemed both outlandish and frightening. According to one young Macedonian woman who was there, "I and my friend were the only two women on the beach, surrounded by these Wahhabis. They were staring at us, and we felt nervous and decided to leave. What is going on? Are we living in Saudi Arabia? What are people going to think of our country if this continues?"[28]

Islamists see Macedonia as an inviting target because of its internal weaknesses and changing demographics. Muslims currently constitute 30 percent of the population and are reproducing much more rapidly than Christians. Although statistics are notoriously unreliable, it is likely that within 25 years the two population groups will approach parity. During the same time, to serve both their needs and their aspirations, better organized Islamic leaders will continue to build mosques and probably at least one more madrasa; an IVZ official suggested that a good place to start would be the eastern town of Stip, where the tiny Muslim population is composed of a handful of Turks. This is why the previous years of infighting between Muslims in this obscure and forgotten Balkan state may be so instructive for the future. If the struggle between Zenun Berisha and his enemies was so fierce over the relatively minor issues of financial, administrative, and property concerns, how will internal battles manifest in the future, when the flock is larger, wealthier, and more diverse?

Indeed, as elsewhere in the Balkans, two simultaneous processes are happening: the "official" Islamic Community is becoming more politically active and relevant, looking to champion its interests on issues like decentralization (according to some officials, the IVZ feels entitled to at least half a billion dollars' worth of Communist-seized assets), and to market itself as the friendly alternative to the Wahhabis. For their part, they will continue to operate in the shadows, until an enabler comes along (as happened with Berisha) or until they have sufficient power in any one place to operate independently. At the same time, they will continue their tight cooperation with radicals in neighboring states, especially Kosovo, Albania, and Bosnia. Macedonian intelligence has linked some of these leaders to weapons smuggling and the infiltration of hostile foreign elements.

As everywhere else, Wahhabism in Macedonia has been supported and funded through a variety of foreign-based charities and accounts, and propagated in on-line chat groups and Web sites. One youth group in Skopje reportedly receives funds from Islamic Relief in the UK, while another in the Struga area receives support from Bosnian charities. The funding for others is routed through Graz,

Vienna, and Linz in Austria, or through cities in Italy and Germany. It usually leads directly back to Saudi Arabia. According to Zoran Mitevski, one ethnic Albanian parliamentarian traveled to Saudi Arabia in September 2006 to negotiate the long-awaited arrival of the IIRO in Macedonia. The notorious charity planned to set up an office and build 30 new mosques in the Lipkovo/Kumanovo area. As in Kosovo, where Islamic Relief and Saudi charities have concentrated on the historically most radical rural areas to indoctrinate, so to in Macedonia are the Islamists concentrating on remote, insular, war-affected places. The hilly Lipkovo region, essentially a no-go area for non-Albanians, also falls under the influence of southeastern Kosovo and has seen numerous violent incidents even after the 2001 war. Radical Islam is consolidating its grip here with the ongoing construction of scores of new mosques.

However, as in Bosnia, Kosovo, and Albania one major question remains: To what extent will the radical Islamist doctrine become pervasive in Muslim society? At first, noting the largely Western style of Muslims in Macedonia, this possibility seems unlikely. However, it is undeniable that the role of Islam is becoming increasingly prominent in everyday life. In late 2005, a representative of the Muslim Scholars League disclosed that the number of Muslim pilgrims setting out for the Hajj that year had "increased by hundreds."[29] The League, which sponsored some 700 Macedonian pilgrims, is led by Sheikh Yusuf al-Qaradawi, a strong supporter of suicide bombing who said that Muslims "must rage, and show our rage to the world" in the wake of the controversy over Danish cartoons of the Prophet Mohammad.[30] Boys as young as six or seven go regularly to worship in new mosques built in the double-minaret Saudi style. The archaic practice of arranged marriages for 12-year-old Muslim girls has actually increased in poor western Macedonian villages between Debar and Struga. Attests Zoran Mitevski, "The object of [Wahhabi] attack is the rural mountain areas, which are more narrow-minded, with low education levels and where a traditional patriarchal system is still firmly in place."

The demonstrated lack of intelligence regarding activities in such places worries foreign observers. "Especially when you get up in these mountain areas, where the villages are hard to get to and the society is very closed, it is a great mystery," says one French former peacekeeper in Macedonia. "In some of these places, Saudis have built mosques, but it is impossible to tell what influence they have gained, because there is no one—not us, not the Germans or British, not even the Americans—who has [intelligence sources] in any of these places. We really have no idea."[31] Given this dearth of information, it is only the rare bit of data or anecdotal account, such as the hikers' tale of mujahedin on Mt. Kitka in September 2005, that allows the occasional glimpse of light into an otherwise opaque and closed world.

As elsewhere, the Wahhabis prey on ignorance, superstitions, and local fears to manipulate believers, changing their methods to suit the environment. To scare Muslims into joining the radical sect, a 2004 report citing intelligence sources stated, rural, sometimes illiterate, Albanians were reportedly being told that "the state wants to destroy their religion and prevent them from having children." In urban areas, on the other hand, recruiters glorified the life of the mujahedin, "asking them to worship Islam and saying that everyone who fights in the name of Allah and dies will become a *shahid* (martyr) and go to paradise, where he will enjoy all the pleasures that he couldn't have in this life."[32] The recruiters also assured that jihadis who fight without fear feel no pain if they are shot. Independent intelligence sources had noted a few months previously that Chechnya jihad videotapes circulating in the Skopje neighborhood of Gazi Baba conveyed the same propaganda and depicted the true *shahid* as always dying with a smile on his face, ready to embrace the afterlife with Muhammad.[33]

According to the 2004 report, small groups of 20–30 mujahedin had become associated with several Skopje-area mosques, including the infamous Yahya Pasha, the Tutun Mosque, and one in the impoverished Roma slum, Suto Orizare, as well as in the villages of Kondovo and Ljubin. The article, which confirmed other reports that the Wahhabis were being paid to belong to the group, claimed that Austria was the ultimate source of radical funding and added that the fundamentalists typically met in empty rooms at nightfall, after the evening prayer, making strange movements and lubricating themselves with a sort of oil "which they claim is holy water."

Despite the veil of secrecy surrounding much of their activities, the fundamentalists are perfectly open about their appearance, with heavily bearded Wahhabi men and their black-clad, fully covered wives no longer a rarity in part of Skopje. And a visit to mosques such as Yahya Pasha reveals a strange cast of characters indeed: men dressed in Saudi tribal headgear, legions of worshippers in enormously wide but short baggy pants, and bushy-bearded look-alikes for the Jordanian mujahedin Khattab, the late former leader of the Chechen jihad, whose jihadi biographical DVD is sold inside the mosque bookstore. When asked to comment on such activities, a Russian embassy spokesman in Skopje stated that, while they were aware of such things, they had no influence or ability to stop the distribution of such materials—a reality far removed from the paranoid Muslim image of Russia as that all-powerful secret force behind every anti-Islamic act, real or perceived, in the Balkans today.[34]

Despite the disappearance of former Mufti Zenun Berisha from official power in the IVZ, Albanian Wahhabi groups in Macedonia have thus proven resilient and simply used independent sources of funding from foreign Islamic states, as well as involvement with political parties and private Albanian security firms, travel agencies, Islamic charities, and other groups to continue staking out their turf. In Skopje, radical preachers at Yayha Pasha Mosque, well-connected with Kosovo radicals like Ekrem Avdiu, preach about the pains of hell that could befall the nonobservant Muslims, while in Tetovo intelligence teams have expressed concern about the Macedonian activities of other Kosovo jihadis like Samedin Xhezairi, who allegedly has developed strong networks with Turkish, Bosnian, and Albanian extremists in that city and in Skopje, utilizing innocuous facilities like cheap hotels as logistics bases.[35] Even mundane events like football

matches have acquired religious overtones, such as the November game between
Russia and Macedonia in Skopje, where Albanian Muslims chanted "Chechnya,
Chechnya," while Russians and a few Serbs in the audience countered by shout-
ing that Kosovo was Serbian.[36] Meanwhile, Wahhabi groups continue to aggressively push their own "solutions" on Muslim society, as with the botched
exorcism attempt that left one man dead in the Macedonian Muslim village of
Labunista in early 2007.[37]

However, evidence shows that, as everywhere else in the Balkans, the official
Islamic community on occasion takes part in supporting radical groups. Wahhabis themselves implicate the IVZ itself in sponsoring outside forms of Islam.
According to the aforementioned Tablighi Jamaat member in Macedonia, the
IVZ itself invited the Pakistani group members to the country in June 2005. In
conversation, most officials state that their goal is merely to uphold the tradition
of Ottoman Islam of the Hanafi school. However, this is not exactly the truth.
This and other evidence confirm that certain factions of the IVZ would like to
see foreign varieties of Islam take root in Macedonia. It is also indisputable that
senior figures from within the IVZ supported, in one form or another, the Izetbegovic government's radical Islamist policies in Bosnia during the 1990s.

The Tablighi Jamaat, both in the Balkans and elsewhere in Europe, is starting
to raise concerns among Western intelligence agencies who consider penetrating
the missionary group to be a key priority. "The Tabligh is a very complicated
problem but a real concern," states French terrorism expert Claude Moniquet,
who attests that the movement is active in Macedonia and, especially, Kosovo
and Bosnia. However, he says, there is still no direct proof that Tablighi Jamaat
is involved with terrorism, "in Europe at least." For Moniquet, the main current
danger of the movement is its radical fundamentalist nature; even more so than
Saudi Wahhabism, the Tabligh "advocates a 'real' and 'pure' Islam, which by
definition is radical...and it plays a great role in the 're-Islamisation' of the Muslim youth in Europe and in converting non Muslim." Many young Muslims
active in jihadi circles in Europe have been "in touch with the Tabligh, [either]
'coming back' to Islam or being converted through Tabligh-controlled mosques,"
Moniquet reveals. This fact lies behind why, in the expert's view, "important
intelligence and security agencies such as those of France consider Tablighi as
a subversive movement which they must monitor and penetrate."[38]

No wonder, then, that Italian military intelligence, another one of the most
interested Western services in the exploits of Macedonian Muslims, would show
heightened interest in known Islamists from the southwestern Torbeshi villages,
over a year after the Tablighi Jamaat proselytizers arrived in June 2005. While
visiting their Macedonian colleagues in September 2006, the Italians brought
up the subject again. According to one participant, "they were especially interested to know more about [Macedonian Muslims] from Labunista, Podgorci,
Oktisi and a few other of the Struga-area villages, those working in Italy or maintaining relations with radical groups there. The Italians fear these people are
being influenced towards jihad by foreign imams in the northern Italian cities

where they work." Three months later this participant, a ranking military intelligence officer, would state that information supplied by the Macedonians had helped Italy in its coordinated raids in the Treviso-Trieste area in early December 2006, which resulted in the arrest of several Bosnian and Macedonian jihad supporters.[39]

Indeed, according to the same DBK agent involved with the June 2005 investigation, several of the Torbeshi leaders most active with the Tablighi Jamaat and Wahhabi movements had strong connections with known Bosnian Wahhabi leaders such as Safet Kuduzovic and Mohammad Porca. One of them had visited the latter in Vienna where, according to the written testimony of outspoken Bosnian former Wahhabi Jasmin Merdan, Porca has created one of "the most ultra-orthodox" Islamic communities in Europe. The Macedonian Muslim leader had also come under scrutiny from the Italians for his efforts, along with the Bosnian Wahhabis, to expand Islam among Bosnian and Macedonian migrant communities in Italy. A December 1, 2006, report from the Italian news agency, ANSA, disclosed that some 150 agents had taken part in counterterrorism raids on 38 different locations, which resulted in the detainment of several Macedonian and Bosnian Muslims involved in radical activities. Treviso, a small city near Venice that Macedonian and Western European intelligence sources had singled out long before, loomed large in a police investigation that also cracked down on radical cells in Trieste, Bergamo, Gorizia, Pordenone, Siena, Udine, and Vicenza.

Led by the Trieste branch of DIGOS, Italy's political crime unit, the police operation materialized following long surveillance of radical mosques, Internet chat groups, and Web sites. The police rounded up foreign devotees of bin Laden and al-Zarqawi, with suspects in the Marca Trevigiana (Treviso area) "being by nationality Macedonian," including an imam in Susegana, a town of 10,000 located 37 kilometers from Treviso.[40] The size and scope of the operation revealed the alarming dimensions of the terrorism threat that has emerged in only a few years along with Balkan Muslim economic migrants from Macedonia and Bosnia. Nevertheless, although experts consider Italy, along with England, to top the list of European terrorist targets, the Balkan dimension of the threat will continue to be underreported unless an attack materializes.

When asked, the Macedonian fundamentalists openly attest that Italy presents rich opportunities for them. One 35-year-old Muslim cleric, organizer of local Islamic youth groups in the southwestern villages, the Wahhabi "beach party" in Struga, and some of the nearby mountain "weekend houses," enthusiastically predicted the future creation of a Sharia state in Italy. Seated before several local Muslim men listening attentively in a dusty village tea shop, the bearded imam invoked the greatness of jihad and solemnly attested: "Prophet Mohammed, grace be upon him, predicted that Islam would be victorious in Constantinople. This came true in 1453 with [the Ottoman invasion of] Mehmet the Conqueror. And, as you will see very soon, his other prediction, that Rome too would be ours, will also come true—not necessarily by force, this time also by conversions. But in the end, Italy will be an Islamic state."

CHAPTER 5

The Ottoman Legacy and Turkey's Deep Shadow

In a formidable show of their unquestioned strength, Turkish security forces fanned out across the most historic quarter of Istanbul, creating a vast cordon around their famous guest, Pope Benedict XVI, who was concluding a four-day visit to the secular but deeply Muslim country that he had previously offended in comments that seemed to depict Islam as a violent, irrational religion. The German pope was visiting the greatest building in Christendom, the former Byzantine cathedral of St. Sophia, and the sublime Blue Mosque across the fountained park of Sultanahmet. A single fear—that the highest representative of Western Christendom could somehow fall victim to Islamic radicals—guided this police operation of November 30, 2006. Some 25 years before, a Turk linked with the criminal underworld and shadowy state security services, Mehmet Ali Agca, had tried to assassinate his predecessor, John Paul II.

In 2004, the charismatic John Paul officially apologized to the Greek Orthodox Patriarch Bartholomew for the Western sack of Constantinople exactly 800 years before. The Latin knights of the Fourth Crusade, ironically, did more damage to the Byzantine capital and its precious possessions than the Ottoman Turkish conquest would in 1453. They ruled for a total of 57 years, until 1261, when Constantinople was liberated by Michael VIII Palaeologos, founder of the last Byzantine imperial dynasty. His fourteenth century descendant, Emperor Manuel II, would unwittingly cause great grief for the pontiff in 2006, when his obscure 1391 conversation with a Persian interlocutor on Islam was referenced by Benedict XVI in a lecture at a German university. The Muslim world went wild; the erstwhile Cardinal Ratzinger, who had opposed Turkey's EU membership bid in 2004, deeming Islam to be "in permanent contrast" to Europe's Christian heritage, apparently felt that Muslim innovations on Christianity included only things "evil and inhuman, such as [Mohammad's] command to spread by the sword the faith he preached." The worldwide protests and demands that the Pope cancel his upcoming trip to Turkey made the faux pas (by a pope who according to his adopted name should be well-spoken, no less) seem to be Byzantium's revenge for the Latin conquest of 1204.

Or was it? Some maintained that it could not have been accidental that Benedict XVI had quoted such an unusual source so soon before traveling to the only Muslim EU candidate, also a major economic power and Western partner in most spheres. By whipping up a frenzy of protest, the allegation (which the Pope insisted he did not support) would seem substantiated, ironically strengthening the Pope's—and the EU's—position by exacerbating latent internal Turkish divisions at a moment when Turkey's failure to open its ports to a member of that union, the island nation of Cyprus, was bringing its candidate negotiations to crisis point. The island had been divided ethnically between Greek Orthodox Christians and Turkish Muslims since 1974, when the Turkish Army invaded and occupied the northern third of the island, a bombastic move that had followed the attempt by a right-wing junta in Athens to annex the island to Greece. Two decades later, the Turkish troops were still there, by their mere presence creating a status quo that no Turkish government could end without bringing upon itself the fury of nationalists and the military, the same military that had always kept a wary eye on the power of religion in Turkey, and especially the Islamic political factions.

The Saadet (Happiness or Felicity) Party was one of those. A week before the Pope's arrival, on November 22, around 100 of its supporters briefly occupied St. Sophia; among them were ultranationalist supporters of the Grey Wolves, a violent group that had taken part in government-sanctioned assassinations, paramilitary atrocities, and heroin trafficking since the 1970s and of which Mehmet Ali Agca, the would-be assassin of Pope John Paul II in 1981, had been a member. During their takeover, the Grey Wolves ostentatiously prayed in the church-turned-mosque-turned-museum. When Pope John Paul II had merely made the sign of the cross upon entering in 1979, it sparked an uproar among Turks; his German successor wisely decided to avoid following suit. Although it promised to bring a million people into the streets of Istanbul to protest the Pope's arrival, Saadet managed only 25,000. The party had been created when the Fazilet (Virtue) Party was broken up under army pressure in 2001. Another, less extreme, breakaway faction, the Justice and Development Party (Adalet ve Kalkınma Partisi, hereafter referred to as the AK Party), won a landslide victory in the November 2002 elections, led by a moderate Islamist reformer, Recep Tayyip Erdogan.

On November 26, 2006, the protesters turned out in force, watched over by circling police helicopters and 4,000 heavily armed officers backed by armored vehicles. Recai Kutan, Saadet's chairman railed that "for Western civilization to develop it needs an enemy and the Pope openly says that this enemy is Islam." A protester's English-language depicted "the pontiff's face on the head of a pig, blood oozing from his mouth," and read, "Go home Pope."[1] Nevertheless, the papal visit went ahead and was deemed a success—especially when Turks were surprised to see the pope and Istanbul Mufti Mustafa Cagrici praying together in the Blue Mosque. Yet Turkey's relations with the EU were not significantly improved. Neither was the public standing of Patriarch Bartholomew, who had invited the pope in the first place; for Turkish nationalists long suspicious of the alleged dangers of the Greeks, the Pope's stated desire to reunite the Eastern and Western faiths after almost a millennium of schism only confirmed that the secret goal of the scheming prelates was an eventual resurrection of the Byzantine Empire.

These tortured complexities, all captured in one single event, reaffirmed the thesis that there is no country of greater importance to southeastern Europe, to the Balkans, and even to the West today than Turkey. To understand why this overwhelmingly Muslim nation of over 70 million, which has only 7 percent of its territory in Europe, may nevertheless play the leading role in shaping the future of all Europe, a brief foray into the country's history is required. Since sweeping down onto the Anatolian plain from Central Asia in the eleventh century, the Turks have played an integral shaping role in European history. The empire that began with the conquest of Byzantine Constantinople by Mehmet II in 1453 lasted, in various forms, right up until the First World War. At its peak in the seventeenth century, the Ottoman Empire extended from the Atlantic on the North Africa coast east to the Arabian Peninsula, from the Caucasus Mountains to the Balkans and the Hungarian plain. In 1683, the Ottomans reached the gates of Vienna for the second time, before being slowly driven back. Yet while Western Christendom was saved, much of the Balkans remained under the Ottoman yoke until the early twentieth centuries. Driven almost completely from Europe by the combined armies of Serbia, Greece, and Bulgaria during the 1912–1913 Balkan Wars, Turkey almost lost the Anatolian coast as well, when the Great Powers partitioned the Turkish heartland into zones of control after World War I. Yet when a Greek invasion meant to liberate the Greek-inhabited coastal city of Smyrna in 1922 became too ambitious, a dashing young general named Mustafa Kemal drove the Greeks back, and the contours of modern Turkey were defined.

Following the conflict, a mutual population exchange in 1923 uprooted millions of Greeks and Turks from lands they had inhabited for hundreds and, in the case of the Greeks, thousands of years. This codified ethnic cleansing essentially left Greece and Turkey religiously "clean" as well, the former becoming almost completely Orthodox Christian, and the latter almost totally Muslim. The only two areas excluded from the exchange were Greek Thrace and Constantinople (subsequently, Istanbul). The former was regarded by the Turks as a buffer zone for the latter, which was also for the Greeks a foundation of Greek culture and commerce, and the seat of the Ecumenical Patriarchate. However, since the 1923 population exchange the Turkish minority in Thrace has remained, whereas the Greek one in Istanbul has been almost completely driven out, especially during the 1950s.[2]

In rebuilding a shattered country, Mustafa Kemal—soon to be known as "Ataturk," or Father of the Turks—took a hard look at the reasons for the once-great Ottoman Empire's collapse. The military veteran relocated his capital from Constantinople, famous for its decadence, intrigue, and earthly temptations, to the uninspiring central Anatolian town of Ankara. Previously a member of the Young Turk reform movement that had compelled Sultan Abdulhamid to reinstate constitutional law in 1908, Ataturk was obsessed with importing Western political, cultural, and scientific ideas. He regarded Islam as a detrimental and anachronistic force blocking national progress, and thus did the previously unthinkable by banishing it from governance. Ataturk boldly replaced Islamic rule with a secular republic; the army was to defend the new order from any would-be usurpers, both foreign and domestic. At the same time, to mold a population that had only ever known multiethnic syncretism, Ataturk standardized the Turkish language, put a new emphasis on Turkic culture, and nurtured the development of a robust nationalism.

For Mustafa Kemal, this was a point of pride. During Ottoman days, when the affairs of state and commerce were often in the hands of Greeks, Armenians, or other ethnic groups, to be "Turkish" was synonymous with provincialism and ignorance. Ataturk sought to change that. He replaced what had been for almost two millennia a multiethnic commonwealth ruled by a military theocracy (first Byzantine Christian, then Ottoman Muslim) with a nation-state ruled by a military democracy. It was one of the most audacious and sweeping overnight transformations of a country ever attempted. For over 80 years, the experiment has worked, though the constant pushing and pulling of contradictory forces continue to make Turkey one of the most fascinating, complex, and unpredictable countries in the world.

The most controversial and far-reaching of Ataturk's reforms was the decision to banish religion from public life. Today, as the position of Islam not only in Turkey but across the world continues to become increasingly acute, the chronic showdowns between the self-appointed guardians of Ataturk's secular republic, the military, and the civilian government with its tendencies to be sympathetic to the Islamic faith (and the voters who profess it) assume greater significance. Over the past 30 years, military coups and legal action have kept "pro-Islamic" politicians in their place. The Turkish balancing act between religion and the republic has had its ups and downs. The country has banked on the image of Turkey as the "bridge between civilizations," between the Islamic East and Christian West, highlighting the usefulness and moderating impact of such a position in its bids to win the support of the United States and Europe.

The appropriate role of Islam in politics has long been debated in Turkish society. At times, religion has taken on greater prominence, but going too far has also resulted in crackdowns from the protector of the republic, the military. The most visible example of Islamist curtailed was that of Necmettin Erbakan, leader of the Refah (Welfare) Party government that lasted a little over a year, from 1996–1997; its attempts to reorient Turkey towards the Islamic world led to the party's forced dissolution in January 1998; it was accused of unconstitutional behavior. Despite this setback, Refah members formed a new pro-Islamic bloc, the Virtue Party. In June 2001, this too was banned by the state. From its ashes emerged the AK Party, led by a moderate reformer and former mayor of Istanbul, Recep Tayyip Erdogan. The AK Party won November 2002 elections, immediately sparking debate over creeping Islamism in the government. A constitutional amendment was required before Erdogan could become prime minister.

However, though many AK Party members, such as Erdogan and Foreign Minister Abdullah Gül, were former Refah officials, the government did not give critics much ground upon which to criticize it, sticking to a platform of economic and social reform in the interests of future EU accession. Turkey's economy had collapsed the year before and the public demanded change. According to Turkish scholar and political analyst Mehmet Kalyoncu, the AK Party's victory was "an outcome of the Turkish public's reaction to the previous political rot in Turkey."[3] A gradual recovery was accomplished under Erdogan's first three years in office, bolstering the nation's confidence. Nevertheless, certain forays onto less secular grounds—such as failed initiatives to criminalize adultery and ban the sale of alcohol in city centers—alarmed European officials previously assured that Turkey's liberal reform course would continue unimpeded by Islamic factors. For Turkey, the major challenge has been to convince the EU that membership for over 70 million Muslims—something that would give Turkey the second-largest, and eventually the largest, number of European Parliament seats—would not result in "Islamist" legislation for Europe.

Despite the frequently raised concerns over the place of Islam in Turkish government and society, Kalyoncu stresses the need to distinguish between Islamism, per se, and religiosity, between the politicization of Islam and the private expression of religious belief. Distinguishing between the reign of Erbakan a decade ago, when a pro-Arab foreign policy was deliberately put forth, and the relatively pro-Western government of the modern AK Party, the scholar cites a late 2006 survey conducted by the TESEV (Turkish Economic and Social Research Foundation), which found that most Turks believe that there is no current "Islamist threat" today. "They believe there is rather increased religiosity that manifests itself in an increased number of mosque attendants. Nevertheless, the public does not view piety as contradictory to their Western way of life and democratic values...[but] view the freedom of expression and practice of Islam as consolidation of democracy in Turkey in its true essence."[4]

While the Islamist protests that preceded the pope's visit in November 2006 were heavily publicized, the percentage of Turks openly supportive of Islamic parties is, indeed, relatively small (in 2002, Saadet took only 1 percent of the vote). Opposed to the more conservative Islamic factions, however, is one large and somewhat unusual Islamic movement, which has become politically influential in modern Turkey—that of Fethullah Gülen, a charismatic and elderly ex-preacher who since 1998 has been living in comfortable exile in Pennsylvania. A reclusive but wealthy leader, Gülen preaches an idiosyncratic form of Islam, associated with the esoteric Turkish Nür movement, throwing in healthy portions of demagoguery.[5] He and his creed have inspired suspicion in Turkey. Following years of preaching, a scandal broke out in 1998 when it was claimed that Gülen was advising supporters to work slowly and patiently to create an Islamic state in Turkey. He then moved to America, citing health problems, and was tried in 2000 for conspiracy to overthrow the state. Despite its cult aspects, the "Gülen Movement" emphasizes education and liberalism, factors that have made it seem an appropriately sanitized version of Islam for the secular republic of Mustafa Kemal.

The Gülen movement has provided one solution in Turkey's search to find a suitably liberal form of Islam to show the West. And the pro-Islamist government of Erdogan's AK Party, which legally exonerated Gülen in 2006, indeed, backs it. The political clout of Gülen's faction in Turkey was revealed in June 2004, when one of its own, Ekmeleddin Ihsanoglu, was elected to a four-year term as Secretary General of the Organization of the Islamic Conference (OIC). It represented the first time a Turk had headed the organization, one of the most powerful positions in the Islamic world. The prime minister had lobbied for Ihsanoglu. According to the BBC, "The Turkish government presented Mr. Ihsanoglu as a reform candidate, both in terms of the organisation and the wider Islamic world."[6]

Despite its liberal appearance, the Gülen movement has aroused the suspicions of the powerful Turkish military. It fears that the religious group would like to weaken the Turkish military's grip on political life and even create some sort of an Islamic state. One of the group's alleged goals has been to infiltrate the Turkish military with its own sympathizers, in order to try and take it over from within; the army similarly inserts its own spies in Gülen-owned schools. For its part, the United States seems to be seeking to maintain the tension between the Turkish political/religious establishment and the military to ensure that neither group is allowed to dominate. The end result is an Islamic movement that, while undoubtedly eccentric and, to many Turks, ludicrous, is at least not anti-American and not linked to al Qaeda.

Fethullah Gülen has, however, not limited his aspirations to Turkey, and his schools are found throughout the world, often in places of interest to Turkish foreign policy. A former student in one of Gülen's schools in Turkey, Emre Yilmaz, is a young Kurd originally from the southeastern city of Diyarbakir. He agrees with the conception that Gülen is trying to push a "new Ottoman Turkish style of Islam," to enhance Turkey's sphere of influence in the Central Asian republics and in its old Balkan colonies. And despite the movement's perceived opposition to the Turkish military, Yilmaz notes, "They never criticize the army when it bombs Kurds." Amidst the tortuous complexities of modern Turkey, this tacit complicity in the bombing of fellow Muslims may account for why Gülen is relatively tolerated by the army: "as long as you hate the Kurds, you still have a place in Turkish society," avers Yilmaz. He recalls how, in the eternal give-and-take between the forces of religion and secular nationalism, the teaching he was given at the Turkish Gülen school was in essence a front for reinforcing insular Turkish nationalism—despite the movement's self-proclaimed image of an educated, liberal Muslim philosophy. He states:

> The Gülen teachers made a lot of problems for me. They didn't want me to be interested in foreign people or languages, but to be Turkish. Because I had loved studying English in school, they told my father, a very devout imam, that I was in danger of losing my religion and perhaps of even becoming a Christian! It was a lie, but my family believed them and became very angry.[7]

Reiterating what others have said—ironically, Turkish nationalists more than anyone—Yilmaz maintains that Gülen's entities serve the interests of the United States in Turkey. He believes that their sensitivity to public suspicion of being excessively Islamic or insufficiently Turkish is what led to negative experiences such as his. Further, while they are, indeed, Muslims strongly against al Qaeda, the former student attests that during his time in the school, the Gülen teachers, like more radical Islamists, frequently attacked Russia over its war against Muslims in Chechnya behind closed doors. "They sent people to teach in schools in the Caucasus," he adds. "Perhaps some of them ended up fighting there."

On the other end of the ideological spectrum from the Gülen movement was Turkey's major Islamic armed group, Turkish Hizbollah (not related to Hizbollah in Lebanon). It was reportedly created by the Turkish military and the MIT in the 1980s, to help divide rebelling Kurds in the southeast. In all, up to 20,000 Islamic fighters, most of them Kurds, were indoctrinated and organized surreptitiously into proxy terrorist and assassination squads. Composed of devout and often uneducated rural men from the southeast, Turkish Hizbollah was used as another weapon in the army's own scorched-earth campaign against the PKK (Partiya Karkerên Kurdistan, or Kurdistan Workers Party), a vaguely Marxist armed group fighting for an independent state for Turkey's 20 million Kurds. The PKK uprising began in 1984, and by the time it subsided with the Turkish government's capture of PKK leader Abdullah Ocalan on February 15, 1999, the conflict had left some 30,000 dead with over 3,000 villages destroyed. Throughout the 1990s, however, Turkish Hizbollah murdered over 3,000 businessmen and ordinary civilians, pulling off assassinations and terror attacks that were sometimes too dangerous for official Turkish forces to be involved in directly. This monstrous creation was modeled on America's apparent success in Afghanistan, where it had created the mujahedin to fight the Soviets.

The participation of the state in supporting the holy warriors was confirmed in February 2000 when former Prime Minister Tansu Çiller admitted publicly that she had ordered Turkish Hizbollah to be armed by the military starting six years earlier.[8] Çiller justified the jihadis as a necessary part of Turkey's own war on terror. The former *New York Times* bureau chief in Istanbul, Stephen Kinzer, recounts the scandalous admission:

> When newspapers reported that weapons found at Hizbullah hideouts had come from a military arsenal in the southeast, Tansu Çiller, who had been prime minister when most of the "mystery killings" were committed, proudly admitted her responsibility. "Yes, it was my signature on the order to deliver those weapons," she said. "We met and made a decision. We decided that terror was the main issue and that whatever was necessary to stop it would be done." To the suggestion that she might have exceeded her authority by hiring one terror gang to fight another, she replied simply and no doubt accurately: "The military chief of staff, the governors, the police—everyone worked together on it."[9]

As the war with the PKK raged throughout the 1990s and the infinitely more powerful Turkish Army eventually got the upper hand, the Turkish Hizbollah (supported partially by Iran as well) started diversifying its activities, bombing liquor stores, music clubs, and other "non-Islamic" structures. Despite its attested fervor and appalling methods of torture and killing, which included burying people alive, the rank-and-file of the radical group were largely average, rural Kurds —as were their victims. Indeed, as Emre Yilmaz recalls from former conversations with Turkish Hizbollah veterans in Diyarbakir, many fighters did not know that they were being used as puppets by the Turkish state. When they found out, they were mortified—and furious. One former Kurdish fighter told him how the realization set in:

> We had been instructed to kill the PKK and similar people because they were allegedly bad Muslims. But then we started seeing our friends getting killed. We said "hey, what's going on? We know them and they are not bad Muslims!" Eventually we learned that it was the Turkish government controlling us, and so two MIT spies inserted into Hizbollah were discovered and killed. Soon after that, they killed our leader in Istanbul, and the army bombed our camps. That was the end of Hizbollah.[10]

Indeed, in a four-hour gun battle on January 17, 2000, broadcast live on television, police succeeded in killing Turkish Hizbollah leader Huseyin Velioglu in an Istanbul safe house. The Turkish government undertook a yearlong series of counterterrorist operations against the radical Islamic group it had created, resulting in the detainment of 2,000 individuals and hundreds of arrests. Police also discovered the grisly remains of scores of people who had been tortured and killed by the jihadis. In the end, the Hizbollah movement had to be destroyed because it was on the verge of getting out of control, with its connections to Turkish state security coming out into the open. After the government crackdown scattered Hizbollah to the winds, the most devout and determined fighters escaped to Iran for shelter, religion, and sometimes military training. Today, some of these are still fighting for Islam—but now against the U.S. Army in Iraq. The Turkish experiment with Hizbollah just reinforces the argument that Islamic radical groups can never be controlled by their creators—as the United States learned with the Afghan-Arabs and, later, the Bosnian mujahedin.

A covert program as cynical, deadly, and creative as the one that spawned the Turkish Hizbollah could only have been accomplished by a state possessing a powerful security apparatus, capable of operating according to a no-questions-asked, oversight-free code of independence. Frequently referred to today as Turkey's *Gizli Devlet* ("Deep State"), this security apparatus was created by the United States and NATO early on in the Cold War, when the potential threat of Soviet invasions inspired them to create covert paramilitary forces—quite often composed of right-wing radicals and, indeed, former Nazis and other Fascists, most famously with the Gladio movement in Italy, all across Europe.[11] The Turkish contribution to "NATO's secret armies," the Counter-Guerrillas, was a part of the Turkish Army's Special Warfare Department, housed in the U.S. Military Aid Mission building in Ankara. The Department "received funds and training from U.S. advisors to establish 'stay behind' squads of civilian irregulars who were set up to engage in acts of sabotage and resistance in the event of a Soviet invasion."[12] The secret army also operated closely with the MIT and was supplemented by a nationwide "youth group," the Grey Wolves, established in 1969 under the aegis of the Nationalist Movement Party (MHP) of Alparslan Türkeş, a Counter-Guerrilla member and ultranationalist politician who embraced fascism and dreamed of creating the *Turan,* a pan-Turkic state stretching as far as China.

Military coups in 1971 and 1980, bookended by chronic massacres of civilian demonstrators throughout the 1970s, were all led by Counter-Guerrilla/Grey Wolves elements. Immediately after the 1980 military coup that brought the Counter-Guerrillas leader, General Kenan Evren to power, American CIA Ankara station chief Paul Henze reportedly cabled Washington exulting, "our boys have done it." At that time, the Grey Wolves had 200,000 registered members and 1 million sympathizers nationwide. While Colonel Türkeş and other Grey Wolves were arrested, those who volunteered to fight against Kurdish and Armenian groups were released. As the war against the PKK heated up in the 1980s, the secret armies turned to "black ops" such as torturing and killing Kurds while disguised in PKK uniforms. They also began to turn increasingly to heroin and weapons smuggling, with Grey Wolves leaders given permission to traffic narcotics by the intelligence services in exchange for their cooperation on other issues. A 1998 Turkish parliamentary report revealed that "security forces were responsible for many of Turkey's 14,000 unsolved murders and disappearances in recent years."[13]

Indeed, modern Turkey is situated not just on the crossroads of civilizations, but on the world's most important drug crossroads. Most of the Afghan heroin imported into Europe passes through this vast country. The role of the state, though deliberately obscured, is all pervasive. According to Sibel Edmonds, a former FBI translator and whistle-blower on governmental corruption who is also of Turkish origin, "these [heroin trafficking] operations are run by mafia groups closely controlled by the MIT (Turkish Intelligence Agency) and the military. According to statistics compiled in 1998, Turkey's heroin trafficking brought in $25 billion in 1995 and $37.5 billion in 1996. That amount makes up nearly a quarter of Turkey's GDP." By 1998, at least 15 MIT officers had been killed in the vicious internal battle between the police and the intelligence service over control of the lucrative business. "Only criminal networks working in close co-operation with the police and the army could possibly organize trafficking on such a scale," concluded Le Monde Diplomatique.[14] Edmonds attests that "the Turkish government, MIT and the Turkish military, not only sanctions, but also actively participates in and oversees the narcotics activities and networks."[15]

Edmonds points to the 1998 incident in which Turkish police were discovered using Turkish embassies in Europe to facilitate drug smuggling and the saga of Huseyin Baybasin, once known as "Europe's Pablo Escobar." This Kurdish drug baron jailed in Holland was at one point responsible for 90 percent of the heroin smuggled into Britain—a business that had been enabled by cooperation with Turkish officials. According to immigration tribunal records and a newspaper investigation, Baybasin was granted asylum in England in 1995, in exchange for informing the British Customs & Excise service about Turkish officials involved in heroin trafficking. After being arrested in Holland soon thereafter, Baybasin attested that he had enjoyed "the assistance of Turkish embassies and consulates while moving huge consignments of drugs around Europe, and that Turkish army officers serving with NATO in Belgium were also involved. 'The government kept all doors open for us,' he said. 'We could do as we pleased.'"[16] According to a senior UK Customs officer, the government could not arrest the Turkish kingpins "because they are 'protected' at a high level." Baybasin claimed, "I handled the drugs which came through the channel of the Turkish Consulate in England."[17]

A shocking car crash on November 3, 1996, near the town of Susurluk, on the Izmir-Istanbul road, revealed in one sudden flash the tight connections within the Gizli Devlet. Pulled from the mangled wreck of a Mercedes were a Kurdish parliamentarian linked with terrorist militias, the head of Turkey's counterterrorist police, a beauty queen, and her lover, the former Grey Wolves leader and drug smuggler Abdullah Catli. Pistols with silencers and machine guns, plus false diplomatic passports, were found in the trunk of the car. The only survivor, Kurdish MP Sedat Bucak, was a tribal chief who had been awarded a huge tract of southeastern land by the government. Bucak's task was to guard it with his private army, and he "thus acquired the power of life and death over the area's inhabitants."[18] Catli, it turned out, "was a heroin trafficker on Interpol's wanted list [and] was carrying a diplomatic passport signed by none other than the Turkish Interior Minister himself." Further, Catli had been involved in the assassination attempt on Pope John Paul II in 1981, personally giving would-be assassin Mehmet Ali Agca the gun.[19] Two months after the crash, "a court in Germany found that Tansu Çiller, former prime minister of Turkey, had been protecting heroin traffickers, an accusation that prompted official protests from Ankara."[20]

Catli had also led a special team of hired killers who allegedly worked from a "list" kept by Prime Minister Çiller. After his fatal crash, she hailed him as a "great patriot." Catli took certain liberties with his work, racketeering people by warning them that they were on "Çiller's list," but promised that in return for payment he could get their names removed. "Having pocketed the money, he then went on to have them kidnapped and killed, and sometimes tortured beforehand." Another covert assassin, Ayhan Çarkin, implicated in 91 murders committed in the Kurdish southeast, presented his MIT interrogators as having said:

> We know about that, and nobody is holding that against you. But why did you kidnap Omer Luftu Topal [the casino king]? On your own account? Do you know that you are serving a political master? Namely Prime Minister Tansu Çiller and Mehmet Agar, director-general of the national police.[21]

The key factor that had led to such a sordid state of affairs was the Deep State's transformation after the fall of the Soviet Union. It became a much wealthier and more sophisticated entity, a true multinational corporation with an enormous geographic and economic remit. East of Turkey's Anatolian heartland stretched a series of former Soviet republics, all united by a common Turkic culture. For nationalist politicians and aging fascists like Alparslan Türkeş, Central Asia thus represented a sort of manifest destiny for the greater Turkish nation, the long-awaited chance to fulfill Turkey's historic mission promulgated since the MHP's nationalist rhetoric of the late 1960s. Further, the new republics contained vast quantities of untapped wealth—oil, natural gas, and mineral deposits—and bordered on Afghanistan, the major producer of the world's opium. The combination of such natural resources and strategic positioning (between Russia, China, Afghanistan, Iran, and Turkey) made the Central Asian states, as well as the Caspian Sea and Caucasus, key to what was soon being referred to as the "New Great Game."[22]

The Turkish Deep State and Islamic groups, especially the Gülen movement, had mutual interests in opening up Central Asia to Turkish influence. Economic interest went hand-in-hand with political, cultural, and religious influence. Saudi Arabia, for example, was making determined efforts to bring Central Asian Muslims, who had been deactivated from their faith during the Soviet period into the fold, and it was in the U.S. interest to see that "moderate" Turkish Islam as represented by Gülen would prevail. Besides, every major world power, as well as regional ones had strong interests in developing the energy corridors of Central Asia. Throughout the 1990s, the Clinton administration based its foreign policy to a great degree on "pipeline politics" in the Caspian and Central Asian regions. In 1998, then-U.S. Secretary of Energy Bill Richardson summarized American policy and Caspian oil, stating, "We're trying to move these newly independent countries toward the west. We would like to see them reliant on western commercial and political interests rather than going another way. We've made a substantial political investment in the Caspian, and it's very important to us that both the pipeline map and the politics come out right."[23]

The Turks' fascination with the former Soviet republics (in which Russia, too, was determined to retain influence) was colored by their ethnic kinship affiliations with the Azeri, Kazakh, Uzbek, and Kyrgyz peoples, all cousins in the great Turkic family extending from Mongolia to the Balkans. Some imagined that by strengthening alliances with its ex-Soviet cousins, Turkey could become a superpower in the emerging world order. Particularly fond of the idea was Turgut Özal, Turkey's prime minister from 1983–1989, and then president until his death in 1993. Özal waxed enthusiastically of a new Turkish sphere of influence stretching "from the Adriatic to the Great Wall of China," promising billions of dollars in training, loans, and investments for the Central Asian republics. In 1992, the former Counter-Guerrilla and Grey Wolves leader Alparslan Türkeş visited Azerbaijan, where he was treated as a hero and supported the successful presidential bid of Azeri Grey Wolves sympathizer Abülfaz Elçibay.

The Turkish security apparatus soon proved indispensable for American efforts to counter Russian influence in the region. In fact, one of the original purposes of harnessing the MHP/Grey Wolves pan-Turkic ideology in the 1960s had been precisely to weaken the Soviet Empire through appealing to pan-Turkic identity and unity. Of more immediate usefulness, gathering intelligence by proxy, by "outsourcing" it to the Turks, was much easier than for the Americans to do it themselves. Using its ethnic and linguistic kinship with the Central Asian peoples, the Turkish MIT would become the CIA's eyes and ears on the ground, in the process carrying out shadowy and very lucrative operations for the Americans, spying on the Russians and Islamists and moving guns and drugs. "The CIA could not have operated there like the Turks, who had the cultural and linguistic knowledge," states Sibel Edmonds. "Further, unlike the CIA, the MIT is not reined in by legislation. They are willing to cross more lines...Imagine the scandal if something like Susurluk happened in the US with US officials—they may be corrupt, but they couldn't get away with something of that magnitude. But that is the difference: the CIA wants to keep their hands clean, while Turkey uses military planes to transport drugs on a daily basis."[24] This enhanced role offered both profit and prestige to the Turks, now finding success on a much larger stage. According to Edmonds, dozens of Turkish and Kurdish businessmen became "overnight millionaires" because of the heroin trade, operating through innocuous-sounding front companies in Central Asia.

Simultaneously with the civil war between the government and the PKK—and the use of Turkish Hizbollah by the MIT—the closely related Grey Wolves were sponsoring another mujahedin cause, this one for external use: the jihad in Chechnya against the Russians. The war there elicited the sympathy of Turks on religious grounds, and the Grey Wolves raised funds, ran training camps, and channeled fighters to Chechnya from Turkey. Yet by the end of the 1990s Istanbul itself was the scene of multinational jihadi intrigue, as Iran and Saudi Arabia vied for control of Turkey's pro-Chechen nationalist groups. Some

3,000–5,000 mujahedin were passing through the country; CNN correctly noted that "their movements across Turkey certainly could not take place without at least the tacit consent of the Turkish government. Indeed, it is no longer a secret that the main training camp for the Chechen fighters is at Duzce, a town between Istanbul and the Turkish capital of Ankara."[25]

Led by the Grey Wolves, Turkish fighters had also volunteered to help their ethnic kin in neighboring Azerbaijan, when war erupted there in 1992, in the mountainous border territory of Nagorno-Karabakh, nominally an Azerbaijani province but having an Armenian majority. At first, Russian armaments helped the Armenians establish de facto control and expel tens of thousands of Azeris. Turkey responded by arming the Azeris and by sealing the border with Armenia. There had never been much love between the two; the Armenians accuse Turkey, in its previous Ottoman incarnation, of genocide against 1.5 million Armenians during and after the First World War. Turkey fiercely contests the accusation, which has become a potent political issue, especially in the diaspora. The U.S. Congress nearly passed an "Armenian Genocide" bill in 2000, but squashed it after being threatened with losing Turkish government military contracts; the French Parliament showed no such misgivings on October 12, 2006, when it antagonized Turkey by making it a crime to deny the "Armenian Genocide." On January 30, 2007, Congressional lawmakers introduced a bill, House Resolution 160, that if ratified would symbolically recognize an Armenian Genocide. Turkish officials again intoned darkly about the adverse effects such legislation would have on bilateral relations, at a time when Turkey was becoming an increasingly key player in American security policy in the Middle East.

In 2004, Turkey's war resumed against the Kurdish PKK after the latter called an end to its 1999 cease-fire. The American invasion of Iraq the year before had given the Kurds a safe haven from which to operate, and increased the fears of the Turkish military. The American invasion was hugely unpopular among Turks, who rightly understood that toppling the regime of Saddam Hussein would provoke a civil war and, most dangerously, renewed troubles with Kurdish separatists, who had quieted as Ankara began to offer more rights, in line with its EU obligations. Since the war in Iraq, however, the conflict has returned. Through 2006, over 200,000 Turkish troops remained locked down in the southeast, engaged in sporadic battles with the Kurds, and frequently chased them across the Iraqi border. In addition, the MIT continued to exploit its connections with the ethnic Turkoman population of northern Iraq, fueling Kurdish suspicions of Turkey's alleged interest in controlling the region.

The Turkish military, accused since it utilized Turkish Hizbollah two decades ago of stage-managing domestic terrorism for its own ends, endured further criticism when it turned out that a November 2005 bombing of a Kurdish bookstore in Semdinli, near Diyarbakir, had been conducted by plainclothes MIT agents hoping to blame it on the PKK. In a May 2006 report, *The Economist* voiced concern over Turkey's future in pointing to this incident, the alleged torture and threatened imprisonment of 80 Kurdish children involved in protests after a

PKK funeral in March, and a tough new antiterrorism law that "could spell a return to abuses at the height of the PKK insurgency in the 1990s, when hundreds of writers were imprisoned, thousands of detainees were tortured and many were slain in extra-judicial killings by security forces."[26]

Further, the Turkish-Kurdish conflict may be developing in more complex and dangerous ways. In southeastern Turkey, "many unemployed Kurds, disillusioned by the government, the EU and the PKK alike," the magazine reports, "are turning to Islam. Turkish Hizbullah...is re-organising throughout the south-east under new labels. Its influence is palpable in the shanty towns round Diyarbakir, where unemployed youths say that 'Islam should rule the world.'" With a military returning to the black ops of the 1990s, a demonstrable threat of spillover from Iraq's civil war, and Iran's alleged nuclear weapons program continuing to provoke fears through 2006, the last thing Turkey needed was a new Islamist insurrection.

In the Balkans, on the other hand, Turkey's role is less volatile. A mixture of factors, including its Ottoman cultural and religious legacy and political and geostrategic concerns, have inspired its interest in the Balkan states since the end of the Cold War. Even long before, as was mentioned in Chapter 2, the prototype of the ethnic Albanian militant movement was created, in 1982 in Izmir. A decade later, the Turkish leadership would grant Tirana's defense officials access to top-secret NATO information at its bases long before the latter deserved authorization, in 1992, and it also housed the fugitive Albanian Islamist and former spy chief, Bashkim Gazidede, after the first Sali Berisha government crashed in 1997. From his safe haven in Turkey, Gazidede proved invaluable in helping the MIT with Turkish-Albanian espionage and sabotage operations against Greece.[27] He was allowed to remain in Turkey until pressure (reportedly, American) caused the Turks to expel him in December 2005. Turkey was one of the most active participants of all NATO members in the Kosovo intervention of 1999, hosting KLA training camps and flying many bombing sorties, seeing the war as symbolic revenge against Serbia, the Christian power that had all but driven it from the Balkans 87 years earlier.

Years before the NATO intervention, Turkey had courted Balkan pro-Islamist political leaders from Serbia, for example in 1997, when the Refah Party government was secretly funding two Bosnian Muslim parties in the western region of Sandzak. In Bosnia itself, Turkish interests—economic, religious, and, during the 1992–1995 war, military—have long been vital. Commercial and religious cooperation is extensive and, interestingly enough, Bosnia has become a favorite destination for hundreds of Turkish female students desiring to study while veiled. In this Balkan beachhead of Islam, they can enjoy more overt displays of their Islamic faith than at home.

Indeed, Turkey's fundamental legacy in the Balkans lies in its gift, starting from the fourteenth century and its incarnation as the mighty Ottoman Empire, of Islam to the region. In the absence of such a historical process, the question of the future course of Islam in the Balkans would, of course, not exist today.

For better or for worse, the Turkish heritage is intimately bound up with Europe's course today in light of the religious cleavages and scattered Muslim populations left behind after the Ottomans were expelled from Macedonia during the Balkan Wars of 1912–1913. Today, the Balkan map is a patchwork of religious communities, with Islam in some places concentrated, in others small and diffused. In the modern age of global travel and communications, the oft-cited alleged Islamist goal of a "Green Corridor," in which a contiguous strip of "green" (Muslim inhabited) land stretches from Turkey through Bosnia, Macedonia, Kosovo, Serbia, and Bosnia, is neither believable nor relevant. Nevertheless, it is, of course, the case that foreign Islamic groups, terrorists included, look first to partially or fully Muslim-dominated areas of the Balkans for their radical operations and social colonization projects.

In this light, one of the most interesting and overlooked pockets of Islam in the region lies in Bulgaria, a primarily Orthodox country of 7.4 million on the Black Sea, which has two Muslim minorities, both dating from Ottoman times. Some 1 million Turks, descendants of the Ottomans, live in Bulgaria, primarily near Turkey in the south. A somewhat smaller minority of Pomaks—Slavic Bulgarians converted to Islam during Ottoman times—is settled also in the south, along the Rhodope Mountain region bordering on Greece. While there has long been friction between Turks and Bulgarians due to the notable political clout of the former, the Turks are generally peaceful and "traditional" in their Islamic observance. However, Turkey's request in 2006 to "export" 110 observant female students to a medical university in Plovdiv, on condition that they could study veiled, caused concern. Some 80 percent of the national academic council was opposed to the request, and university head Georgi Paskalev expressed his confusion in stating, "I never had a case like this before and don't know how to proceed."[28]

At about the same time, three young women lost in a court battle to study while veiled. They had been backed by the Association for Islamic Development and Culture, "an NGO founded by Muslims educated in Jordan." Indeed, foreign Islamists have established a strong though still subtle presence in this largely Christian former Communist country, building 700 new mosques. Arab foundations and charities have created new Koranic schools and offered scholarships to young Bulgarian Muslims to study Islam abroad, while Saudi organizations are funding increasing numbers of Hajj pilgrimages. The Sultan of Oman personally invested $400,000 to renovate an Ottoman mosque.[29] In this regard, local and Western intelligence services are most concerned by Bulgaria's other Muslim minority, the Pomaks. Like their Macedonian Muslim Torbeshi kin, the Pomaks have been historically alienated from the majority Bulgarian Orthodox Christian population and are thus more susceptible to outside influence. Because religion constitutes the chief factor in their identity, these poor, pastoralist Slavic Muslims have become prime targets for Arab proselytizers seeking to make inroads in Bulgaria, the European Union country with the largest indigenous Muslim population.

Other shadowy NGOs have recently been exposed as fronts for radical Islam. On February 20, 2007, four persons in Sofia and the southwestern town of Blagoevgrad, and connected with the Union of Bulgarian Muslims, an extremist group founded in 2006, were arrested "for propagating radical Islam and inciting religious hatred." Two of the group's Web sites, which published Chechen jihad propaganda and called for the replacement of Bulgaria's secular state with one ruled by Sharia law, were also shut down. According to Yavor Kolev, the head of a special unit for fighting organized crime, the group was led by a 51-year-old former Sofia mufti, Ali Kheiriddine, who had been collaborating with a Jordanian, Ahmad Mohammad Moussa. The latter had been expelled from Bulgaria in 2000 "for establishing a local branch of the Muslim Brothers, a radical Islam organization."[30] Commenting on the arrests, Bulgarian Islamic scholar Simeon Evstatiev warned that "[radical] Bulgarian Muslims will become part of a global, trans-national network...not only with the Muslims from the Middle East, but also with the European Muslims."[31]

The Union of Bulgarian Muslims was neither the first nor the most dangerous extremist group to have been uncovered in the country, however. In early 2005, Bulgarian investigative journalist Yana Buhrer Tavanier published lengthy reports indicating that a terrorist-linked Wahhabi charity, Al Waqf-Al Islami, had built several new mosques in the country's northeast. The Dutch branch of the charity, which once organized a seminar attended by six of the 9/11 hijackers, had also sent Bulgaria's leading Muslim cleric, Fikri Sali, to Saudi Arabia in July 2004, where he received funds "from dubious Middle Eastern sources" to build "mosques and schools that promote the radical teachings of Wahhabi Islam." Although in 1999 Al Waqf-Al Islami representative Abdulrahim Taha was expelled from Bulgaria, the investigation discovered that "Al Waqf never pulled out of Bulgaria" but actually that "its activities seem to be expanding." The charity was reregistered in 2002, "without any reference to its Islamic character or religious activities," and was said to be led by a 41-year-old Syrian, Muafak al Asaad, who co-owned a Bulgarian firm along with the expelled Taha.[32]

According to the investigation, the Wahhabi mosque-building in Bulgaria has been overseen by a Saudi citizen, Sheikh Abdullah Abdul Aziz Soreya, who started making annual visits to the country in 1993—allegedly to treat "knee problems" in a health spa, but actually to build mosques and pay off imams. His local collaborator, Muafak al Asaad, represented Al Waqf-Al Islami, through its building and renovating mosques in villages and towns such as Razgrad, Bisertsi, Todorovo, Brenitsa, and Stefan Karadzha. A former student told the journalists that "if a lesson lasted 45 minutes, 30 minutes of it would be devoted exclusively to jihad [or holy war], in particular the jihad against infidels and against Turkey...For these people, anyone who is not one of them—a Wahhabi—is an infidel."[33] As elsewhere in the Balkans, the incursions of the Wahhabis have led to intimidation and an internecine struggle for control of religion and Islamic Community-owned property.

Another Islamic boarding school, built in 1997 in the village of Delchevo, is run by a secretive Turkish order, the *Suleymanci,* named after Suleyman Hilmi Tunahan, a religious figure born there in 1888—ten years after the Russian Army defeated the Ottomans in Bulgaria. In Turkey, the Suleymanci possess 1,700 student halls, with almost 100,000 residents, and "today operates at least one Koran course in every Turkish town."[34] In Germany, where a large Turkish diaspora lives, the order has 20,000 adult members, associated with 320 cultural centers, at which 60,000 children study. Religious fervor being somewhat less in Bulgaria, the order there attracts primarily widows with children and poor families drawn to the idea of free housing and tuition for students. According to a Bulgarian imam associated with the school, the method is simple: "We travel from village to village to enroll them. Most of them are poor kids—children of divorced parents, or orphans, or their mother's in Holland and their father in Turkey." The best of the students were sent to Turkey for further training. A girl who did not enjoy her experience at the Delchevo Suleymanci school depicted a setting very similar to what could be expected from the Wahhabis. "They wouldn't let us out to have coffee, or watch television, or talk to boys," she said. "We were reading and studying [the Koran] all the time. We wore headscarves, long skirts and long sleeves in the hot weather."[35]

Bulgaria's experience shows that not only Arab Islamic groups are interested in the struggle for former Ottoman lands. Turkey-based Islamic movements, more so than indigenous Balkan Turks, also seek to control the development of Balkan Islam. Along with the Turkish government's many cultural and architectural projects, designed to refurbish and renovate signs of the Ottoman past, movements like the Suleymanci also keep up Turkish Islamism. So to does Fethullah Gülen, who has established a network of posh private colleges in the former Ottoman Balkan states, enticing high-school and university level Muslim students (and not only Muslims) with state-of-the-art, well marketed private schools that offer access to the modern world, while very subtly reinforcing its trademark "moderate Turkish Islam"—a tactic that has enhanced the value of the Gülen movement in the eyes of Turkish foreign policy planners who see, as was the case in Central Asia, the schools of the eccentric old spiritual leader as a means for the covert spreading of "Turkishness" against competing Islamic forces such as the Saudi Wahhabis and non-Muslim schools established by Western countries.

However, similar to the testimony of the Kurdish former student at a Gülen school in Turkey cited above, it seems that in the Balkans some are being used to spread more radical doctrines behind the scenes. A former student of a Gülen school in Struga, Macedonia, claims that on several occasions "the brightest and most interest students" were given extracurricular lessons in radical Islam. The witness, an ethnic Turk who did not want to be named, claimed that in the Gülen schools of Struga and Gostivar this practice is going on "after hours, in small and specially selected groups of teenage boys...the teacher would introduce them like secret initiates into a cult, praise fundamentalism and so on."[36]

Whether or not this practice represented institutional policy or, more likely, a local deviation is unclear; however, the story offers a revealing glimpse into how even the most benign "moderate Islam" can sometimes be used to mask more radical activities.

Even conceptually, Turkey's historical legacy is still deeply affecting Balkan political and social realities. The Ottoman past is praised and vilified, sometimes in the same sentence, by the region's varied peoples, an ambivalent situation that reflects the ever-shifting relationship of individuals and societies with history itself. While previous generations of Western historiographers accused the Ottomans of having had a corrosive and retarding influence on the Balkans, essentially truncating its development and isolating it from the non-Islamicized West, modern scholars tend to be more forgiving. Whether it stems from political correctness or careful revisionism, historians today have tended to stress the cultural and technological contributions of the Ottomans, and to invoke evidence in defense of the idea that life under the Ottoman millet system, in which Christians were essentially second-class citizens, was really not so bad.

In the Balkans itself, the debate today remains fierce. The notion of triumphant liberation from odious Turkish oppression and occupation is central to the national narratives of almost each country in the region. Only some Bosniak Muslims, and certain other Slavic Muslims and Albanians, argue that the Ottoman Empire represented a sort of golden age that should be resurrected. While for Balkan Muslims Ottoman civilization represents legitimacy and normality, for the far more numerous Christians, the long centuries of Ottoman occupation are portrayed as an unfortunate, twisted, and violent disruption of their preexisting societies, whether Byzantine Orthodox or Roman Catholic. There are very few still alive who remember daily life under the Ottomans, but the wildly differing—and equally true—stories of both happiness and misery under their rule continue to resonate in tales passed down among families, popular legends, and even school textbooks.

Indeed, the Turkish state today remains very sensitive regarding how its Balkan past is remembered. A senior Turkish diplomat in Skopje once lamented the fact that Macedonian schoolchildren were still being taught that their ancestors had been brutalized and humiliated by their Ottoman overlords, something that was, at least during the turbulent revolutionary period from the 1890s to 1912, a perfectly accurate description. "Why can't Turkey and the Balkan countries all just agree on a common school curriculum that is fair to everyone's history?" he said. "It would help minimize destructive nationalism."[37] While such a policy is neither feasible nor desirable, what with its implications for the limitations of free thought, it does indicate the Turkish government's concern to shape the way in which the West perceives its Ottoman European legacy, as such perceptions may have subtle influence over Turkey's "European-ness," and thus its suitability for EU membership.

Although the Turks have been accused of historical crimes against Balkan Christians, the modern reality is much different. By and large, non-Turkish

Muslim populations created during the Ottoman occupation were more involved in the most turbulent Balkan events of modern times than were the Turks, whose reputation for peacefulness and tolerance has been acquired due to their distaste for the wars that gripped the region from 1991 to 2001. Indeed, in Kosovo Turks have on occasion even been expelled by their own Albanian co-religionists. Here and in Macedonia, they have been victims of an aggressive and chauvinistic assimilation program; by virtue of the fact that they are Muslims, the Turks are supposedly "really" Albanian. For Turks, who find their culture's contribution to history somewhat more impressive than that of the Albanian mountain tribes, the affront is irritating. Hakan, a young student in the Macedonian village of Vrapciste, a stronghold of 3,000 Turks who nevertheless lost municipal control to Albanians due to high politics, colorfully retorted to one Albanian's argument: "I told him, 'we have more gay people in Turkey than you [Albanians] have people in the whole world!'" While an exaggeration, it is yet one that illustrates the self-confidence that Balkan Turks, unlike other Balkan Muslims, possess today. This self-confidence has had a mellowing effect and kept them from engaging in the madness of ethnic war that has gripped so many of their neighbors since 1990. However, the fact remains that in Kosovo and Macedonia, the Albanians hold the balance of power, and have used it against the Turks, as local Turkish leaders bitterly note.[38]

Despite their marginalization and continuing obsolescence, the Balkan Turks are still relevant as a stabilizing force, ethnically and religiously, upholding the Sufi school of Islam, which is often regarded as the most peaceful and spiritual of Muslim sects in the region. The Ottoman Turkish legacy holds the key to the future of Islam in the Balkans, and its relation to non-Muslim societies in another way as well. It is inextricably linked with the crucial, preliminary question of what the Balkans was, is, and should be. Was the arrival of the Ottomans and a new religion, Islam, just an unfortunate disruption of Christian life, or did it represent the high point of Balkan culture? Is it something that should be reembraced or banished from memory—or perhaps superseded altogether by secularism or by alien forms of life, such as soulless Western consumerism, or Wahhabi Islam?

The answer to these questions will have very tangible ramifications for the future shape of the region. Every Balkan state except Greece and Turkey endured four decades of Communist rule, in one form or another, from the end of the Second World War until about 1990. During this time, the authorities seized private property from individuals and institutions alike; some, such as the Orthodox churches and Islamic communities, had owned vast tracts of land and numerous urban structures. With the end of Communism and the region's disintegration into small, weak nation-states, the contentious issue of denationalization has sparked controversy everywhere. And this is where the Ottoman legacy becomes so important. Individuals and institutions seeking restitution base their claims to rightful ownership on documents created by various pre-Communist governments. However, their arguments for legitimacy are inevitably colored by their perspective on Balkan history. The only thing everyone can agree on was that the Communist property seizures were wrong. But what previous status quo, then, is the "authentic" one? To which historical precedents can today's claimants argue for their "rightful" ownership of Communist state-seized property?

Unlike in the West, where most Muslims are immigrants or the offspring of immigrants, the long centuries of Ottoman rule in the Balkans allowed Muslim migrants and converts alike to stake out their own claims to legitimacy and ownership on all-important historical terms. Their descendants today thus are not demanding their due based, as in Europe, on "universal" principles of human rights, but rather on claims of historical ownership equivalent to or greater than those of their Christian neighbors, whose restitution arguments rest on the same vexed grounds. This complex issue has been afflicted by acrimonious disputes not only between but within religions, such as the ongoing drama in Macedonia's Islamic Community regarding what faction will control, and so profit from, Community-owned properties.

Some examples of modern property restitution, such as the return of Balkan Jewish shops, synagogues, and whole neighborhoods destroyed by occupying Nazi collaborators in World War II, reflect in clear and irrefutable terms the rectification of unprovoked injustices. The most notable such success to date has been the restitution of property belonging to Macedonia's Jewish community, which lost 98 percent of its population during the Bulgarian fascist occupation.[39] However, few cases are as clear-cut. A Muslim community, and even a Christian one, might point to old Ottoman records to justify a property claim, or perhaps to documents from, say, prewar royalist Yugoslavia. For Serbs, Albanian-dominated western Kosovo (more exactly, "Metohia," a Greek term denoting church-owned lands) had previously been a major possession of the Serbian Orthodox Church during Byzantine times. If the Muslims can cite claims of historic ownership when turning to Ottoman records, why can Christians not do the same when holding up even older Byzantine documents?

Of course, in the modern world right rarely influences might. The final results of denationalization are inevitably decided by eminent domain, "squatter's rights," political control, and corruption. Few have respect for justice. Even the Jewish community in Macedonia, with its undeniable moral right to its Nazi-destroyed properties, had to act fast to keep Skopje's rampant construction mafia—with which high politicians and banks have since been linked—from building on its recovered property sites.[40] In a region with such deep history and so many successive civilizations, the recourse to historical precedence quickly disintegrates into relativism and thus, partisan politicking. Yet even aside from the political process of denationalization, the current war for religious influence seen with the creation and destruction of churches and mosques has profound implications for the future.

Unfortunately for non-Muslims, and for the many Muslims who resent fundamentalist Wahhabi mores, the aggressive campaign to build garish, Saudi-style mosques and disseminate Wahhabi propaganda continues unchecked. Cleverly,

Islamists have even tried to use the thesis of historicity to their advantage when it comes to religious facilities. Some local Muslims seem to have been enlisted for this too. A September 2006 conference in Pristina, dedicated to presenting the facts on five centuries of Albanian Islam, emphasized alleged "pre-Ottoman Islam" in Kosovo. One participant, the Kosovar professor Qemajl Morina, had already been broadcasting this Saudi propaganda for years; in a January 2003 UNMIK radio show, for example, Morina claimed that Islam was originally brought to Kosovo by Arab Saracens, from the ninth to the fourteenth centuries.[41] This audacious attempt to undermine the Ottoman legacy in the Balkans shows that the Saudis are ready to use all means, methods, and local propagandists to fight the surreptitious war with Turkey for the soul of Balkan Islam.

The second relevant issue here is the controversial one of population growth and demographic trends—notoriously difficult to predict because of the myriad factors that go into them, including the effects of urbanization, modernization, emigration, and a changing EU policy on immigration. Nevertheless, it can still be said that Muslim populations are, generally speaking, growing more rapidly than Christian ones throughout the region. In Kosovo, for example, the Serbian Christian population has drastically declined since World War II, with some 150,000 Serbs leaving from 1945–1990 and another 250,000 forced to flee since the NATO intervention of 1999. As has been attested in previous chapters, experts believe that the complete ethnic cleansing of Serbs from Kosovo, now less than 10 percent of the population, is all but inevitable. At the same time, however, Kosovo's Albanian Catholic community is showing slight gains, though Albanian Muslims will continue to make up the majority.

In Macedonia, demographic statistics show that Muslim Albanians account for 89 out of every 100 births in the country.[42] And in Bulgaria, the government fears that Christian Bulgarians will make up less than 60 percent of the population by 2050, as Muslim Turk and Roma populations continue to increase; a recent study revealed that "60–70 percent of all newborns in 2003 and 2004 came from the country's non-Slavic minorities."[43] Muslims tend to marry much younger than Christians and to have a much lower rate of divorce. While Wahhabism and other forms of foreign Islam are not widespread, they are encouraging polygamy, more appealing given the extended periods of time that many young Muslim men spend working away from their families in Western Europe. Everything from poverty, alcoholism, and other health problems to the exigencies of modern employment (women in some foreign-owned Macedonian firms have been hired on the condition that they do not have children for up to four years) have helped to keep the Christian birthrate down. As in Russia, the Serbian Orthodox Church has urged Serbian women to have more babies, and various church leaders have suggested paying Christian families to do so.

In short, it seems that Muslims, already outright majorities in some countries and political "kingmaker" minorities in others, are still expanding and will thus continue to enjoy all of the political, social, and economic benefits that this position entails. While it was once better to be from the majority population, the imported arrival of Western "human rights" and minority concerns has made minority status an economically and politically valuable position in certain countries. Some argue that other factors that tend to reduce the birth count will eventually have a leveling effect, such as urbanization, improved educational opportunities, and economic migration. However, these processes take considerable time and may take effect only after it is "too late" for the Christian populations to avoid returning to their Ottoman status—that is, second-class citizens in their own countries.

At the same time, many individuals of whatever ethnicity or religion seek to leave for the West at their first opportunity, in the hopes of a brighter economic future. The desire to get out has provoked Balkan peoples to use whatever means are available to them, from the legal to the illegal. At times, this has meant shamelessly contradicting national sentiment. Macedonians resent the chauvinistic denial of their national identity by neighboring Bulgaria, which considers them Bulgarians "in denial"; however, when the imminent EU member Bulgaria came out with an offer of passports for anyone who could prove their Bulgarian ancestry, well over 10,000 of them applied.[44] In Kosovo, Albanians seeking to escape from their underdeveloped backwater through 2006 showed no qualms about purchasing passports from a country—Serbia—which they allegedly hated and which they were trying to break off from, for the simple reason that Serbian documents allowed them greater freedom of movement abroad than did UN-Kosovo identity papers.[45]

However, Europe's hardening stance against immigration, already manifested in restrictive laws in countries like Switzerland, has brought an unpredictable factor into play. The Balkan states, including Turkey itself, all seek to join the European Union; to date, only Romania and Bulgaria have. One of the major roadblocks lies not with them but with Western Europeans and their hardening stance on immigration, which is seen, rightly and wrongly, as the source of all evils—from rises in crime to unemployment to Islamic fundamentalism. European Union "enlargement fatigue" seems to have taken hold in many countries. Should Western countries begin mass deportations of mostly Muslim refugees, asylum seekers, and economic migrants back to the Balkans, as has been threatened on several occasions, the results could be catastrophic for Balkan economies, especially in rural areas that have long relied on the remittances of their kinsmen working abroad. The economic collapse that would certainly occur, augmented by the sudden arrival of angry young Muslim men feeling themselves betrayed by Western civilization, and with opulently funded foreign Islamic organizations suddenly the only game in town—this not improbable vision augurs ill for peace, stability, and for the suppression of foreign-funded radical Islamist movements in the former Ottoman lands of the Balkans.

CHAPTER 6

Fixin' to Lose

It was a clear autumn day in a Kosovo cornfield, and the three soldiers of the Texas National Guard were swapping tales from back home. Inevitably, they were about hunting and fishing adventures involving charging stags, monster catfish, and sucking snake venom out of one's arm. One lanky, lighthearted soldier told about his swampy, snake-filled east Texas lake, where sometimes uninitiated sightseers would get the bright idea to boat over to those cute little baby alligators, snatch 'em up, and try to bring 'em home. "Only thing is, they don't see that big, mean-lookin' mama alligator, and she don't like it too much, someone messin' with her babies," the Texan drawled. "And if you're in a nine-foot boat, and there's a twenty-foot gator comin' at you—boy, you're fixin' to *lose!*"

This hard vignette symbolizes precisely the West's predicament with the war on terror in the Balkans. It cannot go after the little gators, for fear of the big gators. As for the big gators, their snapping jaws have to be appeased with handouts. As if to make up for this failure, the West has simply dropped its nets for whatever innocuous animal happens to get tangled up in them, hardly bothering to "drain the swamp," as President Bush famously pledged to do around the world in the wake of 9/11.

While this might seem a harsh indictment, it is nevertheless true, especially in places that have long been under the control of unaccountable peacekeeping operations, such as Kosovo and Bosnia, as well as in Macedonia, Romania, and Bulgaria, where political interference, black ops, and economic intimidation have time and again singled out the wrong people for persecution. While there have been some successes, these have been mostly thanks to local governments faced with more acute threats than those the foreigners have to worry about.

Moreover, the decision to trawl the dark and murky depths has resulted in some fairly amoral, if concealed, behavior from Western governments in this so-called war on terror.

The reasons why the West is fixin' to lose in the Balkans are manifold. They stem first of all from the weaknesses inherent to all peacekeeping missions, such as an emphasis on careerism naturally resulting in local political appeasement, gross negligence and dereliction of duties, unprofessional disinterest and unaccountability, and the frequent internecine struggles between and within allied nations determined to pursue individual interests at the expense of the greater good. Aside from peacekeeping, the failure to prosecute the war on terror efficiently owes as well to the political machinations and economic intimidation of foreign powers, typically in collusion with the chosen factions of local governments. A former CIA deputy chief of base in Turkey, Philip Giraldi, attests that "the US government, the British, and the Germans are well aware of the Islamist presence in the Balkans." However, he adds, these powers "have done little to counter them apart from supporting corrupt local governments and training law enforcement." Giraldi goes further. "The war on terror is a mistake in every sense," he states. "It empowers the terrorists and makes them heroes in their own cultures. It is inefficient and it seeks a military solution to what is an intelligence and police problem."[1]

Some experts also argue that a reliance on technology over human intelligence has hampered Western, and particularly American, efforts in the war on terror in the Balkans. Says Serbian counterterrorism specialist Darko Trifunovic, "We feel that the US often puts too much emphasis on satellites and other technological methods. First and foremost, we believe in human intelligence. It was a classic HUMINT (Human Intelligence, that is, the use of people rather than technology to garner firsthand intelligence) operation that the Bosnian Serb Republic authorities ran when they thwarted the attempted bombing of Pope John Paul II's funeral in 2005." According to Trifunovic, the typical Muslim informer is "motivated by money or disappointment with the movement."[2]

The cumulative outcome of these structural factors and politico-economic policies is that the West has misallocated vital resources and deliberately ignored or allowed itself to be distracted from real threats for reasons that can only be described as self-serving, corrupt, or "politically correct." Yet this is by no means meant as a condemnation of all, or even most, of the brave men and women combating terrorism in the Balkans, whether for international institutions or their own local governments. Their testimony gives rare and damning insight into what has gone wrong over the past decade in the Balkans—and also how it can be changed, before it is too late.

Many currently serving officials troubled by what they have seen are afraid to speak on the record, waiting until their retirement and pensions are ensured before setting the record straight. Others are more forthcoming. Michael Stephen Harrison, the former British soldier and a UNMIK Field Coordinator for Protection of Minorities, expresses disgust at the disinterest he has seen in regards to the

Islamic threat. "The UN has no idea what's going on," charges Harrison. "They have shown total ineptitude." The employees who actually care have been marginalized, fired, or ignored, says Harrison. He recalls a "senior British military analyst" who resigned in 2002 because UNMIK top brass "refused to listen to his warnings or respect his 30 years of experience. He was one of the best. But they didn't care to hear about bad news." Another casualty of curiosity was the former OSCE Security Officer and whistle-blower, Tom Gambill. "I kept telling Tom to be careful, because he just wouldn't stop telling them news they didn't want to hear," says Harrison. "Remember, these high UNMIK officials have all sculpted golden futures for themselves out of their career here...to make sure they are promoted to a better posting somewhere else, they have to maintain this charade that everything is rosy in Kosovo."[3]

Gambill, who worked for the OSCE from October 1999 to May 2004, believes that his contract was not renewed specifically because of his frequent warnings to higher-ups about foreign-supported Islamist organizations and Albanian extremist paramilitary groups. Although he was a contract employee to an international organization, not the U.S. military establishment, Gambill interacted with plenty of army and intelligence officials from the United States and allied countries. When he brought up evidence and intelligence gleaned from sources in the field indicating a terrorist presence, however, Gambill was usually ignored. During regular security briefings at the U.S. Army's Camp Bondsteel, Gambill had some supporters, but by and large "more people thought I was being a pain in the ass," he cracks. "The peacekeeping motto was, 'don't rock the boat.' So long as everything bad that was going on could be hushed up or smoothed over, the policy was to leave it alone."[4] Gambill's testimony is reminiscent of the situation in Bosnia a few years earlier where, according to the *Jerusalem Post,* the Clinton administration had sought "to keep the lid on the pot at all costs" regarding its role in the Iranian infiltration of the country.[5]

As is shown in Chapter 7, higher international politics ultimately was behind this see-no-evil, hear-no-evil policy. Yet the situation on the ground also required a prudence that frequently bordered on outright cowardice. While the UNMIK and KFOR commanded irrefutable authority from the United Nations and Western governments, as well as huge budgets and well-stocked arsenals, the operative restrictions at work indicated a different day-to-day reality. The international administration that set up shop in July 1999 had to deal with the hardened fighters of the KLA, most of whom were dangerous and some of whom controlled powerful, clan-based organized crime networks, while moonlighting as politicians. Since such men had the capability of causing everything from political liquidations to mass armed resistance at the snap of a finger, UNMIK officials quickly realized it was better to come to an understanding with the ex-KLA than to cross it; "the deal was, you leave us alone, we leave you alone," a former Swedish OSCE official in Kosovo sums up. "It had its benefits, mainly, that we were allowed to live."

Yet not only did the UN tolerate the mafia in Kosovo, it even worked with it. According to a detailed study of the prostitution business in Kosovo by investigative journalist Victor Malarek, American soldiers and police tolerated—and perhaps even profited from—the Albanian mafia's trafficking in young women from Eastern European countries.[6] And then there was the UN's handover of police dossiers compiled by the former Yugoslav regime on KLA leaders and Mafiosi to the Kosovo Albanian leadership, ensuring that the information would never be used against them in any future war crimes trials or Interpol investigations. The paramilitary thugs also found in the files a treasure trove of information on police informants and witnesses, who were summarily executed.

Such overtures were part of the price of admission for UNMIK in Kosovo. No doubt, there were (and are) plenty of "true believers" in the rightness of the Albanian cause, international officials who remained willfully blind despite the widespread atrocities being carried out against non-Albanians. By and large, however, the average UN official in Kosovo just realized it was better for their personal safety to humor the men with guns. This meant not interfering with organized crime syndicates, blocking investigations into their wartime activities and promoting them to high positions of political power. In exchange, UNMIK leaders got to partake in financial and other forms of corruption, as well as special "services" courtesy of the mafia; indeed, author Malarek quotes in his book an UNMIK officer who states that international policemen never had to pay for sex in the mafia-run brothels and bars.[7]

In the early years of the UNMIK occupation, this dubious coexistence was not particularly detrimental to the war on terror, partially because that war did not yet exist and partially because, as Tom Gambill put it, KLA political leader Hashim Thaci "had scared the hell out of the imams," warning them not to call for jihad against the internationals. However, as time wore on, the foreign-funded Islamists succeeded in becoming both more independent and more interconnected within the fabric of Kosovo politics and society. They did not risk crossing the line by attacking internationals. But they did participate in the Macedonian war, create safe havens for foreign radicals, and continue to build mosques and Islamic indoctrination schools while, perhaps most dangerously, also establishing business connections with the Albanian mafia.

Although some suspicious Islamic charities were shut down following 9/11, many others were not. For Tom Gambill, the apparently unrestricted operations of one in particular—the infamous Revival of Islamic Heritage Society (RIHS) —became practically a personal crusade. The RIHS had been linked to al Qaeda and blacklisted by the Bush administration in Pakistan and Afghanistan. It was essential to Ayman Al-Zawahiri's Egyptian Islamic Jihad cell in Tirana in the mid-1990s. Bosnian mujahedin used the RIHS in Zenica as a jihad propagandizing center. In February 2003, RIHS activities were also banned in Russia. And on August 18, 2005, in Bangladesh, terrorists later linked with the RIHS detonated some 500 bombs across the country.

Shockingly, however, the group has not been closed down in Albania, Kosovo, or Bosnia, despite the unaccountable disappearance of some 14 million euros from its Sarajevo bank accounts in 2005. The reason for this hands-off approach, most likely, is that the Arab sheikhs behind RIHS's Kuwait headquarters are involved with the oil and other businesses together with Western political and business leaders.

Although Gambill did not yet have all these facts about the RIHS, he knew from police reports and photos that the group was active in the central Kosovo village of Malisevo and was presumed to be dangerous. The security officer made a point of bringing it up at security meetings and in written correspondence with the U.S. Department of State throughout 2003. However, he ran up against a brick wall. "I had this info [about the charities] all the way back in 2001," says Gambill. "But the State Department didn't want to hear about it." He recalls:

> I brought it up at every meeting I went to that included [the U.S.] military, but *nada*. Many of the American KFOR guys were there for their six months—you know, get the ribbon, do a few good deeds, and go home. And those who confided in me didn't want to rock the boat with their superiors...the thinking was, "hey, we're here for only six months—let's get the job done as assigned and get home."[8]

Cases such as that of the RIHS attracted attention, says Gambill, from a handful of "motivated" American security officials who "wanted a piece of the action." However, he says, "they were held back in some cases by orders from those higher up in the pecking order. This was much to the disgruntlement of the lower echelons—lieutenants, captains, some majors...the same thing with the CivPol [UN Police]." When Gambill presented photographic evidence of the RIHS presence in Kosovo, and waved the UN decree outlawing the group, the FBI representative at the time was "somewhat peeved." Later, he claims, "I was verbally attacked via e-mail by an American major...He said that I was not qualified to make comments, and that neither my information nor comments were accurate. However, the comments he was making were erroneous... and completely unwarranted. After forwarding his comments to my point of contact on the American base, he (another major) was taken back at this kind of behavior."

In early 2003, an American colleague at the OSCE complained to Gambill's division head, claiming that the whistle-blower "was sending out information contained in OSCE classified reports, which was incorrect," according to Gambill. "I got my information from non-classified sources and correctly triangulated my information before writing anything and distributing. In other words, I always obtained the same information from at least three different sources that were unrelated but consistent. This then qualified as reliable information. I also used a disclaimer, just in case. So his complaint was inaccurate and made for personal reasons, as I learned after I confronted my manager about the report and source."

Yet most who dismissed Gambill's concerns, he contends, only claimed to be experts—though they visited Kosovo once or twice a year:

The ones who did not believe my reports were many internationals who argued that these things [Wahhabi penetration, etc.] didn't occur in Bosnia, and that therefore the Islamic fundamentalists were not a threat. They claimed that there were no organized efforts on the part of the Islamic fundamentalists and that the [Albanian] rebel groups causing trouble were not a significant concern. That line came from many of the US military commanders who came through the region once every six months. There was no continuity in the passing of intelligence from one unit to another—ever.[9]

These realities have been only too evident throughout the Bosnian and Kosovo peacekeeping missions, where arrogant, careerist diplomats and military men claim to know the situation on the ground better than do those working there. Yet these were the people shaping policy—by listening to the underlings who said what they wanted to hear and ignoring those who, like Gambill, had a less flattering story to tell about the aftereffects of the Western intervention.

Quietly, however, some of the whistle-blower's colleagues were thanking him for his contributions: "In several meetings of the combined group (U.S. military, UN, and CivPol), just as many commended me for the information that I brought to the table," he recalls. "I was told that my sources and reports were 90 percent accurate and were appreciated. In one case, a commander came to me after a meeting and commended me on my participation in all his meetings and gave me a unit coin for my contributions. It was done quietly, of course."

Gambill's interest in dubious charities like the RIHS won support from sympathetic security officials, who provided him with further "accurate reports and bits of info that helped to substantiate the info that I was putting out." He began receiving photos and police documents confirming the presence of the group. One of these reports, dated July 26, 2003, recounts that UNMIK police in Malisevo had discovered a Tirana-registered RIHS vehicle, drive by a Kosovo Albanian and a Kuwaiti. Both had UNMIK ID cards, and their vehicle was registered to the Tirana branch of the RIHS. The pair told the officers that "this is a humanitarian organization and they have representative offices in many cities in Kosovo and they visited an Islamic office in Malisevo. The purpose of this organization is to take care [of] orphans in Kosovo."[10]

A second police report, dated September 20, 2003, mentions a different, Kosovo-registered RIHS vehicle driven by an Arab in nearby Orahovac and reveals that the RIHS had asked Human Appeal International (HAI), a Dubai charity based in the English city of Manchester, to fund and build a mosque in the town—"the third mosque they [HAI] have constructed in Kosovo."[11] On HAI's official Web site, however, mosque-building is not listed as one of their humanitarian activities—though orphan sponsoring is. Two days after this second police report was made, on the other side of the world Australian television was citing FBI information indicating that among its other activities, HAI was a fund-raiser for Hamas.[12] The charge led to an arrest of a Hamas activist in the West Bank two years later.[13] Of course, the UNMIK authorities took no notice.

In fairness, some of the limitations of the war on terror in Kosovo have been due to the structural limitations of the UN mission itself. Because most civilian employees and all military units are deployed on six-month or one-year assignments, the regular rotation of personnel over the past eight years has crippled UNMIK's intelligence capacities. Albanian and Serbian are very difficult languages, and most of the foreign employees and soldiers sent to Kosovo have knowledge of neither. It is not hard to see why failure becomes a distinct option. In Kosovo, the situation since 1999 has been of a culturally ignorant, frequently changing international staff supposed to control a virtually impenetrable group of KLA successor organizations—from the UN-sanctioned KPC police and pseudomilitary Trupat Mbrojtëse të Koseves (TMK, or Kosovo Protection Corps, KPC) to the shadow secret services kept by the major Albanian political figurers. On top of that there are the Arab and other Muslim charities and organizations, as well as the Serbian and Turkish organized crime elements.

The chronic changeover of civil and military staff meant that whereas the locals had learned early on how to understand and manipulate the internationals, the latter were always starting from square one. The learning curve only got steeper, with too few personnel staying more than a year. Worse, as Gambill lamented, senior Western security officials visited only every six months or so. "The UN didn't really understand what was going on—and they didn't want to know," he charges, citing cases such as higher-ups' apparent disinterest in investigating six Albanian-American radicals with stated foreknowledge of the 9/11 attacks. "There was no continuity of mission, or pass-on intel." The endless stream of fresh-faced, ignorant personnel posed no threat to Kosovo's powerful criminals and extremists. Peacekeeping in Kosovo became a thankless and truly Sisyphysian labor.

To field an American intelligence agent possessing any one of the relevant languages, let alone a more helpful combination of them, would require training that simply was not and is not available. On its Web site in early 2006, KFOR put out an advertisement for an "intelligence analyst" to work in Pristina. The only language required was English; Albanian, Serbian, Turkish, or Arabic were not so much as mentioned. As the Bush administration has focused on Afghanistan, Iraq, and Iran, the Balkan war on terror has become all but forgotten. As Michael Harrison reminds, "All of our intelligence assets have been shipped to Iraq. We've provided a window of opportunity, and now it has become essentially carte blanche for the Islamic extremists." Instead, the United States has had to rely on "buying" local informers, whose testimony is often factually challenged by hidden interests.

Indeed, as not only Harrison but also Serbian and American military officials attest, the American military was, by mid-2006, not even responsible for collecting its own intelligence anymore. According to a U.S. military official based at Camp Bondsteel, "We farmed it out to the Romanians," referring to a Romanian brigade under U.S. command in southeastern Kosovo. "But they don't do such a bad job—at least far as we know." Some, like Harrison, are more damning. "Oh, it's still standard intel procedure—a round-table working group once a month, like always—but now it's not even the British or US doing their own job. It's like flying a plane without a pilot!"

With the best intelligence staff now shipped out to Iraq and other fronts in the war on terror, the United States has had to rely more and more on its old relationships with the Albanian mafia to keep abreast of the situation. British analysis firm Jane's reported in September 2006 that UNMIK has allowed "illegal" private intelligence agencies run by ex-KLA leaders of Albanian political parties to operate unhindered, "because of assistance given to the USA and its allies in keeping tabs on potential Islamist militancy in the region."[14] According to an American intelligence expert with extensive experience in the Balkans, "What this means, in other words, is we've picked the devil we know over the devil we might not know...of course, we're relying on [the Albanians] to demonstrate good faith with their intel. But often, I suspect, they've taken us for a ride."[15]

Indeed, Harrison recalls an episode in which UNMIK's Team 6 Anti-Terrorist Unit "got supposedly hot info about Islamic activities. They geared up and made a raid on what turned out to be an empty cow-shed in a field." One of the Texas National Guard soldiers recalled a similar story, in which a U.S. aerial drone shot photos of a smuggling operation en route from the Macedonian border into Kosovo's southeastern town of Vitina. "We knew exactly what café we should be at, where the guy would be. But after we had this information about it, they waited two hours to send us down there," the Guardsman states. "So by the time we got there, he had unloaded whatever was most important, and there were only socks and chocolate left on them donkeys."[16]

Faced with this stultifying apathy and, perhaps, complicity with criminal and terrorist activities on the part of the authorities, some like Gambill have sought to air out their grievances. Others have taken matters into their own hands. This has ultimately ended in failure. One American special police investigator recalls how, in early 2006, several wanted men—North African Islamists—with passports from a Western European country were sheltered in a Kosovo apartment belonging to local Islamic fundamentalists. "A police buddy and I staked out this building, and interviewed some people," he said. "We had photos and good information that showed these guys should be dealt with. You think anyone [in UNMIK] cared? No chance. Why do you think I'm leaving?"[17]

Further, the officer charged that the Kosovo Albanian government leaders—the same ones that, according to Jane's, are supplying the United States with "intelligence" on Islamic extremists in the province—have blocked investigations and staffed the civil administration with the often underqualified friends and relatives of known Islamists. "The Kosovo Department of Justice won't act on [counterterrorist information], because the people inside the institution are from the 'other side.' It's very frustrating—and a very dangerous thing for the future." Michael Harrison refers to another case later in 2006, in which an undercover investigator from a Central European country posed as a mafia figure interested in buying rocket-propelled grenades (RPGs) from an Albanian Islamist.

"No one cared. No one [in UNMIK] gives a shit. We have terrorists here, and the Wahhabis coming in from everywhere. Instead of doing something about it, you have the Germans donating 30 tons of weapons for Kosovo's future army, the TMK, now in storage." Tom Gambill added in the fall of 2006 that a NATO internal map from 2003 listing some 17 illegal paramilitary and terrorist training camps was "still currently valid, to the best of my knowledge."

The danger of Kosovo becoming a terrorist transfer zone has been increased since the internationals handed over border control duties to the local Albanian authorities. What this means, in essence, is that there is no longer a border with Albania itself. While border policing was hardly stellar during the period of UNMIK's direct control, it has now effectively vanished. For the United Nations, relinquishing control of Kosovo's borders is just another of the scheduled "transfer of competencies" from international to local rule. In Macedonia, too, where an experiment in ethnic coexistence has left the western third of the country largely in the hands of former NLA leader Ali Ahmeti's men, there is no appreciable border with Albania either. According to one Macedonian military intelligence officer, even though small militant groups are "smuggling heavy weapons in every day from Albania," there is no will to stop the trade, "because all the local police are Albanian, they are in it together, and they don't talk [to outsiders]." [18] The officer feared that the well armed groups could act to destabilize the country in the case of any failure to make Kosovo independent—indicating the complex trap the West has made of the region through its interventions.

Aside from the criminal neglect of UNMIK authorities in the war on terror, far more serious and hostile actions that can only be described as power plays by the world's most powerful nations have also occurred. The EU accused some of its member states, as well as non-EU Balkan aspiring members, of harboring "secret prisons" for the CIA's extraordinary rendition program, in which suspected terrorists are kidnapped and sent to American "black sites" for questioning under extreme physical duress. The program, which essentially began in Albania under the Clinton administration, has been criticized by groups such as Amnesty International and Human Rights Watch. In a report published on November 29, 2006, the European Parliament charged that 11 European countries, including Macedonia and Romania, had colluded with the CIA in its extraordinary rendition program, opening their airports and facilities for the American government's covert war on terror. According to the report, "at least 1,245 CIA-operated flights flew through European airspace or stopped at European airports." Poland and Romania were singled out as likely former hosts of secret detention camps. [19] The Swiss military's Onyx satellite interception system reportedly intercepted a fax from Cairo to the Egyptian Embassy in London in November 2005, which "confirmed the presence of CIA detention centers in Kosovo, Bulgaria, Ukraine, and Macedonia." [20]

The event that brought greatest grief to the last was the controversial case of Khalid el-Masri, a German citizen of Lebanese background who claimed to have been removed from a bus after entering Macedonia from Serbia on December 31,

2003, and taken to a secret location in Skopje where he was beaten and interrogated for three weeks before being handed over to the Americans. Then, el-Masri claimed, he was shipped to Afghanistan on a CIA "ghost plane" and interrogated again for another four months. Finally, after it was decided that el-Masri was innocent, he was dumped in a field in Albania, before being flown back to Germany by Albanian authorities.[21] Embarrassingly for the CIA's powers of deduction, the Lebanese man was guilty only of having the same name as one of bin Laden's henchmen. Supported by the American Civil Liberties Union, Khalid el-Masri sued the CIA and its former director, George Tenet. However, the case was thrown out in May 2006 by a judge who, while conceding that the unfortunate victim of mistaken identity should be entitled to some form of redress, stated that it should not be through the courts: "Private interests must give way to the national interest in preserving state secrets."[22] In November 2006, el-Masri's lawyers petitioned a federal appeals court to hear the case, arguing that there was no longer anything secret about it. At the time, el-Masri also planned to appear before Democratic senators on the Senate Judiciary Committee investigating the Bush administration's rendition program and chronic invocation of the State Secrets Act to block lawsuits such as his.[23]

While the powerful U.S. government could afford to ignore cases such as el-Masri's without much trouble, things were much different for little Macedonia, trying to please both its American minders and the European Union, which it aspired to join. Macedonia's steady process of reforms ran into a snag when the European Union made an issue of the el-Masri case—and the refusal of Macedonian police officials to cooperate with their investigation. Like the other Balkan and Eastern European countries implicated in the renditions scandal, the Macedonian government was being torn by two powerful forces—allegiance to the Americans and full disclosure in front of the Europeans. Unlike other implicated countries, such as Poland, Macedonia was not yet an EU member and thus had less protection. Stuck in this deeply unenviable position, the country lost valuable time and energy, and earned another demerit from ever-critical Brussels. Having arrested and tortured the wrong man, the United States was flamboyantly fighting a fraudulent war on terror, compounding this mistake by simultaneously ruining Macedonia's standing with Europe. In short, it was a lose-lose situation, and one that made no one any safer from the real terrorists.

As two additional cases also reveal, nowhere in the Balkans has the war on terror been more opaque, more deceptive, and more prone to manipulation than in Macedonia. One particularly brazen abuse of powers occurred to secure U.S. business interests and score political points. In December 2003, the Macedonian company Mikrosam, a leading manufacturer of highly specialized machinery and equipment for the composite industry, was blacklisted by the U.S. government, along with its owner, inventor Blagoja Samakoski. Accused of engaging in "missile technology proliferation activities," Mikrosam was banned both from importing American items under the jurisdiction of the Missile Technology Control Regime (MTCR) and the U.S. Export Administration Act and from exporting such items to the United States for two years. Mikrosam was further prohibited for two years from acquiring U.S. government contracts involving the same items. A U.S. State Department official told the media that Samakoski and his company had sold "dual-use items capable of being used to develop a missile with a range of 300 kilometers and capable of carrying at least a 500-kilogram payload...to a non-MTCR member."[24] When the sanctions were renewed in April 2004, the State Department named the "non-MTCR member" as Iran.[25]

The sanctions were disastrous for Mikrosam, which has since 2005 been completely rehabilitated. They effectively crippled the company's business with the United States, forced it to lay off half its work force, and tarnished the image of the company and its president, who was at the time recovering from a massive stroke. There was one problem, however: the case was a total fraud. Dreamt up by opportunistic officials in the U.S. Embassy in Skopje and political appointees in the Macedonian secret service, the sanctions directive rested on false allegations and was motivated by mixed desires for economic punishment, political revenge, and shameless career advancement. It showed how political opportunism wedded with economic self-interest could ruin the reputation of a legitimate business, whose major crime, it seems, was in having been too competitive on the open market with American firms. Predictably enough, American diplomats crowed about this great victory in the war on terror and held up the case as an example of their eternal vigilance against the proliferation of weapons of mass destruction, while the same Macedonian officials benefiting from the crackdown pretended to show contrition and promised to tighten their export-control measures—with the help of American technology and know-how, of course.

The lack of supporting facts in the government's case is probably what kept the international media from taking much interest in the Mikrosam sanctions. On the other hand, the media at the same time failed to probe the veracity of the allegations. By default, therefore, the company remained guilty by implication. Mikrosam owner Samakoski is a respected inventor who has personally and through his company won major prizes for technical achievement and inventions in Macedonia as well as internationally, from the Belgian government, among others. Dr. Samakoski, whose children have undertaken higher education in America and subsequently been employed with leading American corporations, was at the time of the blacklisting also president of the Macedonian-American Chamber of Commerce. In short, he was hardly the anti-American terrorist supporter the sanctions insinuated him as being.

Initially, Dr. Samakoski maintains, it was his political criticism of "the corrupt Macedonian government" led at the time by the Social Democratic Party (SDSM) that inspired Zoran Veruseski, then-chief of the Macedonian secret service, "to manufacture a case of lies against me and Mikrosam, which was used with the full knowledge of [former] US Ambassador Lawrence Butler to promote the unproven allegations and institute sanctions." American diplomats in Skopje and Washington jumped at the chance to play their little role in the war on terror. Yet the claim that Mikrosam had done business with Iran was a blatant deception. "Mikrosam and I have never ever done any business with Iran," attests Dr. Samakoski. "This lie was conveniently manufactured in Skopje and was used in the US Congress, for internal US politics and for career-building in the US State Department." At the same time, he points out, "according to the American press, Halliburton makes business with Iran through Bahrain, of about $2 billion [annually], while Mikrosam has never ever exported anything to Iran."[26]

The second factor leading to the sanctions was economic. Dr. Samakoski and other critics of the U.S. action suspect that Mikrosam became a victim of its own success. It had successfully won a contract with a Pakistani bus company, following a fair and competitive tender in which the other main bidders had been an American and a German company. According to Dr. Samakoski, this angered the Americans, as did his unwillingness to share unconditionally the strategies that had made his company the leading high-tech firm in Macedonia. "During the initial discussions in 2003, a US Embassy official, [then-Deputy Chief of Mission] Eleanor Nagy asked me to reveal our commercial strategies," he states. "But she offered no guarantees that they wouldn't end up in the hands of our competitors, both American and German." Ironically, the U.S. Embassy in Skopje had established several projects—employing, of course, American consultants—designed to teach Macedonia about the virtues of competitiveness; however, when a company from this tiny and inconsequential country actually dared to compete in a tender coveted by the Americans, it was time to crack down.

An even worse sin on the part of Mikrosam was the company's release of a new invention that interfered with an industry-wide pricing schedule. Mikrosam's filament winding machine, based on a Windows platform and with "off-the-shelf" components, was offered for almost 40 percent cheaper than similar German and American models. Mikrosam thus interfered with their projected prices for the next generation of machinery. As is common with most similar industries, the companies have the technology, but release it incrementally to keep prices and profits steady. Mikrosam's devotion to free market competitiveness wreaked havoc with their plans.

Oddly enough, the sanctions came without warning. According to Dr. Samakoski, "Ambassador Butler knew about our exports to Pakistan six months in advance, yet never bothered to mention anything about them." Before the sanctions, he says, Mikrosam was visited "more than five times by US Embassy officials, including Ambassador Butler, and before him [his predecessor] Mike Einich. During their visits, none of them bothered to mention any laws about dual-use equipment. Similarly, no Macedonian official ever warned Mikrosam of dual-use equipment nor has so far instigated an investigation into our production...Mikrosam cooperated fully, answered all questions openly and maintains an open invitation to both the Macedonian government and the US government [to come]."

Indeed, in light of the severity of the alleged threat to international security, the U.S. Embassy's conduct regarding the Mikrosam case seemed remarkably blasé, as Dr. Samakoski's recollections attest:

Mikrosam invited, many times, officials from the US Embassy in Skopje to visit our company and clarify all points of disagreement. During the inquiry and after the sanctions, the US Embassy under Ambassador Lawrence Butler and Mr. Victor Myev never came to visit and inspect our facilities and machines. Yet Mr. Myev, who was responsible for dual-use equipment in the US Embassy in Skopje, frequently went paragliding in Krusevo, 20 kilometers from Prilep, passing Mikrosam along the way. But he apparently never had the time to visit us or warn us about any possible real or faked misconduct.[27]

Jason Miko, an American with long experience in the Balkans in the nongovernmental sector, in the private sector and in political consulting, is familiar with the Mikrosam case and Dr. Samakoski, whom he has known for more than six years. Seconding Dr. Samakoski's allegations, Miko states that he attempted to help him by "facilitating dialogue" with the former economic officer at the U.S. Embassy in Skopje, but that this officer "did not want to talk about the case."[28]

The subsequent failure on the part of the American or Macedonian authorities to take further legal action against the company was telling. "Before, during and after the sanctions, we have cooperated with all law enforcement, [and] all of our exports are subject to dual-use commission and customs regulations," says the Mikrosam president. "We have had no objections and no rejections, and we haven't broken any laws to this day. Our production program was and remains publicly [displayed] on the Internet." Indeed, states Dr. Samakoski, "to this day there have been no formal investigations, proofs or cases against Mikrosam in any court of law proving the illegal sanctions instituted by the US Embassy in Skopje under [former] Ambassador Lawrence Butler. Can you see the similarities with the el-Masri case?"

In addition to secret renditions and politico-economic deceptions, murky manipulation of the war on terror in Macedonia has involved police counterterrorism actions. The controversial "Rastanski Lozja" affair of 2002, in which seven foreign Muslims were killed by special police, represents either a crass deception on the part of a former Macedonian government or a high-stakes covert operation plotted by Western intelligence services to damage the credibility of that government. In either case, it would represent a disturbing abuse of the war on terror for political purposes. The first hypothesis has become conventional wisdom, whereas the second has never really been investigated; however, as will be seen, compelling testimony from witnesses makes a case for such covert hostile interference.

On March 2, 2002, a special police unit conducted a predawn raid in a vineyard to the northeast of Skopje, a place called Rastanski Lozja. Interior Minister Ljube Boskovski, from the then-ruling nationalist government led by the VMRO-DPMNE party, quickly held a press conference to show the results of the raid: seven dead South Asian men (they turned out later to be six Pakistanis and one Indian citizen), armed with a variety of weapons, Islamic literature and paraphernalia, and even uniforms of the Albanian NLA paramilitary. According to Boskovski, the dead men were terrorists bent on attacking Western embassies in

Skopje. He hailed it as a great success for Macedonia in the war on terror, then less than six months old. In retaliation, the Macedonian consulate in Karachi would be bombed by terrorists nine months later.[29]

Western governments, media, and the Macedonian political opposition were more cynical, however. The BBC noted that "Western leaders have in the past been sceptical about reports of foreign Islamic militants operating in Macedonia," thus subtly cast aspersions on the official account.[30] This was cemented three weeks later in a BBC report by journalist Nicholas Wood who, citing "senior US diplomats," claimed that "they no longer think the men had any terrorist connection and a senior migration expert says he believes the men may have been illegal immigrants...It seems clear though that the government claims about a terrorist plot are unfounded, leaving many to question the motives behind the Ministry of the Interior's story."[31] Such coverage only added to Western perceptions of the Georgievski government as an unpredictable and nationalistic menace to the country at a sensitive time.

After the parliamentary elections of September 2002, the incumbents were defeated and the new ruling coalition under SDSM made a priority of prosecuting leading police officials associated with the raid (Boskovski himself did not appear, having already been shipped to the Hague regarding an unrelated incident from the war of 2001). However, four officers involved with the raid, including special police leader Goran Stojkov, spent almost a year in jail before and during their trial. The BBC's retelling of these developments made little note of the internal political war between SDSM and VMRO-DPMNE, which was, far more than any concern for ethics in police conduct, the issue at stake behind the government's legal actions. Further, the media reports obfuscated the real situation, in the process smearing the Macedonian government as an institution, although the regime was a different one than had carried out the Rastanski Lozja operation. Nevertheless, the BBC reported simply in late April 2004, "Macedonian officials have admitted that seven alleged Pakistani militants killed in March 2002 were in fact illegal immigrants shot in cold blood to 'impress' the international community."[32]

In April 2005, the four men charged in the affair were acquitted by the Macedonian courts due to inconclusive evidence and statements from two other police witnesses who had been "turned" by the prosecution. The pair "claimed they had been forced by police to give false testimony...and pressured by senior officials, including [former Prime Minister Hari] Kostov, to sign a statement blaming the others. The defense attorney said the whole affair was simple revenge on Kostov's part. Boskovski had, as interior minister, summoned Kostov for an interview about alleged financial crimes during Kostov's time as manager of [Commercial] Bank."[33] The policemen, their relatives, and political supporters from the VMRO-DPMNE party regarded the verdict as proof that Macedonia had an independent judiciary after all.

Even the ruling SDSM, which had brought the charges, was relieved that the case ended without convictions, as the general public's support for the accused was eating away at its popularity. While the state prosecutor vowed to appeal, in the end mainly Muslim groups and some Western officials were the ones to protest, implying that the courts were probably corrupt and had weakly bowed to nationalist pressure. However, no one from outside bothered to take the defense's testimony seriously, despite the fact that it showed, at the very least, that the "evidence" for an alleged police massacre of innocent refugees was confused and contradictory. Indeed, it is possible that a far more sordid deception was carried out at Rastanski Lozja on the part of the Western governments than anything the Macedonians could have come up with.

Throughout the 1990s, Macedonia was finding its feet as an independent state and Western support was strong—especially during the Kosovo crisis when Macedonia took in over 400,000 Kosovo Albanian refugees. However, when the country was no longer needed for Clinton's military adventures, it was forgotten, and the long-term consequences of Kosovo—an emboldened pan-Albanian Balkan insurgency—were ignored. Back in the final years of Yugoslavia, Goran Stojkov had been part of a unit trained by the British SAS. According to him, good counterterrorism cooperation with the West continued right up until the 2001 war. In 1999, this career counterterrorism specialist became the head of security for then-president Boris Trajkovski. With the outbreak of war in 2001, he became the head of the Rapid Reaction Force assembled from "all of the best people we could find," he says. "It was an emergency situation."

However, according to Stojkov, the elite unit—like Macedonia itself—became a victim of larger Western politics: "As soon as we started having success, the [Americans] became nervous that [the government] might win." On the other hand, the regular army's heavy-handed shelling tactics and trench warfare—"like something out of World War I," lamented one Macedonian military analyst— guided by old, Communist-era generals had mixed results, failing to eliminate the furtive rebels and resulting in civilian casualties. Nevertheless, numerous independent sources maintained that the United States intervened covertly to maintain a stalemate situation, which would allow it to be a vital third-party arbiter. America thus allegedly began secretly supporting the NLA from its Kosovo base, Camp Bondsteel, through logistical and communications support as well as secret arms airdrops to Albanian-held mountain villages in northwestern Macedonia. According to Canadian war reporter Scott Taylor, who visited the NLA's mountain command post at Sipkovica in August 2001, Albanian fighters confirmed that NATO had been supplying them with weapons.[34] The former deputy intelligence director, Zoran Mitevski, claims that NLA leader Ali Ahmeti was escorted by U.S. military helicopters based in Kosovo to inspect his troops in the Macedonian hills.[35]

For Macedonians, the nadir was reached in June, during a three-day battle at the Skopje-area village of Aracinovo, where NATO ordered the Macedonian Army to stop its operations and then spirited the heavily armed Albanian fighters off to freedom. It was allegedly done to save the national airport and perhaps the city itself from Albanian rockets. However, the public was shocked when it was reported that Islamic fighters and 17 American military contractors from the Virginia-based Military Professional Resources Incorporated (MPRI) had been found amongst the NLA's ranks. At the same time that the Macedonian government had hired MPRI to train its own men, it appeared that the mercenary company was also being employed by the Albanians. From that moment, the humiliated and disappointed Macedonian public's worst suspicions seemed to have been confirmed: America and NATO were in full favor of the Albanian guerrillas. Thus it was no surprise that, in the long-term, the unhelpful Macedonian wartime government, led by the nationalist VMRO-DPMNE party of Prime Minister Ljubco Georgievski (a close ally of Boskovski's) would have to go. This is the context in which the mysterious shootings at Rastanski Lozja should be understood, if the second version of events was the true one.

In late August 2001, a NATO peacekeeping force arrived in Skopje. It attempted to build confidence by collecting the NLA's weapons with Operation "Essential Harvest," though conceding that only a tiny fraction (3,875 pieces) of the Albanians' total arsenal would be collected. Most of them were unserviceable and outdated; indeed, according to a Canadian NATO soldier involved in the operation, the oldest rifle collected dated from 1849.[36] The patent absurdity of the situation was comically brought to life when the Skopje Museum asked NATO to donate the weapons to the museum's collection rather than destroy them. The military alliance did not see the humor in the situation, however. Indeed, as a Swiss report attested, NATO was making intense efforts to collect as many weapons as possible—while troubling the NLA as little as possible. In early September, border police in Slovenia intercepted 48 tons of weapons being smuggled in from Austria. "The shipment contained several hundred thousand old, hardly usable weapons, similar to those now being collected in Macedonia," read the report. "This is why Slovenian police did not rule out the possibility that the weapons were meant to make NATO's Operation Essential Harvest in Macedonia even more successful."[37]

After the terrorist attacks of September 11 in America, the beleaguered Macedonian government tried to ingratiate itself with the West by pointing to the connections—some real, some spurious—between the Albanian paramilitaries and Islamic terrorists. The effort was by and large a failure, and the West continued its standoffish approach, especially leery of Interior Minister Boskovski, and his special police force, which had burgeoned and been renamed the Lions. It was, according to critics, a less disciplined force than when it had been the Rapid Reaction Force under General Goran Stojkov. While the experienced Stojkov still commanded it, Boskovski's enemies claimed that he had infiltrated the ranks with common criminals and thugs. In November, three Macedonian special policemen were ambushed and killed while attempting to secure a suspected mass grave containing Macedonians killed by Albanians during the war in the Albanian-held village of Neprosteno. After the firefight, the Albanians also briefly held 100 Macedonians hostage. A Skopje newspaper claimed that an American diplomat had invited the Albanian militants in advance to prepare a "welcoming party" and was thus partially responsible for the carnage, though it could not be proven.[38]

In the eyes of the West, the Georgievski regime, and especially Interior Minister Boskovski, represented a greater danger than did the supposedly disbanded NLA. Ahmeti and his men cleverly knew how to say exactly what the West wanted to hear about their alleged commitment to human rights and a multiethnic Macedonia. The Western powers took a three-pronged approach to damaging the government, in the hopes of replacing it the following year: first, by pointing out its demonstrated corruption through bombastic reports and announcements from the interventionist think tank, the International Crisis Group, and anticorruption watchdogs; second, by consolidating the transformation of the NLA's Ali Ahmeti from paramilitary leader to a legitimate political contender; and third, by ensuring that the government could not capitalize on the fact that a decade of Western intervention in the Balkans had left the region, and its secessionist armies, infested with radical Islamists. It was this third approach that may have constituted the Rastanski Lozja affair.

It is not clear exactly when, or even if, the U.S. and British governments decided to set up the Macedonian government by making them believe they could help fight terrorism. Stressing that he is strictly a counterterrorism professional, Goran Stojkov separates what he was told from what he experienced. According to him, Macedonia's counterintelligence service, the DBK informed his team of classified reports from British MI6 regarding potential Pakistani terrorists in November or December 2001—in other words, just when the perceived noncooperative stance of the Macedonian government was starting to infuriate its Western overseers. The British disclosed that a terrorist cell, then in Pakistan, was coming to the Balkans. By January, the group was said to have reached Turkey, and the Turkish government corroborated the information. By early February, the men were in Kosovo, with plans to infiltrate Macedonia, warned MI6. According to Stojkov, the original plan was for an elite unit known as the Tigers to intercept the Pakistani group; however, "they were specialized for urban operations, and therefore it would have been risky to passers-by if we intercepted them inside the city. So it was decided to leave the operation to our unit [the Lions]."

According to Stojkov, the police operation had been prepared approximately one month beforehand. The British had been able to track the Pakistanis for so long, he was told, because they had an infiltrator within the cell since it had left Pakistan. "I'm not interested in the politics," the police general states. "I can only say what I saw and who I was with." With him during the operation on the night of March 1, 2002, claims Stojkov, were some 34 heavily armed special police officers—as well as two British intelligence agents. Taking up positions near a vineyard just north of Skopje, the police waited for the Pakistanis, using night-vision goggles to locate them. "The two British agents told us not to shoot one of the guys—that is, their man inside the group," recalls Stojkov. At least as far as he had been told, the Pakistanis really were terrorists. Stojkov also claims that a gun battle did indeed ensue—with all of the terrorists killed except, of course, for the British mole, who was recovered by the two agents and promptly escorted away. With the operation concluded successfully, Interior Minister Boskovski sought the praise of the West. Instead, he was soon being accused of politically motivated murder, and the police team that had acted on his orders had to take the fall. Goran Stojkov's remarkable testimony raises questions as to the veracity of the accepted truth regarding the operation.

Stojkov himself, who has sued the state for the year he spent in prison, claims to have no interest in supporting Boskovski. "Politicians and intelligence agents are both in a line of work I consider disgusting," he maintains. "I am not interested in political games. I am a professional. I just do my job." If the implications of his story are true, they would indicate a stunning Western betrayal of a supposed ally in the war on terror. On the other hand, if the whole incident was indeed the depraved work of an opportunistic interior minister, it would still lead to essentially the same conclusion—that the operation had involved the manipulation of the war on terror. Either way, the murky Rastanski Lozja shootings and its judicial aftermath indicate how the threat of terrorism in the Balkans has been manipulated to serve political purposes.

Taken together, these stories paint a deeply ambivalent picture of Western efforts in the war on terror in the Balkans. From the lethargic and negligent "see-no-evil" complacency of the UN in Kosovo to the incompetent kidnapping of the wrong man in the el-Masri case, from the economic strong-arming of Blagoja Samakoski to the murky manipulation of international intelligence and terrorism in the episode at Rastanski Lozja, the West has time and time again wasted valuable time and resources in dubious, politically determined activities that amount, in effect, to a base betrayal of regional and Western security. While plenty of real terrorists continue to roam free and unimpeded in the Balkans, these threats are largely being ignored in favor of cat-and-mouse games and political intrigue.

In some cases, however, Western interventionist experiments in the Balkans have been fueled simply by the inability of disorganized and often contending national and multinational security structures to cooperate. While "intelligence-sharing failures" have famously and frequently been cited in the case of American services such as the CIA, FBI, and the Pentagon, less has been reported about the situation in Europe—one that is infinitely more complex, with a multitude of services, both hierarchical and overlaying, in all of the European countries, as well as the EU security apparatus, NATO, Interpol, and all the liaison teams between each of them. This mind-boggling variety has vexed the practical possibility of any real inter-European cooperation. Even if the individual services and countries did not have their own rivalries and turf wars, the sheer number of them would impede smooth teamwork. Indeed, the European Union has no counterpart to the U.S. Department of Homeland Security. As one retired MI6 officer with strong contacts in the active intelligence community states, "The various national authorities all serve their own mostly obfuscated agendas first, discarding [mutual] interests, and therefore creating an entirely unpredictable outcome...worsened still more when you throw into the mix the individual Balkan governments, and some surrounding rival powers, e.g. Turkey and Greece."[39]

In the Balkans, the fact that EU countries look after their own interests has meant an infinite extension of the game of intrigue and deception famously played by the Great Powers a century ago, during the dying days of the Ottoman Empire. The internal fractures between and within EU countries and their agencies, as well as the lack of a coordinated, union-wide counterterrorism strategy, threaten Europe's ability to counter the Balkan terrorist threat in an efficient and competent manner. A prime example of how this disconnect has expedited terrorism occurred in Kosovo, where, as was discussed in Chapter 3, the German BND knew about the March 2004 Albanian riots several weeks before they happened, but failed to inform the German KFOR military detachment. The BND, as well as the CIA, had working relations with a known Islamist instigator, Samedin Xhezairi or "Commander Hoxha," an Albanian Muslim in Prizren with reported al Qaeda ties, and a main organizer of the pogrom against Kosovo's Christian Serb minority. The BND had been tapping Xhezairi's phone, but whether to protect its informant or for some other reason, failed to pass on intelligence gained from these wiretaps. German military units were thus caught unprepared and could only watch helplessly as the Muslim rioters destroyed numerous homes and churches, ethnically cleansing the Christian Serbs.

This noncooperation should come as no surprise, according to the British intelligence source. "The BND wasn't and still isn't really forthcoming with relaying information to the German military," states the retired agent. "[Former BND director] August Hanning's old shop serves a political purpose, whereas the military are committed to assisting the UN, NATO and so forth. That creates an internal German conflict of interest for embedded military within intel structures of these organizations...The left hand doesn't know what the right hand is doing, and vice versa."

This disorganized front goes a long way to explaining why covert "sponsorships" such as the likes of Samedin Xhezairi can go so dramatically wrong. In the case of Germany, six different "intel interests," with little coordination between one another, are operating at any given time. These include national agencies such as the BND and the BVS (a domestic law enforcement body under the Justice Ministry), as well as intelligence liaison missions to international bodies, such as NATO, the United Nations, the European Union, and the CIA. According to the former MI6 officer, this disorder and similar conditions in other EU countries have created a situation that is "beyond hopeless":

> The UN team is split up into another four intelligence-gathering components, each with their own military and civil employees. The CIA liaison has on the one hand a bunch of "Commander Hoxha's" to keep track of, and on the other the obligation to not only inform Washington of everything, but also local national authorities and all

the NATO commanders. That in and of itself is a real logistical challenge. Meanwhile, Hanning, when he was at the BND, actually manipulated situations in the [Balkan] region to his advantage, deploying a rather large operational force. As for the EU liaisons, they are there because they like to keep abreast of...of... nobody really knows. Once in a while, they toss some intel in, but it mostly complicates a situation that is already at a panic state of insolvable.

One meeting report from [2004] states that Germany was represented by 16 different people—some of them even not aware who the others were. Then add Austria, which thinks of itself as a separated part of Germany, all the while relaying anything they pick up also to the Eastern European countries. In short: there's still no clear-cut intel authority, and activities/ops are spread all over the place, by and large without control.[40]

The same situation predominates across the EU. Each country has not only its own "national interests" to safeguard against rival allies, but also its own intra-agency and inter-agency turf wars to wage. With numerous non-EU countries operating in Kosovo under the aegis of UNMIK and KFOR since 1999, all with their own agencies and internecine feuds, the probability of total confusion and anarchy only becomes more likely. The small semblance of order remaining in Kosovo owes to the fact that the UN has allowed former KLA leaders and the mafia to control society. It is no surprise, then, that when it comes to something as dangerous and complex as dealing with a transnational but decentralized Islamist movement, even the most powerful countries in the world are stymied.

Today, this chaotic situation has moved from the unfortunate to the scandalous, with the CIA, MI6, BND, and others eager to build "special relationships" with Islamic extremists bent on killing Christians, attacking Western targets, and creating a fundamentalist caliphate. Almost three decades after the CIA put Osama bin Laden in charge of the Afghan jihad against the Soviets, the West still has not learned its lesson: that no matter what they promise or how nicely they behave, the fundamentalists are merely using them for their own purposes. In assuming that religious fanatics can be bought off, appeased, or even enlisted for a limited use, Western intelligence agencies imperil not only themselves but all of Western society.

Nevertheless, old habits die hard, and it is by no means certain that we have seen the last of the practice. At the same time, the old familiar faces of Balkan jihad have not gone away—far from it. Despite U.S. pressure on Bosnia to deport former mujahedin, old leaders like Abu Hamza appeared regularly on Bosnian TV throughout 2006, railing against the evil West and threatening the government with consequences if it tries to expel Bosnia's jihadi "saviors." In addition to Xhezairi, Ekrem Avdiu, the Kosovar jihadi sprung from a Serbian jail due to UNMIK pressure in 2001, remains a "vital" player in Kosovo's Wahhabi movement. "He's still sending a lot of Albanian imams to Saudi [Arabia]," attested the U.S. special investigator in October 2006. "Matter of fact, eight came back in the last two months...two new mosques have gone up, with money brought in from al Qaeda."[41]

In Mitrovica, Kosovo's ethnically divided northern city, says the investigator, "you got every Friday up to 500 Albanians getting the anti-American, jihad preaching from Avdiu's boys...the moderate imams are scared as hell, they're looking for help. Avdiu is going in and saying, 'look, you're not praying right.' And US intel has no idea of the scope of the Islamic problem. The higher-ups don't even want to address it." Indeed, longtime UNMIK employees in Kosovo who have watched the process disintegrate over the years express disbelief at how the Western media and politicians can get away with calling the intervention a success. As has been recounted, the direct link between Kosovo Albanians and terrorist plots, up to and including the London July 2005 attacks, has materialized in the form of arrests.

Outside experts point to procedural flaws for why the war on terror, as carried out in the Balkans, is failing. Former CIA agent Philip Giraldi maintains that "the CIA is not geared up to run long-term seeding operations that would be required to disrupt terrorist cells, so it relies on generally unreliable local partners to do the hard work." This comment sums up perfectly the West's legacy in the Balkans. Temporary trysts with dubious partners—typically, drug dealers, arms smugglers, and "polite" jihad fanatics—have led to a volatile reality of militant groups, organized crime, and the constant threat of terrorism. The failure to develop "long-term seeding operations" in the Balkans owes also to the lack of any coherent long-term general strategy from the Western powers, always looking to "downsize" their missions and get out.

In this light, the testimony of European experts, such as the ESISC's Claude Moniquet, is revealing. In Macedonia, NATO's postwar peacekeeping mission was followed by a much smaller EU police training mission, PROXIMA, which existed from December 2003 to December 2005. However, this "was too short to produce real and reliable intelligence," maintains the French expert. "To establish an intelligence operation on a subject like Islamism, in a country like Macedonia, is a question of three to five years for professional intelligence officers." In the view of this French terrorism expert, while the EU mission "produced some intelligence on organized crime, [there was] nothing really useful on Islamism."[42]

By contrast, one group does have an organized and simple strategy for the region—the Islamist proselytizing network hailing from the Arab states, Iran, Pakistan, and elsewhere. The perceived distance and foreignness of the Balkans, even for Western European countries, lends an "out of sight, out of mind" quality to it. The examples of successful seeding operations mentioned by experienced individuals such as Giraldi thus tend to have been carried out on the territory of states with homegrown terrorist problems. Thus, the kind of counterterrorism operations "that would eventually bring victory," says the former CIA agent, can be seen in what "the Brits did so successfully in northern Ireland, the Spanish against the Basques, and the Italians and Germans against their own indigenous terrorists. We seem to have lost that hard-earned wisdom."[43]

For the American special police investigator in Kosovo, a formidable ex-military man with long experience in the Balkans, the sluggish response of Western security services in the Balkans to the terrorist threat is vexing. "I saw some of the same shit in Bosnia, not going after the terrorists, letting 'em hang out and stay comfortable," he says. "But seeing this stuff here in Kosovo—it really ripped me out of the old red-white-and-blue, you know what I mean? Now I just want to go home, stock up on ammo, sit back and wait."

CHAPTER 7

Global Economics, "Certain Foreign Relations," and the War on Terror

The ISI bid first. The two representatives of Pakistan's national intelligence service put up $150,000 in cash for the three CDs, stolen from a U.S. nuclear laboratory by Turkish spies masquerading as scientists.

The latter thought about it for a moment. But the offer was not good enough: "Let us hear what our Saudi friends have to say." After more than doubling the ISI's offer at $375,000 in cash, the Saudis spirited away the top-secret technical information, like pollen on the breeze, ending up God knows where.

One might think that such a scandalous and serious crime would be investigated immediately by the U.S. government. According to Sibel Edmonds, the former FBI translator who recounts the vignette in a new interview, investigations into affairs such as this have been routinely blocked at the behest of preserving "certain foreign relations." Hired a few days after 9/11 to translate FBI wiretaps from Turkish into English, the Turkish-born Edmonds was unceremoniously fired in March 2002 for reporting to her superiors about endemic sloth, corruption, and even foreign espionage within the bureau. Then-Attorney General John Ashcroft also slapped Edmonds with a gag order, preventing her from speaking about anything she knew, under the little-known State Secrets Act. Although she has testified before congressmen in private sessions, Edmonds is still not allowed to tell her full story in public, meaning that the high officials who she believes are betraying American national security continue to act with impunity. Her numerous court challenges, getting as far as the Supreme Court itself, have all been dismissed according to the same argument—that to allow her to speak would "endanger certain foreign relations" and harm national security.[1]

Such testimony reveals that the global war on terror is not being compromised simply by mediocrity, indifference, and the oft-cited lack of intelligence sharing discussed in Chapter 6. Rather, it is being aggressively exploited by well-connected individuals, crime syndicates, and military and government officials all seeking to profit from stoking conflicts around the globe. And so the most major political decisions, economic moves, and "certain foreign relations" are, all too often, bound up with the forces that make terrorism possible. At times, the politics can be hard to understand. The economics is easy to understand, but hard to justify ethically. The foreign relations are for the most part not understood at all because they are conducted in the shadows. All of these realities bode ill for the war on terror.

Where all of these factors merge is first and foremost within the shadowy underworld of global organized crime. The numbers are truly staggering. In her book *Terror Incorporated,* Italian economist and terrorism expert Loretta Napoleoni revealed that the total global narcotics business in 2003 was worth "$400 billion a year; another $100 billion is produced by the smuggling of people, weapons and other goods, such as oil and diamonds."[2] In 2004, the opium harvest in Afghanistan, supplier of 90 percent of the world's heroin, surpassed 3,600 tons. The 206,000 hectares cultivated symbolized "the largest amount of heroin or of any drug that I think has ever been produced by any one country in any given year," stated former American counternarcotics official Robert Charles.[3] For 2004, the final street value of the heroin reached a staggering $36 billion. Yet even after NATO's pledges to crack down, figures have since skyrocketed. In September 2006, senior UN drugs control officer Antonio Maria Costa revealed the Afghan opium harvest had "reached the highest levels ever recorded, showing an increase of almost 50 percent from last year."[4]

For these drugs to reach European and American markets, they must pass through a series of countries whose stability is very important to the West, almost all of which face serious present or future challenges from Islamic fundamentalists and even terrorists. By virtue of their very existence, all that the Islamists need do is to establish a presence in these countries. To ensure economic and political stability, and to keep fundamentalism from taking overt political power, the West must at the very least tolerate the widespread criminal activities that are preventing these countries from economic collapse, and thus a descent into anarchy, as was seen in Albania in 1997 after Western creditors grew alarmed at how unsustainable, government-linked pyramid schemes were multiplying. It was only through massive laundering of mafia funds that the government was able to maintain the charade. When the scam was revealed, and the pyramid schemes crashed, the government crashed along with it. The resulting anarchy and ransacking of the state arsenals by paramilitaries made the war in Kosovo a fait accompli. The West has not made the same mistake twice.

Yet were it so simple as that. The Islamists in Central Asia, Turkey, and the Balkans are not only holding the West hostage with the implicit threat of state and economic failure, should the latter crack down on regional trafficking, they are also building terrorist empires through their direct involvement in organized crime. In 2004, *Time* discovered an Afghan al Qaeda network behind the trafficking of locally produced heroin "to buyers across the Middle East, Asia and Europe, and in turn is using the drug revenues to purchase weapons and explosives."[5] These weapons are now being used, among other things, for a revitalized Taliban's war against NATO troops and the Afghan government, and against U.S. ally Pakistan next door. According to Interpol, some 40 percent of Afghan heroin and morphine passes through Iran—a fundamentalist Muslim country trying to acquire nuclear weapons.[6]

Next, the heroin passes through Turkey, which according to Edmonds is used by the al Qaeda network "to obtain and transfer arms to its Central Asian bases, including Chechnya."[7] Canadian police detective Stu Kellock, once head of UNMIK's Regional Serious Crime Unit in Pristina, Kosovo, described one smuggling route that passed through the Balkans to the West. Afghan heroin came through Turkey, crossed Bulgaria, and then the Albanian-majority Presevo Valley of southern Serbia, finally reaching Kosovo and the Albanian mafia: "Once inside [Kosovo], the drugs would be transported across to northern Albania," Kellock attested, "through the [former paramilitary] KLA stronghold of the Drenica valley, to places like Tropoje for distribution, either north by land or across the Adriatic to Italy."[8]

Balkan trafficking, therefore, can be led and influenced by Islamic fundamentalists a world away. "Even if Kosovo Albanian [mafia bosses] are not radical Islamists, they still hold the key for heroin crossing the Balkans," says Belgrade University terrorism expert Darko Trifunovic. "They depend on al Qaeda's Afghan supply network. And these suppliers may well tell the Albanian mafia, 'if you want the drugs, don't touch our [Islamist] boys in Kosovo.'"[9] Indeed, direct links between the Kosovo mafia and Islamic terrorists were discovered when, in September 2006, Norwegian police arrested Arfan Qadeer Bhatti, a Pakistani planning attacks on the Israeli and American embassies in Oslo. Bhatti, it turned out, had long connections with Princ Dobrosi, a Kosovo Albanian previously arrested in the Czech Republic and Norway for drug dealing.[10] The Pakistani had recently visited Dobrosi in Pristina, as well as Pec, an Albanian nationalist stronghold in western Kosovo, where he visited the growing radical Wahhabi community.[11] "Pec has gone completely Wahhabi," avers Dusan Janjic of the Belgrade NGO Forum for Ethnic Relations. "When high [Western] officials meet you privately, they say they are so worried about radical Islam—but their reports don't show this."[12]

Indeed, Balkan black humor seems to have proven infectious; informed British police, says Janjic, privately refer to Kosovo as the "Republic of Heroin." Satellite phones seized during an American raid on an al Qaeda smuggling house in Kabul "had been used to call numbers linked to suspected terrorists in Turkey, the Balkans and Western Europe."[13] Sibel Edmonds neatly puts the whole picture together:

> Turkish networks, along with Russian, are the main players in these fields; they purchase the opium from Afghanistan and transport it through several Turkic speaking

Central Asian states into Turkey, where the raw opium is processed into popular byproducts; then the network transports the final product into Western European and American markets via their partner networks in Albania. The networks' banking arrangements in Turkey, Cyprus and Dubai are used to launder and recycle the proceeds, and various Turkish companies in Turkey and Central Asia are used to make this possible and seem legitimate.

That the mass media has failed to put all the puzzle pieces together, Edmonds contends, is because major organized crime is too lucrative to be ignored, by either the "bad guys" or the allegedly good ones. To really investigate the heroin trade would mean following the drug route from Afghanistan to the West— something that would implicate the CIA, NATO, the Turkish and Central Asian governments, as well as the mafias that control Western-supported Balkan rulers, especially in the all-important powder keg of Kosovo; alienating the local chiefs there could spark a region-wide war. Not only is the full story too challenging for the attention span of Western news consumers accustomed to a 24-hour news "cycle," it is also too embarrassing for the powers that be.

Further, organized crime is also too important to the economic stability of many key states for the rules to apply universally. This is where high politics again comes into the picture. In sometimes volatile Turkey, for example, heroin profits equal a quarter of the gross domestic product (GDP). Without the money from drug profits that are laundered or reinvested locally, the Central Asian governments would collapse. Indeed, says Sibel Edmonds, "The stability of Central Asia is very important for the US. Everyone there has a dictatorial government, but everyone is happy...A massive amount of money is being spent to keep everyone happy. American officials are happy. [The Turkish] MIT is happy too. Nobody's going to rock the boat—it is sailing along well enough."[14]

In the Caucasus and the Balkans, governments have enthusiastically geared their entire administrative processes towards NATO and EU membership. Yet both regions are major corridors for illegal trafficking of all kinds and the rule of the mafia has created zones of protected activity, where bullets and bribery have replaced the rule of law and where criminals—as well as their terrorist partners—can plot in safety. And, since an endemic culture of smuggling and patronage also holds sway, political activity is reduced to a chronic factional battle for control of the levers of power—that is, the power to manage what comes in and out of the country, and to profit from it accordingly. With the exception of internal ethnic politics, party platforms are relatively indistinguishable. Even between rival ethnicities everybody is, in the end, "pro-Western." And so, for the sake of local political stability and leverage, Europe and America never interfere with the major criminal players, who are often identical to or associated with politicians and state security officials—in other words, the policymakers and frontline fighters in the war on terror. This is not to say that every regional politician or security officer is corrupt; far from it. Yet the large-scale criminal enterprises are undeniably allowed to flourish because the political status quo they ensure is necessary for Western overseers to enact their policy in the regions.

Indeed, fulfillment of the West's policies in the Balkans has inevitably required cooperating with mafia-connected regional leaders. Although Montenegrin Prime Minister Milo Djukanovic was implicated by the Italian government in a massive cigarette trafficking operation together with the Italian mafia, he was not touched; this owed partially to the fact that "Montenegro was an important ally against [Yugoslav President] Slobodan Milosevic until his fall in 2000."[15] In November 2006 the veteran leader retired after a democratic enough 17 straight years in power, having finally guided his statelet of 650,000 souls to independence from Serbia—a necessary conclusion of the West's chronically hostile policy towards the latter. Following his party's victory in the elections of September 10, 2006, Djukanovic handed over control of the newest country in Europe to party colleague Zeljko Sturanovic. Nevertheless, as opposition leader Novak Radulovic contended, "Djukanovic with his local bosses and tycoons will remain the real prime minister in [the] shadows."[16]

In Kosovo, where a UN administration replaced Yugoslav rule following the 1999 NATO bombing, the need to placate the province's mafia-connected men of strength manifested acutely in the UN's "don't-rock-the-boat" policy. Detective Kellock recalls a "very interesting statement made to me by a *very* senior police officer" following his team's conviction of a powerful Kosovo Albanian criminal. The statement went "along the lines of 'we did not know whether or not *to allow you* to continue your investigation—we were pleased that you did and the result that was obtained.'" Nevertheless, states Kellock, "secret meetings, innuendo and comments made to me made it very clear that some [high officials] were not pleased with this situation." Indeed, despite its purported stance of "moral, ethical and legal compliance with UN Resolution 1244," top civilian UN leaders "would do so only if it served their interests in Kosovo."[17] Senior UNMIK officials have ordered the destruction of files that indicate higher-than-reported numbers of attacks against minorities.[18] They also systematically fired or relocated employees who speak out or contradict the official line. And a long-time European official in Kosovo claims to have seen an UNMIK police dossier on Ramush Haradinaj, a major KLA figure turned politician, "stamped across the front with the words, 'awaiting political decision.'" To arrest powerful mafia and paramilitary figures in Kosovo would not only flatten the economy and increase the risk of a regional war, it could also prove very embarrassing, bringing to light unflattering details regarding the involvement of American and European officials with Kosovo's criminal underworld.

High international politics and economic ambitions become still more acute in the Caucasus, Central Asia, and especially the Balkans, where the goals of the West and multinational corporations are diametrically opposed to—yet at the same time, curiously symbiotic with—an equally multinational and ambitious Islamic caliphate project. To understand exactly why this is so, one must look deeper on the vexed regional map, beneath the thin veneer of countries, national identities, and unique populations, who are in any case never consulted on the major issues regarding their future. To conceal the powerlessness of the locals, however, Western governments and the media have gone out of their way to present the opposite image, through an obsessive coverage of allegedly self-empowered "democratic reform," color-coded revolutions, and so on. Yet the mere fact that democratic elections are held by no means ensures that human rights, social equality, and fair governance will hold fast.

For the West and the multinational corporations, beneath the layer of nation-hood, on the raw topographical map, there emerges a complex maze of transport corridors, pipeline routes, oil and mineral deposits, arable land, water supplies, and sites of other natural resources—you could not call them people, in the sense that they are told (as being individuals blessed by the West's supposed Enlightenment values), but rather consumer markets and labor forces of various salary levels. At a different level of the map, the one pertaining to faith and society, foreign Islamists for their part gaze upon a sea of populations to be organized and expanded according to their aggressively expanding religion.

Both conceptions are exploitative, and both rely on the manipulation of nationalism and the social ills that reify it. Today, despite the fact that we are living in a supranational, globalizing world, the anachronistic devotion to the ideal of the nation-state remains potent in the Balkans, among Albanians and others too, a quixotic emotion that has been cynically manipulated by outside powers, before, during, and after Yugoslavia's implosion in 1991. Ironically, every Balkan "independence" drive has simply led to a new dependence—nowadays, on foreign creditors, political overseers, and international institutions. The West's divide-and-conquer approach to the Balkans has yielded numerous attractive results for foreign investors, in everything from prime seaside real estate in Croatia, Montenegro, and Bulgaria to dirt-cheap investments in major Serbian industry, as well as telecommunications and media markets everywhere. One would have to be extremely naïve to believe that these investors, through their governments and financial institutions, do not exert leverage over the "democratically elected" governments of Europe's brave, new "independent" states.

As everywhere else, the goal of Western governments and the multinationals in the Balkans is to monopolize wealth and the processes of wealth creation, legal and illegal. Overarching strategic plans for the regions are based on what is now referred to as "energy security," that is, the West's unfettered access to and transportation of Caspian oil and minimization of its dependency on Russia for petroleum and gas. From statements made at NATO's November 2006 summit in Riga, Latvia, it seems that the next incarnation of that alliance will be as a guardian of said energy security—increasing the chances of a military showdown with Russia, Iran, and even China. At a subregional level, control of drinking water sources, plentiful in the Balkans, is another concern of the West as it prepares for the expected future scarcity of the world's most essential commodity.

On March 23, 1999, in a surprisingly frank and very revealing admission, then-President Clinton justified NATO's dawning intervention in Kosovo thus:

When I ran for President in 1992, one of the things I said over and over and over again was that in the 21st century the dividing line between foreign and domestic policy would blur...

And I supported the idea that the United States, Canada and our European allies had to take on the new security challenges of Europe of the 21st century, including all these ethnic upheavals on their border. Why? Because if this domestic policy is going to work, we have to be free to pursue it. And if we're going to have a strong economic relationship that includes our ability to sell around the world, Europe has got to be a key. And if we want people to share our burdens of leadership with all the problems that will inevitably crop up, Europe needs to be our partner. Now, that's what this Kosovo thing is all about...it's about our values.[19]

This breathtaking vision for a new globalist world order has, however, its less appealing side effects. In the Balkans, with its bitter recent experiences of war, poverty, volatile state-building, and painful economic transition, Western control over all political, economic, and social developments has directly exacerbated the terrorist threat. Already afflicted by all of the characteristics that facilitate terrorism—state corruption, healthy militant movements, organized crime and its synergistic relationship with the legal economy—the Balkans has suffered from Western strategic shortsightedness, often in the banal pursuit of individual career ambitions, among diplomats, negotiators, and employees of UN peacekeeping missions. Further, the execution of Western policy has by necessity led to dubious partnerships with war criminals and mafia bosses. In the name of supporting a convoluted and hypocritical interventionist policy, the West has enabled decidedly unsavory characters. When juxtaposed with the wildly differing policies of Islamic states, the West has ironically created all of the conditions for radical Islam—a force that threatens Western security, especially in Europe—to take root. While it cannot be said that through its interventionist policies the West deliberately set out to create a patchwork of Islamist safe havens in the Balkans, it also cannot be denied that interventionism has led to precisely this result.

In short, Western interventionists in the Balkans have become desperately wedded to a policy of disaster. A large part of the blame, of course, must fall on policies devised deliberately, such as the Clinton administration's aiding the mujahedin in Bosnia, or its toleration of the Berisha-Gazidede regime in Albania despite its close ties with foreign terrorists and massive corruption. While ignored in the mass media, the underlying reason for the modern political instability, wars, and explosion in organized crime in the Balkans today has historical roots: today's situation is but an extension of the age-old game of intrigue, brinksmanship, and local favoritism played by the "Great Powers" of yesteryear to enhance their influence in the region. For Europe, this interventionism has always proven suicidal, as with the turbulent years up to and including the First World War.[20] World War II also saw needless suffering on a massive scale in the Balkans, simply because of the machinations of ambitious Western leaders. Today's Great Powers have still not learned their lesson—nor have Balkan political leaders lost their appetite, it should be said, for winning power and wealth through doing the bidding of foreign masters. The truth is that the people of the Balkans have never been left alone to sort out their own affairs: the Cold War, which did not even last 50 years, represents the longest period in which the region has known peace for at least the past two centuries.

Indeed, the Ottoman occupation, which some, especially Muslims and revisionist historians, consider the prime example of multicultural coexistence, and thus a sort of peaceful golden age of Balkan civilization, actually saw numerous conflicts that intensified as the empire grew weaker in the nineteenth century. The crackdowns on civilians that accompanied the Serbian uprising of 1803, the Greek War of Independence in 1821, and the various revolts leading up to the Russian-Bulgarian war against the Turks in 1877–1878 merely prefigured a 44-year-period in which the Balkan countries were almost constantly involved, in one way or another, with war, which only ended with the final elimination of the Ottoman Empire from the face of the earth in 1922. However, soon thereafter arrived World War II, less than two decades later. After the Cold War, there were the modern Yugoslav wars from 1991 to 2001. In this context, it is almost a miracle that the region has kept intact as well as it has.

The great war of today, according to the Bush administration, is the global war against terror, in which the Balkan states are expected to do their part. In this light, the most fundamentally surreal dimension of the West's Balkan misadventures must be that specific policies have directly benefited Islamic fundamentalism, as attested by the Western support for Muslim-dominated secessionist movements and paramilitaries with demonstrable ties to terrorists and mafia groups in Bosnia, Kosovo, Albania, and Macedonia. The Clinton administration's support for the foreign mujahedin in Bosnia, as has been recounted, opened a vital window of opportunity for Islamic terrorist organizations to deepen and diversify their operations in all of Europe—directly expediting the 9/11 attacks and the 2004 Madrid bombing. The Bosnian support was allegedly necessary to prevent a "Greater Serbia." However, "what the West seems to have forgotten," states Darko Trifunovic, "is that long before the [2001] terrorist attacks against America, the Bosnian Serbs were fighting against jihad, a literal jihad ordered and funded by Osama bin Laden, in their own country. Former mujahedin have told me that bin Laden personally ordered them to fight Christians in the Balkans—and later, to expand in Europe, especially Italy and Spain. The West is now paying the price for supporting the mujahedin against the Serbs."[21]

In another way, the West has also become a victim of its own success in the Balkans. Ironically, the creation of liberal democracies in docile, pro-Western nation-states also enables the rival development of radical Islam within them. Whereas these countries are constantly going through one election or another, leading to yet another new government working sporadically, in fits and starts and for a limited mandate, the Islamist movement has one mandate, one goal, and indefinite tenure in office. The same effect is also seen with the proliferation of new borders in the Balkans, and the deleterious effect this has had on efficiency and use of time. To get anything done between states, meetings have to be arranged, and scores of protocols, documents, and agreements first have to be signed. The frequency of changes in governments, and the lack of a real supranational organizing entity equivalent to the EU, inevitably means stagnation and slowdowns.

By contrast, the Islamist movement, which is fundamentally one with strong political ambitions and which sees the region as a borderless potential state entity, with the Muslim Ottoman Empire as a precedent, has an informal organizing entity in its own ideology. Unlike Balkan democratic governments, it is hampered neither by temporal nor efficiency-related problems. In its organizational structure and activities, the Islamist movement manifests as a supranational regional colonizer—and, thanks to organized crime and its Arab sponsors, a very wealthy one at that. The bastard twin of the global economic order represented by multinational corporations, financial markets, and institutions, Islamism preys on the intrinsic weaknesses and inefficiencies of the new Balkan order to achieve its objectives.

Pan-Islamism is also currently exploiting social problems that are the by-product of crooked globalization. For example, Hafiz Sulejman Bugari, a radical imam from Vratnik in Bosnia, has reportedly helped bring heroin-addicted young Muslims from Serbia's Sandzak region to special rehabilitation clinics in Sarajevo; when the former addicts return, "almost all sport Wahhabi beards and dress and appear to adhere to a fundamentalist form of Islam."[22] The same phenomenon has been reported in Skopje, Macedonia, where according to local Muslims the young are even being fed with heroin in order to give the Wahhabi movement a reason to save them. Of course, should a formerly heroin-addicted young Balkan acolyte of radical Islam bomb a Western embassy somewhere, it is unlikely that the media, which has chronically failed to put together all the pieces of the sordid story of heroin transport from Afghanistan to the Balkans, will draw the appropriate conclusions.

In the big picture, it is certain that quixotic, anachronistic nationalism, the inefficiency that comes with democracy and ingrained political fracturing will continue to define Balkan society for the foreseeable future. At the same time, radical Islamic groups are becoming more organized and more pervasive, it might be argued, precisely to the extent that liberal democracy continues to consolidate itself in the region. An increase in active Islamic worship and self-identification amongst the Muslim populations, in addition to the explosive demographic growth registered in these populations themselves, means that the influence of Islam on local politics is unavoidable and will only increase. Already, there are plenty of examples, such as the Wahhabi-instigated disturbances in Macedonia in 2005 and 2006, which caused friction between the Albanian parties, the rise of voluble pro- and anti-Muslim blocs as well as internal Muslim splinter groups in Bulgaria, Turkey, and Albania, the dangerous influence of Saudi Arabia in Kosovo, and the volatile rise of the Wahhabis in Serbia's Sandzak region.

Nevertheless, despite all the warning signs, the West has pressed on with its plan to make "all the pieces fall into place on the map," as one veteran Washington political consultant put it. These include the independence of Montenegro and Kosovo, the ethnic federalization and decentralization of Macedonia, and the forced centralization of power in Bosnia and Hercegovina, putting the triethnic country increasingly under Muslim domination. The overriding policy, which can seem opaque, schizophrenic, and hypocritical at times, rests—at least publicly—on the notion that borders will no longer matter in a future European order in which the Balkan states have all been incorporated into the European Union. Yet, for numerous reasons, most of which involve the union's own internal problems and the European public's general antienlargement sentiment, that goal will be realized in a very long time—if ever. As the clock continues to tick, and the European Union continues to hold the Balkan countries at arm's length, the only significant force of opposition, the Islamic international is ready and willing to present itself as the solution to the region's social and economic ills.

Indeed, the myth of EU membership as the cure-all for Balkan nationalist threats and economic torpor is just that—a myth. It is predicated on the notion that the European Union will accept the Balkan countries in the first place, and second of all, that, by the time they do join, the ever more fractious union would still be worth belonging to anyway. Current EU policy in the Balkans is being affected by domestic debates over immigration, which have manifested in the rise of right-wing nationalist parties in several European states and high-profile showdowns over visible Islamic symbols such as the burkha. Many suspect that many European countries' support for Kosovo independence, for example, is largely driven by a desire to return economic migrants and asylum seekers—especially Muslim ones—to their countries of origin, a move that, as was stated in Chapter 5, could crash national economies and lead to ethnic or religious conflict.

The threat of Islamic terrorism to the West has never been greater, and the immigration debate to a large extent reflects Europeans' fear of this. Unfortunately, the rise of organized crime in Europe has only increased the ability of Islamic terrorists and fundamentalists to move freely across the continent, relying on the cooperation between terrorist groups and mafias from Eastern Europe, the Balkans, and Western Europe. In a 2005 exposé of the Italian mafia's direct links with Islamic terrorism, Italian journalist Paolo Pontoniere revealed that "hundreds of Al Qaeda operatives coming from North Africa are being sent to Northern Europe though a maze of safe houses belonging to the Neapolitan Camorra, a Naples-based criminal network akin to the Mafia."[23]

The Camorra, which engages in a rich variety of illegal industries, has always cooperated with "terrorist groups from all latitudes and political persuasions." Now, Italian investigators believe, it is helping al Qaeda "obtain forged documents and weapons for its operatives, who disembark almost daily from ships connecting Italy to the Arab countries of North Africa...in exchange for substantial cargoes of narcotics, these operatives are moved through Camorra's connections from Naples to Rome, Bologna, Milan and eventually to other major European cities such as Paris, London, Berlin and Madrid." According to Michele del Prete, a district attorney investigating the Algerian Islamic Brotherhood in Italy, "the exchange currency cementing those trades is drugs." Neapolitan reporter Dario Del Porto added that in the case of "trouble" from the police, "the Camorra's soldiers will see [the terrorists] off on one of the many trains leaving hourly from the city's main station, or via speed-boat—the same vessels the Camorra uses to traffic cigarettes, drugs and illegal aliens." DIGOS, Italy's political crime unit, pegs the number of al Qaeda operatives passing through or seeking refuge as over 1,000, but the true number could be as high as 5,000.[24]

In the Balkans as well, human trafficking gangs from Turkey, Romania, Albania, and Russia are not picky about whom they will transport. Terrorists, or those fleeing terrorism charges in various states, are easily smuggled across porous Balkan borders and into the preexisting human networks ready to receive them in the West. While most trafficked people are simply poor economic migrants, "hand-in-hand with that are people in organized crime who allow terrorism to be possible," stated Swedish security specialist Magnus Ranstorp. "They move in the same circles and need the same things. If you want to tackle terrorists, you have to tackle the supporting environment, the organized crime rings and the human trafficking rings."[25]

Claiming that Iran is involved still in the terrorism-related activities in the Balkans that it started with the Bosnian jihad of the early 1990s, Ranstorp attested that "the Balkans have become the crossroads where we see the merger of Islamic extremist groups who reach out to organized crime groups." Mioljub Vitorovic, the Serbian special prosecutor for organized crime cases, cites a relevant example of this that indicates the scale of the threat—and the difficulties in combating it, due to the political corrupting power of the crime syndicates. According to Vitorovic, a Bangladeshi Islamist making more than $150,000 per week through a massive human trafficking operation has infiltrated Bangladeshi jihadis into Bosnian terrorist camps and provided cash compensation for the families of suicide bombers in Europe. However, the Serbian prosecutor "complained that the suspect, whom he declined to name, appears to have some high-level protection because he has been able to flee whenever police are closing in."[26]

The Romania-Serbia infiltration route is not the region's most significant, however. By land and by sea, third-world migrants are trafficked across Turkey, reaching Bulgaria or Greece overland. Others leave Turkey by ship, crossing Greece's Aegean Sea to Italy, directly or via Albania. For years, aggressive Albanian traffickers plying the Adriatic in armed small craft have brought tens of thousands of illegals into Italy, sometimes ending up in gun battles with the Italian Coast Guard.[27] During his second term in office in 2006, Albanian Prime Minister Sali Berisha announced that the speed boats used so effectively by the traffickers would be banned for three years, though foreign experts remained skeptical that the ban would have much effect, as the criminals would find other means.[28]

In Turkey, the land bridge between Europe and the desperately poor or war-torn countries of the Middle East and Asia, the ingenuity of the traffickers, and the sheer scale of their operations make eradicating the problem impossible. Year in and year out, media reports reveal how unfortunate illegal immigrants, entrusting their safety to traffickers get killed by landmines while crossing the Greek-Turkish border in Evros, or when the Greek or Turkish coast guards rescue migrants from capsized vessels in the Aegean.[29] The thousands of islets that litter this sea make for perfect way stations along the journey.[30] Bad weather, overcrowding, or both often cause these unfortunate people, purchasers of the most expensive boat tickets in the world ($10,000 per head is not an uncommon price to pay for illegal passage to the West), to lose their lives in the risky pursuit of finding a better life in Europe.

However, as has been said, economic migrants are only part of the equation in the Balkan human trafficking network. Prostitution is a major industry; in most cases, young Eastern European women are tricked by promises of work in Europe by Ukrainian, Moldovan, and Romanian traffickers, and then sold to the Albanian mafia, which has made a killing on the peacekeeper market in Kosovo, but even more so by exporting these unfortunate women to Italy, England, Germany, and other places in Europe where they have their own Albanian networks. Over 70 percent of the London sex trade is run by Albanians, according to the British government.[31] Since the Kosovo war of 1999, when Britons had a generally sympathetic attitude towards Albanians, the dramatic rise of Albanian organized crime in prostitution and drugs has reversed that sympathetic opinion. Yet while the European Union, Western human rights bodies, and London broadsheets have constantly bemoaned the amoral behavior of the traffickers, the fact remains that the latter can only succeed due to Europe's apparently insatiable desire for prostitutes.

For Western security, the greatest direct threat posed by human trafficking in the Balkans is, of course, terrorism. Since the early 1990s and "safe hotel" Tirana, the Balkans has acquired a reputation for being *the* place in Europe where extremists can lay low, circulate, and plot their next moves. The unchecked incursions of radical Islamic organizations and charities, as well as the wholesale production of mosques, has created the infrastructure necessary for hiding and moving terrorists, protecting them from crackdowns such as Bosnia's decision to expel its foreign former mujahedin. While he does not consider such men particularly dangerous, at least so long as they are allowed to remain in Bosnia, Sarajevo security analyst Anes Alic states that the real problem is that "Bosnian authorities do not know the whereabouts of most of them, as many have changed their names and addresses over time. For all intents and purposes, these people are already underground in Bosnia."[32]

Since returning to their countries of origin is a highly unfavorable option for the ex-jihadis, established Balkan escape routes present an invaluable option for both these men and for other, "newly minted" mujahedin. These routes, which traverse Bosnia, Montenegro, Kosovo, Macedonia, Bulgaria, and Albania, are manned by a combination of criminal gangs and leaders from the Islamic movement, motivated by money and a cause—the perfect symbiosis of terror and crime. Former Macedonian counterterrorism chief and deputy director of intelligence Zoran Mitevski retains close links with the active intelligence community and frequently accesses real-time lists of the radical Islamists now being moved from one secure location to another. "With the Bosnian ex-mujahedin, there are three escape routes currently," he attests. "One goes from Bosnia through Montenegro to Albania, either overland or into Albania across Lake Shkodër [shared by Albania and Montenegro]. The second goes from Bosnia, through the Sandzak region of Serbia and into Kosovo, and then into Macedonia or Albania. The third goes from Bosnia, again through these countries but then eastward into Bulgaria. From there, the terrorists either travel by ship across the Black Sea to the Caucasus and Chechnya, or overland into Turkey."[33]

According to Mitevski, the Islamist networks not only provide safe passage, but in some cases provide fugitive mujahedin with false documents and the cover of employment in their charities and other organizations. Thus, while watched charities may no longer be a source of terrorist fundraising to the same degree as they were before 9/11, they remain a threat in their capacity for concealing dangerous individuals. The growth of a radical Islamic movement in the Balkans has also provided an infrastructure capable of hiding Islamist fugitives from EU countries, for example, when large-scale riots and protests have led to police clampdowns.[34] Regional and Western intelligence sources point to informal networks in which homegrown Wahhabi leaders routinely escort Arab donors secretly across the Kosovo-Macedonia border mountains, into "friendly" villages full of new mosques built with the latter's monies. When the aforementioned Euro-jihadis start streaming out of Iraq, the Balkans will be an appealing place to hide away, should they encounter trouble in EU countries. For better and for worse, globalization is bringing people of all sorts closer together.

Immigration and demographic concerns, of course, also color the EU's relationship with perennial candidate country Turkey. With a mainly Muslim population of over 70 million, Turkey as an EU member would have the second-largest number of seats in the European Parliament after Germany and would, European protectionists fear, flood the union with cheap labor and thus exacerbate already rising levels of unemployment. Primarily, the impulse of both the opponents and supporters of Turkey's EU membership has been towards fear mongering. The former warn of the political and economic ramifications of admitting a large and relatively poor Muslim country bordering on Iraq, Iran, and Syria into the European club, while the latter warns precisely the opposite—that exclusion and alienation would make the Turks anti-Western and more prone to seduction from extremist varieties of Islam. As long as both the positions for and against are based on fear and warnings, however, the less emotive and more relevant facts regarding the relative benefits of Turkish EU membership remain ignored.

Wary of current European fears of Islam, the Turkish government has presented the country as modern and secular minded. Ironically, however, adhering to the secular formula prescribed by Ataturk in 1923 means that certain EU-mandated "reforms" cannot be implemented without endangering the secular order itself. A prominent example is the Greek Orthodox theological seminary of Chalki, which has been closed since 1973 and which the EU would like to see reopened in the name of religious freedom. Without the seminary, future generations of Orthodox leaders cannot be trained, meaning that the Patriarchate—in continuous existence since the fourth century CE—is in danger of sputtering out, an unthinkable event for the world's 250 million Orthodox Christians and, especially, for Greeks. Contrary to the conventional wisdom, however, the Turkish reticence over reopening Chalki has little to do with the Greeks. Rather, the Turkish government does not want to give various Islamist factions a logical precedent for making their own demands, should a religion school for the Christians be allowed. To the Turkish political order, a handful of mostly elderly Greeks living in Istanbul is not a threat. Islamic movements, however, are. For the Turks, it is a no-win situation; by carrying out the EU's stated reforms, Islamic movements could become a danger to the secular order, whereas failing to carry out the reforms alienates the country further from Europe, thus automatically increasing the chances of internal unrest and dissatisfaction from nationalist and Islamist forces.

The case of Turkey, whose long Ottoman shadow falls over the Balkans it helped create for hundreds of years, also brings us back to the crux of the West's dilemma today in regards to crime, corruption, and "certain foreign relations." The enhanced wealth and prestige that the country won, as recounted in Chapter 5, from its participation in the new "Great Game" for control of natural resource supplies and energy corridors in the Caspian/Central Asian region, only exacerbated the corruption of the Turkish Deep State—and its hold on America. Developments there a decade ago brought Turkey again to a new and unprecedented level of power and wealth. In 1996–1997, in the aftermath of a new Israeli-Turkish friendship pact, "things suddenly switched," recalls Sibel Edmonds. Very aware of the significant power and influence of the Israeli lobby in Washington, the Turks, who had no significant diaspora lobby in America, sought to learn from their new allies. "Turkey essentially said to the Israelis, 'okay, we want to be like you—show us how it's done,'" recounts Edmonds. "And they hired advisors and consultants from the biggest lobby groups, such as the Jewish Institute for National Security Affairs (JINSA) and the American Israeli Public Affairs Committee (AIPAC). Israel was the mentor."[35]

There were benefits for both parties, recounts Edmonds. With Israeli tutelage and assistance, Turkish officials began to move in ever more elite Washington circles and developed stronger connections with American elected officials, administration figures, influential advisors, and military men willing to champion Turkey's political agenda, military procurement needs, and economic investment programs. At the same time, Israel was allowed to use Turkish military bases, despite the strong and simmering disapproval of Turkey's Muslim population, while in Washington Israeli groups gained access to classified military information available to Turkey in its capacity as a NATO member. The FBI soon became suspicious of the blossoming friendship between the Turks and Israelis, however, and even opened investigations of diplomats, political apparatchiks, and lobbyists, some of which exploded into public view in 2004, with the arrest of Larry Franklin, a Pentagon analyst sentenced to 13 years in prison in January 2006 for passing top-secret files on Iran to Israeli lobbyists in Washington.

In her six-month tenure with the FBI, translator Edmonds rendered numerous documents allegedly pertaining to Turkish espionage in American nuclear labs, drug dealings involving NATO officials, and hostile intelligence gathering against the U.S. government. An embarrassed Attorney General John Ashcroft, citing the need to preserve "certain foreign relations," slapped a gag order on her under the State Secrets Act. Despite the fact that congressmen and an internal FBI inquiry found that her allegations were factually accurate, Edmonds lost her appeal to the Supreme Court—on the same grounds. While the FBI has refused to comment publicly on the allegations Edmonds has made in her whistle-blower lawsuits, several high-profile investigations leading back to the Turkish-Israeli covert alliance that began during the second Clinton administration have been carried out, most notably the Franklin affair. However, says Edmonds, this represents merely "the tip of the iceberg." If there was a full investigation of her case, she maintains, "certain elected officials would stand trial and go to jail."[36]

Indeed, Franklin has been depicted in the media as a relatively small player, perhaps even the necessary fall guy concealing much larger and higher-up crimes. Nevertheless, he represents a link between the Israeli and the Turkish lobbies. "Why would Larry Franklin, an unknown Pentagon analyst, be at almost every ATC [American-Turkish Council] event?" asks Edmonds. "Was he perhaps in the pocket of the Turks?" The ATC is a powerful Washington lobby group whose board contains leading American and Turkish political luminaries, as well as captains of industry in all the major defense contracting, natural resources, and consumer goods producers in both countries. According to Edmonds, people in and around the ATC played a key role in the espionage and criminal activities that, she says, are making America and the world demonstrably less safe—up to and including drug trafficking, illicit weapons sales, and black-market nuclear weapons technology proliferation. According to her, key players in her case and in other cases have included "the same old crowd" of neoconservative hawks and other establishment figures long connected with both the Turkish and Israeli lobbies and the American military-industrial complex.

However, the obvious need to cover up these crimes that affect American and, indeed, global security means that the most powerful leaders and institutions will never be investigated, and that "certain foreign relations" will not be harmed. This extends to a hands-off policy of appeasement when it comes to policy moves by allies such as Turkey and Saudi Arabia. The perfect example illustrating both simultaneously was when, in July 2006, a Turkish court exonerated Yassin al-Qadi, the Saudi tycoon who had been blacklisted by the United States as a sponsor of terrorism through his Muwafaq/Blessed Relief charity, which allegedly funneled millions to Osama bin Laden during the 1990s.[37] The Bush administration was quiet. Further, as discussed in Chapter 2, the CIA's curious release of known Islamic radical Abdul Latif Saleh in 1999, and his ability to ride off into the sunset to Dubai in 2002, most likely owed to the tight business relations between the man Saleh represented in Albania—Yassin al-Qadi—and Western political and economic leaders. Indeed, while the Bush administration froze the Saudi businessman's assets in October 2001, Edmonds scoffs, "The US has not reduced his real assets, which are kept elsewhere, and they apparently will not touch him. So what did this blacklisting mean in the end?"[38]

Indeed, despite the massive and indisputable connections between Saudi Arabia and the 9/11 attacks, U.S. officials have balked at cracking down, as to do so would destroy relations with a close and oil-rich ally. It is well known who was spirited out of America on the only aircraft allowed to fly in the immediate aftermath of 9/11—the relatives of Osama bin Laden. Yet even before that sinister day, at least since the regime of George H.W. Bush, investigations of the Saudis had been forcibly blocked. In the late 1990s, a Saudi defector brought the FBI some 14,000 incriminating Saudi government documents regarding high Saudi officials. Rather than thank the man, the bureau treated him as if he had the plague. Recalled an agent involved with the case, "The low-level agents wanted this stuff because they were tremendous leads. But the upper-level people would not permit this, did not want to touch this material...We do not even want to know. Because obviously going through 14,000 documents from the Saudi government files would anger the Saudis. And it seemed to be policy number one that we don't get these boys angry."[39]

Other examples abound. When Robert Wright, "the only FBI agent to seize terrorist funds [over $1.4 million, belonging to Yassin al-Qadi] from U.S.-based Middle Eastern terrorists using federal civil forfeiture statutes" before 9/11, sought to investigate alleged terrorist-training camps in Chicago and Kansas City in 1998, he was "sabotaged" by higher-ups.[40] Another investigation into the infamous bin Laden-linked Saudi charity World Assembly of Muslim Youth (WAMY) was repeatedly blocked; "the FBI wanted to investigate these guys," said U.S. national security expert Joe Trento, but "they weren't permitted to." After the election of George W. Bush, "agents were specifically told to 'back off.'"[41] After 9/11, the official government investigation censured details incriminating the Saudis. Nevertheless, "our investigators found a CIA memo dated August 2, 2002, whose author concluded that there is incontrovertible evidence that there is support for these terrorists within the Saudi government," wrote Congressman Bob Graham in later disclosures. "We had discovered an FBI asset who had a close relationship with two of the terrorists; a terrorist support network that went through the Saudi Embassy; and a funding network that went through the Saudi Royal family."[42]

Why is this important in the present context? Simply because Saudi Arabia is the chief supporter of the Wahhabi movement that is spreading like a cancer across the Balkans today, and is thus the single largest state sponsor of Islamic fundamentalism, and thus the forces that create terrorism, in the world. The Saudi government, royal family, oil companies, and businessmen associated with them continue to spread intimidation and fear, for now mostly within Balkan Muslim communities, by driving a stake between Muslims with the introduction of their violent and alien doctrines. This, however, is just preliminary to more radical activities, as the attested experience of Wahhabi groups elsewhere in the world indicates. Nevertheless, for the reasons of safeguarding diplomatic relations, the West does nothing.

The need to save precious foreign relations has stymied the cooperation of Western intelligence and law enforcement. Oftentimes, they have been working at cross-purposes, under the disruptive influence of high diplomatic officials. In any case, in the best case scenario, the legitimate economy has entered a relationship with terrorism, all the more so as globalization continues to gain ground. To illustrate how hopelessly and inextricably intertwined the worlds of terrorist financing and the legitimate economy have become, Loretta Napoleoni further points to the cause of Osama bin Laden's prior holdings in Sudan, which happens to be the world's leading producer of gum acacia, a key ingredient in soft drinks. Through his control of a single company, the world's leading terrorist also had a stranglehold on the American drinks industry. When President Clinton ordered economic sanctions on the Khartoum regime, companies like Coca-Cola actively lobbied for gum acacia to be excluded from the sanctions list. In this bizarre but revealing case, continuing to do business with Osama bin Laden was an urgent necessity for the American economy. Were companies like Coca-Cola to lose access to a necessary ingredient for producing their soft drinks, the economic losses would have been in the billions. The multinationals were, essentially, beholden to the terrorist godfather for their livelihoods.[43]

According to Napoleoni, the size of the terrorism-related economy is an astonishing $1.5 trillion—a number that only keeps increasing. "This constitutes an international economic system parallel to the legitimate one. It generates a river of money, which flows towards traditional economies and essentially poisons them," she maintains. "This process weakens states and encourages the formations of state-shells; entities created around the economics of armed conflict sustained by terror groups. As this process evolves, the size of this alternative economic system will increase and with it Western dependency on it."[44]

In the end, there is one inescapable conclusion that emerges from all of the testimony recounted above. It is that so long as preserving corrupt foreign relations take precedence over national and international security, the war on terror will never be won. And when it is the case that terrorism cannot be investigated because blocking its criminal funding channels would cause fatal tremors in the global economic system—this is when we know that terrorism is here to stay.

CHAPTER 8

The Next Generation: Jihad, the Balkans, and the Threat to the West

It happened during Friday prayers, just a few weeks after a shoot-out between rival Muslim political parties that left one man dead in Serbia's Novi Pazar, and just a few months before the discovery, on a nearby mountainside, of a jihadi training camp bursting with weapons. The three Wahhabi vigilantes, armed with wooden clubs, burst in on the imam and worshippers gathered in the "Arab Mosque," in the provincial capital of the Sandzak region, bordering Serbia, Bosnia, Montenegro, and Kosovo. The not very veiled message was that it would be better for the imam's health to start leading prayer correctly—that is, according to Wahhabi ways. With the imam under attack, 33-year-old Habib Fijuljanin reached for his gun, ripping off warning shots. Later, the situation turned bloody when his brother, Izet Fijuljanin, arrived. As the Wahhabis started smashing his car, Izet shot back, wounding his attackers. Hospitalizations, arrests, and a police shutdown of the mosque quickly followed. According to a contemporary report, the November 3, 2006, incident "was not the first at the mosque."[1]

Indeed, the religious situation in this depressed provincial town of western-most Serbia has been explosive for years. And, because of the Wahhabis' persistent gains, it is getting more so with each passing month. The major urban center in an economically depressed subregion that spills over across the Serbian-Montenegrin border, Novi Pazar is a Bosniak-majority town dependent on textiles and smuggling for its material sustenance and on religion for its identity. Over the centuries, it has been variously claimed and occupied by Serbia, Bosnia, Ottoman Turkey, and the Austro-Hungarian Empire. This historically nebulous status, along with chronic poverty and the modern ideological incursions of Saudi Arabia and Iran, has made the Sandzak an unpredictable microregion susceptible to outside influence and machinations. With the urban areas like Novi Pazar populated chiefly by Muslims and the outlying villages by Christian Serbs, the Sandzak could be said to be a Bosnia in miniature. Now, a largely inter-necine, almost nihilistic, war between the Wahhabi fringe and the rest of Muslim and Christian society is making the Sandzak perhaps the most dangerous staging post for radical Islam in the Balkans today.

The region has had a turbulent modern history. The war in neighboring Bosnia strained social relations between Christians and Muslims. Under Milosevic, the latter claimed discrimination, but they also had control over large sections of political and economic life, with the illicit local textile industry, churning out cheap knock-offs of international brands and keeping the Muslims wealthier than their Serbian Orthodox Christian neighbors. In short, discrimination and intimi-dation were mutual and the politics characterized by temporary alliances and deception. However, today the textile industry has languished, adding to the ranks of the unemployed and creating a greater urgency to find financial support from outside. In one of those unpredictable ironies of the globalizing economy, it may, in fact, have been the Chinese that did in the tradesmen of Novi Pazar; according to Serbian investigative reporter Marko Lopusina, a deal between Mira Markovic (wife of then-President Milosevic) and the Chinese government allowed over 30,000 Chinese to set up shop in Serbia over a decade ago. Conse-quently flooding the local market with their own cheap textiles, the Chinese have indirectly exacerbated the economic trends that feed radical Islam—as is now emerging in the Sandzak.[2]

Several turbulent events in this usually sleepy Serbian backwater have raised eyebrows over the past year, both locally and for Western intelligence services that have taken a new interest. At a concert of the renowned ethnomusic group Balkanika in Novi Pazar in June 2006, a group of ten bearded Wahhabi hooligans rushed the stage, trashing the instruments and then addressing the crowd through the microphone: "Brothers, go home," shouted the radicals. "They are working against Islam here. This is Satan's work."[3] Local people, Muslims and Christians alike, were shocked and disappointed by the ability of a violent extremist group to interfere with their cultural life. Some four months later, an even more dis-turbing event occurred when a heavily bleeding woman was rushed to the hospi-tal in Belgrade. She had been transferred from Novi Pazar after her Wahhabi husband had decided to perform a Taliban-style "female circumcision," since, according to Wahhabi belief, "the wife should not enjoy in sex and not be attrac-tive to other men," reported Belgrade's *Kurir*. Mentioning the testimony of mod-erate Muslims and Wahhabis alike, the newspaper added that "in Novi Pazar, Tutin, Sjenica, Rozaj and other places [in Sandzak], Wahhabis treat their wives as slaves. They do not allow any man, except the father, brother and the husband to see the face of the wife."[4]

Indeed, Wahhabi communities have taken root on the Montenegrin side of the newly internationalized region, especially in Bijelo Polje and Rozaje, where the official Islamic Community has less influence and uneducated youth have proven susceptible to fundamentalist teachings.[5] If a new cross border cause can be manipulated by irredentists, the "Sandzak unity" movement would have to be an Islamist one, rather than the largely nationalist struggles of ethnic Albanians in Kosovo and Macedonia. Serbian military analyst Milovan Drecun contends that increasing violent incidents caused by local Wahhabi fanatics throughout 2006 represent "just an initial stage" in an extremist plan for the "violent creation of the so-called Islamic state of Sandzak."[6] He also attested that Montenegrin Wahhabis were tightly connected with similar groups in Kosovo, Bosnia, and Macedonia, and were well armed. Indeed, the "recreational" activities of the Islamic Youth of Sandzak—a public excursion to an island on a lake near Albania—are identical to recent Islamic youth group activities in Macedonia, similarly designed to make an overt display of Wahhabism in tourist areas.[7] The fact that Montenegro's secession from Serbia would, in erecting new borders between Muslims, give extremists a cause to rally around has been noted for years; however, the powers that be chronically failed to see anything dangerous about Montenegrin independence.[8]

Several months before these incidents, a British specialist security publication claimed long-term social trends were behind this ramp-up in radical activity. "Religious schools and an Islamic university are educating increasing numbers of young people, filling a vacuum left by failing republican and municipal administrations," stated a brief from *Jane's Intelligence Digest.* "There are also growing numbers of so-called Wahhabis who follow Islamic practices imported from Saudi Arabia. This group of predominately young men operating outside the traditional Islamic community, Islamska Zajednica (IZ), played a leading role in orchestrating February's flag-burning demonstrations in the region's capital, Novi Pazar, protesting against newspaper cartoons of the prophet Mohammed first published in Denmark."[9]

The flag burning in Novi Pazar not only mirrored similar events in European cities and the Islamic world, putting this unlikely Balkan backwater "on the map" of ideological hot spots. It also coincided with similar events in Sarajevo and Skopje, Macedonia. In the latter demonstration, observers and intelligence sources confirmed the presence of a small number of Bosniaks, adding to suspicions that all three protests had been centrally arranged through the radical leadership in Bosnia, since the ethnic Albanian Muslims of Macedonia have shown less interest in such forms of religious devotion. Sarajevo's influence, in terms of both the mainstream Islamic Community and the radical Wahhabi groups, extends directly to the Sandzak—a "lost territory" for the Bosnian Muslim state. Through economic depression, state disinterest, and a legacy of oppression, Sandzak has become an ideal breeding ground for radicalism.

In a place where religion more than ethnicity defines the majority population, it is no surprise that Islamic leaders run the show politically as well. The leader of Sandzak's Islamic Community, the foreign-trained Mufti Muamer Zukorlic, was brought to power in 1993 by two formerly hard-line Muslim politicians, Sulejman Ugljanin and Rasim Ljajic, who have since split and become the major political rivals in the region. They had strong ties to the Islamist SDA party of the late Bosnian President Alija Izetbegovic and his defense minister, Hasim Cengic, architect of the Iran-Sudan-Bosnia arms and mujahedin pipeline during the war. Since 1993, Mufti Zukorlic has "built up a network of schools, madrassahs, a printing house, an Islamic clothing company, a newspaper and an Islamic university," according to Jane's, which nevertheless does not consider him to be a radical. Under Zukorlic's watch, however, trends toward fundamentalization in dress and culture have increased, from which it is a question of a step of degrees, rather than a total reorientation, to end up at Wahhabism. With the Islamic Community holding "the balance of power in Sandzak," and manipulating its prominent position "to extract concessions from politicians and play a more active role in day-to-day politics," it is clear that political Islam can only grow stronger in the microregion.

This trend in the Sandzak today is a perfect example of what is happening, at a slower pace, in other Islamic enclaves throughout the Balkans. In remote pockets of Bulgaria and Macedonia, Islam is cumulatively becoming a vital political force precisely to the degree that radical Wahhabi minorities become pervasive. New and previously unheard of political questions, social customs, and religious mores are entering the debate all around the Balkans, with the "moderate" Islamic powers—represented universally by the official Islamic Communities of each state or subregion—holding themselves up as the necessary antidote to fundamentalists—while at the same time double-dealing with these fundamentalists. "On the one hand, Zukorlic and the [Islamic Community] can present a danger—that of potential extremism in the shape of Wahhabism," a Serbian local explained for Jane's. "But on the other hand, he can present himself as the solution, that the IZ ensures moderation. What his strategy means in practice is that either way, politicised Islam in our region will continue to grow."

Some, such as the former DBK counterterrorism chief and deputy director of Macedonian intelligence, Zoran Mitevski, accuse Mufti Zukorlic of directly sponsoring a radical Islamic movement with separatist designs. According to Mitevski, Zukorlic has received huge funding from the governments of Saudi Arabia, the United Arab Emirates, and Iran, as well as from al Qaeda-connected charities such as al Haramain and the World Assembly of Muslim Youth (WAMY) to "realize their dream of an Islamic state of Sandzak along the lines of Iran." Despite what he has said regarding the separation of religion and government, the initial stage of the independence drive, autonomy, is, in fact, being directed by Zukorlic. When Serbia was creating a new constitution in October 2006, Zukorlic and local Muslim political leaders (with the exception of pro-Belgrade Sulejman Ugljanin) issued a proclamation against it, demanding that the government "solve" the issue of Sandzak by giving it autonomy.[10] With the precedent of Montenegro and Kosovo (indeed, Mitevski discloses that much of the funds made available to Zukorlic are funneled through Islamic charities in Pristina), Sandzak's Muslim leaders are determined to make this tiny enclave divided between two countries into an Islamic state of its own.

The advance guard for this movement is, of course, the Wahhabis. While the sect is still small, with only a few hundred adherents, it is growing. The violence the Wahhabis have caused, utterly disproportionate to their percentage of the general population, is why security experts and local residents are concerned. Fears of Wahhabi militancy materialized on March 17, 2007, when Serbian police discovered a large cache of weapons in a remote mountain cave outside of Novi Pazar. According to AP, "police found large quantities of plastic explosives, ammunition, face masks, military uniforms, bombs, food, water and other equipment," as well as "propaganda terrorist material, military survival instructions, geographic charts and several CDs." Four Muslims from Novi Pazar were arrested, while one person managed to escape. According to Serbian police, the militant group was organized and equipped by Wahhabi fundamentalists.[11]

The Wahhabis arrived in the Sandzak just a decade ago, from Bosnia, and quietly built a power base with an eye towards more militant future activities, as the March 2007 arrests would seem to show. They came with the support of the radical, mujahedin-connected Active Islamic Youth, and have since been supported by Sarajevo radicals backed by Arab money funneled through Islamic charities in Vienna, as well as through diaspora channels in Sweden, Austria, and the United Kingdom.[12] It is important to remember that this geographical progression of radicalism could not have existed without the deliberate installation of a foreign-funded charity and terrorist network, originally conceived by the West as a lifeline for the beleaguered Bosnian Muslim government of Izetbegovic against the Serbs, created under the watchful eye of the Clinton administration and German and Austrian intelligence.

Today's creeping radicalization further and further from the initial Bosnian core shows once again the folly of their interventionist policy. The Serbian central government, only now recovering from years of Western sanctions and NATO's bombing campaign, can hardly be expected to fund this chronically impoverished Muslim enclave, leaving the door wide open for an Islamic Community and Wahhabi groups, both funded lavishly by outside Islamic donors, to set up state-of-the-art schools, sports facilities, and other alternatives to the state structures.[13] In the bigger picture, the primary causes of Sandzak Islamic radicalization (including, of course, the heroin problem being exploited by Bosnian Wahhabi "rehabilitators") was created by the West, and particularly America, over two decades of shortsighted interventions. When one factors in as well the decline of the all-important textile industry and the resulting increase in poverty among Muslims, another root cause of radicalism, it becomes clear that, whatever partisan sources say about Serbian nationalist repression, the Sandzak today is in the big picture a casualty of globalization and intervention.

Nevertheless, despite the increasing turbulence, the region continues to be ignored by the outside media, with the exception of politically connected incidents, such the shooting of one of Sulejman Ugljanin's candidates during a local election in September 2006.[14] With the world's focus on Iraq, Afghanistan, and the Middle East, few except government intelligence services have the time or resources to pay much attention to Balkan backwaters that, though bubbling along under the surface, have yet to boil over into full-blown terrorism. This is, however, a mistake of judgment that fails to consider the strategic patience and tactics of Islamic extremism. For terrorism is only one tactical weapon in the hands of zealots seeking to reshape societies in their own image, and in many cases it is not even the appropriate one.

To comprehend the real danger of extremist Islamic movements in the Balkans, Western Europe, and elsewhere, one therefore needs to consider how extremist and dogmatic views are being disseminated and entrenched in Muslim societies without a tradition of such beliefs. Whereas the European parliamentary democracies (and the modern Balkan states imitating them) plan their policies and staff their administration according to four- or five-year cycles, with all of the campaigning, elections, and coalition politicking that go along with this system, the management of the Islamic cause is infinitely more simple; its single overarching policy is to spread religion, with any internal disagreements that crop up concerning only the means, not the ends. Further, the new decentralization of the terrorist cause in the post–al Qaeda period has created a grassroots movement in its purest form, a movement in which anyone, anywhere along the global network, can take action without the approval or consent of any leader or law other than that of Islam.

Fundamentalist Islam, unlike Western society, is not predicated on ideals of progress and an ever-brighter future. Its backers rather seek the infinite temporal extension of a bright enough present of daily worship and tightly arbitrated social rules existing since the seventh century. That the desired ideal is to be found in the existing practice in Islam is the most significant difference between Western and Islamic societies, and the one that makes the latter so much more potent: in short, the Islamists can deliver immediately, whereas the West is always positing success and gratification of all kinds to follow an ever-ascending arc of progress and consumption. Further, unlike most Westerners, the Islamists do not view their work as a necessary though annoying departure from their "real life."

The eternal patience of the Islamic movement—a quality present since its earliest days—does not view obstructions as anything more than temporary setbacks. The oft-cited claims that the vast majority of Balkan Muslims are not interested in extremism thus become irrelevant. Nothing if not chauvinistic and stubborn, the fundamentalists simply do not care. So long as the funding spigot from Arab states and other foreign Islamist forces continues gushing with full force, they will continue to push their propaganda, picking up, little by little, more and more adherents. The long-term plan of Osama bin Laden and his peers, for a revived global caliphate, may indeed seem fanciful and unlikely; it is hard to believe that an effectively destroyed al Qaeda could possibly execute this complex plan. However, if nothing else, the "2020 Plan" drafted by the Syrian jihad theorist and bin Laden confidante Abu Musab al-Suri is indicative of the scale and ambition of the terrorist imagination.[15] At the very least, the Islamists' single-minded and constant proselytizing is much simpler, more efficient, and more organized than are the initiatives led by wealthy but dysfunctional Western governments and peacekeeping missions, mired as they are in indecision, chronic changes of leadership and policy, as well as bureaucratic infighting and all-around mediocrity.

In the Balkans, where the West continues to guide the processes of Bosnian, Montenegrin, Macedonian, and Kosovar state-building, the pan-Islamic movement at the same time is steadily and quietly solidifying its base. For the latter, the West's state-building exploits and promises of "European integration" are irrelevant and, in fact, helpful, insofar as they create controversies, government weakness, corruption, and internal divisions that the Islamists are able to exploit for their own purposes. Nevertheless, save for the internecine struggles within Muslim communities, Islamists have not made their presence felt. This is no accident, though it has lulled the region's residents into a false sense of security. The 1998 testimony of the unfortunate Egyptian imam, Abu Omar, before his secret service captors in Albania—that their country represented a "safe hotel" that his group would not like to be kicked out of by making attacks locally—remains more or less true today. Yet while most Balkan residents feel their countries are hardly worth the trouble for Islamic radicals, this view ignores the reality that the Islamists are simply biding their time and cleverly adapting to the prevailing social conditions, in order to strengthen their position. Then, when the demographics and other salient factors are in place, the real battle for dominance will begin.

According to the Belgrade University terrorism expert, Darko Trifunovic, the real obstacle for Balkan counterterrorism efforts today is that "whereas the leadership and clandestine terror cells of al Qaeda and similar groups can all be countered, the spreading of the Dawa (Islamic teaching) cannot be fought by any means." What Trifunovic calls "Dawa infrastructure"—Saudi-style mosques, madrasas, Islamic cultural centers, and youth groups, written and visual propaganda and so on—"is becoming established more and more strongly with each passing year. Their goal is to spread Islam by all possible means, by building up the mosques, carrying out aggressive training, and disseminating propaganda that depicts the Muslims globally as victims of the alleged Western 'crusade.' This Dawa infrastructure is the engine that produces future suicide bombers and mujahedin."[16]

In the context of building this infrastructure, therefore, it is not surprising that under the influence of Mufti Zukorlic in Serbia's Sandzak more municipal funds have been spent on sports halls than on health care. And, while Zukorlic claims to be anti-Wahhabi, the youth group under official Islamic Community control, the Muslim Youth Club (MOK) "is alleged to maintain ties to the Wahhabis, and many of its members sport Wahhabi fashions," reported the International Crisis Group (ICG), noting that in 2002 MOK Wahhabis brandished pistols at a Western NGO presentation partially devoted to reproductive health; as has been the case with the more recent demonstrations and attacks, the suspicion was that "immorality was being taught."[17] One suspects that what Mufti Zukorlic really feared was the possible challenge represented by alternative Western options to the teachings of Islam controlled by local leaders like himself.

The proof of Dawa infrastructure expansion is evident everywhere in the Balkans, in the explosive proliferation of mosques, propaganda dissemination, sports halls, and the NGOs and other youth groups that use them. In Macedonia, Kosovo, Bosnia, Bulgaria, and elsewhere, hundreds of new Wahhabi mosques have been built in the past seven years, while suspicious charities, supposedly shut down after 9/11, have proven very resilient, renaming themselves or simply remaining entrenched. Things that were never before seen, like fully cloaked women in both rural and urban areas, and the very public appearance of Islamic propaganda distribution systems, are suddenly commonplace. On the main tourist shopping street of Struga, a Macedonian town on Lake Ohrid, bearded Wahhabis hawk Saudi literature in Albanian translation, while in Skopje and Tetovo, DVDs of the Chechen jihad and mujahedin killing Americans in Iraq are sold openly in markets or in mosque bookstores. Preachers in Kosovo's so-called "Osama bin Laden" mosque rail against America and Israel.

Nevertheless, the unwillingness of the mainstream media and political establishment to investigate cases that might prove embarrassing for the West's Balkan legacy, as well as an unaccountable, "don't-rock-the-boat" mentality among peacekeepers, has kept these developments largely out of view of the Western public. And it seems there is little that can be done. As one American military official in Kosovo reminds, "We see [the Wahhabis] doing their thing, selling their books, but if they're not doing anything technically illegal, we can't stop them. We know what some of them are driving at, and what they are preaching in the mosques, but we can't do anything except watch."[18]

Despite their apparent license to act with impunity, Balkan Islamists still see fit to take certain precautions—a testament to their strategic and tactical patience. A young Albanian in Skopje recalled how he was approached with a job offer from one of the local Islamic charities: simply for driving back and forth from Kosovo each day (an hour's drive) and bringing back small numbers of CDs and DVDs, he could receive 600 euros per month—three times the average Macedonian monthly salary. According to the man, who did not accept the job, the charity preferred to import its propaganda material thus in a discreet manner not recognizable to border officials: "They thought it was better little by little, rather than by one large shipment which maybe the government would get suspicious about."[19]

The situation with radical Islam is most well known in Bosnia, though perhaps less of a threat than in other parts of the Balkans. Still, in Sarajevo the Wahhabis have control of several mosques, including the city's most central place of worship, the towering, Saudi-funded King Fahd Mosque. "Over the past five years, they have built very few new factories in Bosnia, but 1,000 new mosques have gone up," says Trifunovic. "It is not a revolution, but rather a silent transition." In this conception, the progression of nonterrorist activities, which, however, contain the seeds of future terrorism, include the preaching and brainwashing—war orphans make a particularly potent recruitment pool—followed by "sport activities," which include self-defense classes and training leading up to, and sometimes including, combat training. "By the end, you just need supply the bullet or the bomb."

Indeed, while everyone is talking about "hidden training camps," says Trifunovic, "the truth is that today they mostly don't exist. The modern equivalent is more simple activities in buildings like sports halls, spreading the Dawa and training in sports activities—things that are not illegal and cannot be stopped, but which are providing the basis for radical worldviews and terrorist activity." Indeed, the evidence from recent terrorist attacks in the West has shown that extremists there are also adopting these methods and opportunities to plot terrorist attacks. The clampdown on mosques in Western Europe, for example, has led terrorist planners to recruit cell members in more innocuous environments. "Using youth centres, gyms, whitewater rafting trips and jihadi videos," reported *The Times* of London, 7/7 bombing leader Mohammad Sidique Khan "convinced Germaine Lindsay, Shehzad Tanweer and Hasib Hussain of the need to murder innocent people to defend their religion."[20]

However, mosque clampdowns in the Balkans have been less successful than in the West, and due to logistical concerns and local realities, it is not likely that comprehensive action will ever be taken. Dzevad Galijasevic, the Bosnian politician who accused government figures of supporting terrorism in the country, echoed Trifunovic in stating that "the training camps in [Bosnia] don't exist anymore" and that today's radical recruiting "is going on in the mosques. In general, they recruit the young people." According to Galijasevic, the central Bosnian towns of Teshanj and Zavidovici "are the real al Qaeda centers." A former major of the Maglaj municipality, Galijasevic was threatened in 2000 and again in October 2006 for his outspoken opposition to the former mujahedin and Wahhabis. The politician also singled out the mosques in obscure villages such as Lijeshnici, Novi Sheher, and Kopoce as prime terrorist recruiting centers and accused one Muslim cleric, Izudin Krushko, alleged importer of Egyptian mujahedin, of being their organizer. "At the moment the most Wahhabis, mujahedin and al Qaeda members are in Shericima and Zeljeznom Plju near Zenica, and in Zepcha, in Muhurecim near Travnik, in Bocinja near Maglaj, and in Gornja Moacha between Brchko and Srebrenik."[21]

Considering that Balkan Islamists thus have all channels open to them, the radical message can be imported everywhere from the mosque to the home. Everywhere from Skopje or Sarajevo, DVDs of Dawa preaching in the gymnasiums and mosques of Macedonia, Kosovo, Bosnia, and elsewhere are sold. Thus, increasingly, there is the total maximization of the Dawa infrastructure: the purpose-built sports hall or mosque where the lecture is held; the NGO or youth group that organizes and staffs the event, and the DVD production companies and Web sites that then duplicate and circulate the visual record of the event throughout the Balkans and beyond. The production and funding of such propaganda inevitably leads back directly to a handful of Balkan radical mosques, NGOs, Web sites, production houses, and distribution channels, locally affiliated but with funding and support ultimately coming from Iran, the Arab states, or wealthy Islamic charities in the West.

Finally and most provocatively, Wahhabi activists keen on keeping under the radar also employ a portable Dawa infrastructure, preaching in private sessions at the homes of would-be converts. In Macedonia, for example, intelligence sources relying on Muslim informers cite the pervasive use of jihad videos aired in private homes, as well as ever-more-restrictive rules regarding marriage and the family, designed to increase the Wahhabi flock by expediting conversion and creating a pool of children whose parents will, unlike most Muslim parents today, be enthusiastic about sending them to Islamic schools from the earliest ages possible. The enthusiasm that devotees of sects such as the so-called "Pakistani Wahhabi" Tablighi Jamaat have shown for building "Islamic kinder-gartens" in isolated villages confirm this desire. At the same time, rival Islamic education opportunities, such as the official madrasa in Kondovo and the Turkish Gülen-managed schools in Struga, Gostivar, and Skopje indicate that the battle for the hearts and minds of Macedonia's Muslims is fierce—resulting in ever-expanding efforts to seduce students from all of the country's Islamic factions. And the same phenomenon is happening everywhere else, as Islam becomes politicized and, unlike in Yugoslav Communist times, freed from the restrictions of a single, state-overseen bureaucratic structure. Ironically, it has consistently been the European Union and United States, referencing human rights concerns, who have urged Balkan governments to legalize religious denominations and sects like the Wahhabis, groups that have no historical ties to the region and that could pose a terrorism threat.

The biggest achievement of the Islamic states and other Muslim supporters originally drawn to the Balkans by the collapse of Communism and the Bosnian and Kosovo jihads, has therefore, not been a military one. Indeed, though they inspired fear and committed numerous atrocities, the mujahedin in these theaters played only a very modest role in military outcomes that were essentially decided by America. However, the pretext of helping the Muslim war efforts through military and humanitarian means allowed them to establish, through control centers in European cities such as Vienna, Hamburg, Oslo, London, and Milan, to infiltrate Balkan countries, where they have built countless mosques and other Dawa infrastructure, in an effort to transform Muslim societies. As has been recounted, this process has also involved violent challenges to the official local Islamic leadership in several places.

A long-term goal of global terrorist syndicates, according to experts like Trifu-novic, is to turn Balkan countries into net exporters, and not only importers, of Islamic proselytizing and terror. Resentment of America over its wars in Afghanistan and Iraq, and of Western Europe over symbolic affronts such as the Danish cartoons of Prophet Mohammad and the French ban on burkhas in schools, has become stronger since the "war on terror" officially began in 2001. Although the tangible results of Wahhabi preaching and this new alienation are still few, they are attested by the sporadic reports of Balkan Muslims fighting in Chechnya, Afghanistan, and Iraq written over the past few years. From the demonstrated Bosnian ties to the 2003 Madrid train bombing and the failed attempt on the Pope's funeral by Bosnia-based radicals in April 2005, to the arrest of a Kosovo Albanian in connection with the London terror plots three months later and the Bosnia youth arrests in November, there is mounting evidence to attest that two decades of Western intervention, simultaneously with foreign Islamic proselytizing and funding, have heightened the risk of the Balkans as a breeding ground for terrorism.

Indeed, as the American special police investigator in Kosovo and other sources resignedly admit, the Balkans has become "a two-way conveyor belt" for radical Islam, importing foreign radicals and exporting ideologically vulnerable students and a small number of terrorist supporters. None of this could have been possible without the steady and pervasive creation of a Dawa infrastructure. On the laptop he carries with him everywhere he goes, Darko Trifunovic keeps the files, photos, and videos attesting to over 15 years of mujahedin activity in the Balkans. One particularly alarming set of photos depicts little boys in the company of armed mujahedin. "These were Bosnian orphans trained in mujahedin camps," he says. "Today, we don't know where they are. These kids, now young men, represent the next generation."

Tactically, the pan-Islamist movement cleverly seeks to blend in, like an animal with camouflage coloring, with its surroundings. In the Balkans, where Western rhetoric of human rights, democracy, and multicultural tolerance is practically a religion in itself, Islamic groups have cleverly used this rhetoric against local societies and, by default, their Western sponsors. The vocal Tirana "human rights" group, the Muslim Forum of Albania, for example, exemplifies the current generation of Islamist organizations' covert presentation of a fundamentalist agenda. Protests and rallies over the Danish cartoons, Pope Benedict's comments on Islam, American foreign policy, and other issues are now being justified by activists invoking human rights and interreligious cultural sensitivity. After all, since the West has spent so many years chiding Balkan countries for their mutual intolerance and hatreds, why should Islamist activists not refer to such principles when they perceive their own rights as having been violated?

As elsewhere in Europe, Balkan Islamic groups who espouse a very fundamentalist and intolerant vision for the future society are getting smarter. They are starting to use all the weapons of the West against it, from the rhetoric of democracy and human rights to the vehicles of think tanks and nongovernmental organizations. As they continue to raise their profile, the Islamists have increasingly sought to make their provocations open, discursive, and physically nonviolent. Terrorism is required only when there is no other way, or when Islamic radicals believe they can use it to topple a Muslim state deemed overly secular—a trend that, along with assassination attempts of Muslim leaders, will be seen more and more frequently over the coming years.

Intelligence experts believe that through mimicking the West's "values rhetoric," Balkan Islamists are also following trends simultaneously playing out elsewhere in Europe—and benefiting from the same foreign funding structures. While substantial funds from shadowy sources are readily available, concedes one Washington-based analyst on security matters, "as long as they play the game of human rights, rather than terrorism per se, it is hard to move in." The increasingly sophisticated and expensive organization behind protests and propaganda, such as those that followed the Danish cartoons of Prophet Mohammad and Pope Benedict XVI's September 2006 comments about Islam and violence, has raised concern for European security services. In both cases, successive and well organized protests began, supported by large amounts of flyers and other mass-produced visual material. "How is it possible that defunct and financially bankrupt mosques got their hands on 1.5 million euros to co-organize these protests against the cartoonists?" asks a retired British intelligence officer, citing confidential government sources. "That money was already in place in Europe and got distributed on call. The same with the Netherlands. Their new Muslim activists get funds from somewhere. I'm not really interested in where they got the guns. You can buy those all over Europe. But a million euros? That's not just lying around on every street corner."[22]

In another example, the French urban riots of November 2005, this expert also believes that outside forces had a hand in manipulating rage and unrest for their own purposes. The chronically marginalized young men of North African descent who set fires and destroyed private property in those riots were expressing their discontent with a system they felt to be repressive and unfair. However, "special 'scholars and motivators' were sent in from Sudan, Iran and Tunisia to gear up the incitement and steer this more toward an Islamic protest and away from what were its real factors: social unrest and inequality. These scholars and motivators have the very same paymaster as in the Danish cartoon incident: Iran." Darko Trifunovic, who agrees with this assessment, goes further in suggesting that the clandestine Iranian assistance was meant as a warning to France not to cross Tehran over its nuclear program.

However, others, such as the former CIA agent Philip Giraldi, disagree. "Iran does have some reach in Western Europe (and the US), but it is largely exercised through Hezbollah, which is strongest and best established in Germany," he states. "I do not see the Iranians using their leverage by pushing their adherents onto the streets because they will lose more than they will gain by it. They have much better leverage through their economic relationships with Europeans."[23] To understand the capabilities and operational strategy of the next generation of terrorist syndicates in Europe, and indeed the world, one first must acknowledge the major structural change: the decentralization and autonomy of the new jihadi movement. In only a few years, this transformation has been sweeping and complete. Some six months after the U.S. invasion of Iraq, Giraldi noted:

Prior to December 2001, al-Qaeda was a global organization with a leadership, financial, and logistical structure; training camps; and centralized operational planning. It was able to project its power widely and had relationships with like-minded groups in places like Indonesia and the Philippines. The United States destroyed that al-Qaeda when it drove the Taliban from Afghanistan, but al-Qaeda learned from the disaster and was able to transform itself, becoming in the process largely decentralized and locally self-supporting. Al-Qaeda and other Jihadi groups now operate a terrorist movement without command and control, referred to as "leaderless resistance."[24]

For the Italian economist and terrorism expert, Loretta Napoleoni, who sees some degree of resemblance between the jihadi movement of today and the Marxist-Communist terrorist groups of the 1950s and 1960s, the operative ideology is not simply that of bin Laden and al Qaeda, but more generally "al-Qaedism." A concept "borne of the ashes of al Qaeda, the armed organization that was destroyed after 9/11," al-Qaedism is an extremist creed drawing heavily on an antiglobalist, anti-imperialist ideology, which posits Islam as an answer to these evils and the countries that represent them, and which employs the politics of spreading fear through terrorism to advance this agenda, with the ultimate goal being a renewed caliphate. Although the organized group that was commanded by bin Laden and responsible for the 9/11 attacks is long gone, "because of Iraq, it has been able to grow and mutate into this widespread, decentralized movement. The danger is that in being an international, global ideology, al-Qaedism is potentially everywhere."[25]

Indeed, the April 2006 U.S. National Intelligence Estimate stated that, as critics of the Bush administration's decision to attack Iraq had long argued, the invasion had made the United States demonstrably less safe by providing a new theater for jihadis and a wider cause for them to rally around. Beyond the old organizations of Osama bin Laden and Ayman al-Zawahiri, the Iraq war spawned "a new class of 'self-generating' cells inspired by Al Qaeda's leadership but without any direct connection to Osama bin Laden or his top lieutenants," according to the estimate.[26] Vindicating the testimony of independent experts, future CIA Director General Michael V. Hayden stated in April 2006 that "new jihadist networks and cells, sometimes united by little more than their anti-Western agendas, are increasingly likely to emerge...if this trend continues, threats to the U.S. at home and abroad will become more diverse and that could lead to increasing attacks worldwide."[27] In April 2005, a U.S. National Intelligence Council study concluded that Iraq had become "the primary training ground for the next generation of terrorists, and that veterans of the Iraq war might ultimately overtake Al Qaeda's current leadership in the constellation of the global jihad leadership." This significant trend was acknowledged by Rand Corporation terrorism analyst Brian Jenkins, who noted that the new corps of mujahedin that has fought in Iraq "is just going to go ahead and spread throughout the entire jihadist universe...what we see in Baghdad today is what we're going to be dealing with tomorrow in a whole bunch of places."[28]

One of those places is Europe. Larry Johnson, a former CIA agent and State Department counterterrorism specialist, stated that "Iraq is creating a new generation of jihadis looking for places to live in Europe...they will take up residence with existing communities or form new ones in Europe."[29] Citing Spanish and Italian counterterrorism officials, Loretta Napoleoni notes how Western European governments are becoming "very concerned about returnees from Iraq. These are jihad fighters who possess EU passports, and who may wish to continue to fight in one form or other in the West after having been radicalized in Iraq." Social unrest, discrimination, and perceived symbolic affronts to Islam will more and more frequently be manipulated by outside sponsors of terrorism. The likeliest new "fronts" for the fundamentalist war in Europe include the ghettoes and other gritty urban areas where most of Europe's poor Muslims live. North Africans in France and Spain, Turks in Germany, and Pakistanis in the United Kingdom are only a few of the most prominent Muslim minorities that have been involved in extremist activities over the past decade.

At the same time, surprising new fronts are emerging. "Scandinavia is at the forefront of al-Qaedism today," maintains Napoleoni. "There has been large-scale migration to Sweden and Norway from Syria and Egypt, as well as Iraq and Kurdistan during the 1980s and 1990s, people who have moved recently and experienced discrimination. In Denmark, as we know from the cartoon protests, tensions are rising. In Rotterdam, the majority of the population is Muslim. And Norway is very concerned. There have been massive Saudi investments in Oslo for a Wahhabi madrassah. These are traditionally tolerant countries, registering low or negative growth rates in terms of births, whereas the Muslim population is growing rapidly."

Scandinavia, as well as Holland, is also predicted as a likely terrorist target by the former CIA agent, Philip Giraldi, who predicts "one or more major terrorist attack in Europe each year for the foreseeable future...Britain is clearly the number one target for a future terrorist attack because its multiculturalism has apparently produced more hostile Muslims that anywhere else. It also has many Pakistanis among its Muslim population and they come out of a more radicalized culture with a more intolerant form of Islam."[30] Indeed, on November 10, 2006, Britain's MI6 chief, Dame Eliza Manningham-Buller, disclosed that the authorities were investigating 30 different plots involving 200 domestic terror networks, some that had "links back to al-Qaeda in Pakistan."[31] Barely a decade ago, nonchalant Londoners could pass off the fiery speeches of clerics like the hook-handed Abu Hamza as the ranting of a harmless eccentric and not care, while their government condoned his export of mujahedin (via the Al-Muhajiroun group) to Kashmir, Albania, and Kosovo, among other places. Yet several arrests made since 9/11 and especially since the July 2005 London bombings, which have nabbed Balkan Muslims and British Muslims radicalized by the Balkan jihads, have shown the full folly of this neglect and indifference.

In southwestern Europe, disgruntled urban youth are recruited by returning Iraq and Afghan jihadis. Here intelligence sources point to new alliances between traditional European anti-state entities and others in former European colonies; examples include cooperation between Basques in Spain and in Morocco, and between Islamists in Europe and in former Spanish and Portuguese colonies elsewhere in Africa. Lamenting Europe's increasing tendency towards Islamist appeasement in social policy, veteran analyst Arnaud de Borchgrave warns that the "gradual encroachment of fundamentalist Islam continues apace in the U.K. , Germany, France, the Netherlands, Italy, Spain, Albania, Kosovo and others."[32] Europe's emerging terrorist threat is clearly a complex and multifaceted one.

Generally, there are two things that Western security officials have to fear from the shaping influence of Iraq and other post-9/11 conflicts on contemporary jihad. For one, the structural and ideological decentralization that have occurred since 9/11 have resulted in a popularizing widening of the cause. Second, today's jihadis have received, in the badlands of Afghanistan and the urban jungles of Iraq, the kind of real-life experience that no training camp can replicate. The Bosnian jihad from 1991 to 1995 presented an earlier example of such training in action; however, there the enemy was the ill-equipped Bosnian Serb army, not the unmatched military might of the United States and its allies, the enemy of the day. Western military officials have frequently noted the cleverness, adaptability, and technical prowess exhibited by the Iraqi resistance fighters in their David-and-Goliath struggle. Hezbollah, which could not be defeated by the mighty Israelis in July 2006, set another example that bolstered the confidence of radicals everywhere. Now, the fear is that today's jihadis might return to Europe not only hardened by battle but also possessing highly efficient paramilitary skills. Were a future urban protest in Europe to be topped off not by teenagers throwing stones and torching cars but by trained mujahedeen lobbing RPGs and setting off improvised incendiary devices (IEDs), the political significance of such actions would increase exponentially.

Although many would scoff at the notion of street warfare in a European capital, the scenario cannot be ruled out. Further, there are striking similarities between the urban landscape of labyrinthine, centuries-old European cities and those of Iraq. The fact that European security services have infinitely greater control over their cities than does the fledgling Iraqi government is often repeated; but less frequently stated is the fact that European governments have an infinitely lower threshold for civilian casualties and destruction of infrastructure. Since martyrdom is a distinct plus for jihadis trained in Iraq and Afghanistan, fulfillment of a future political goal—the usual expectation by which extremist groups find self-interest in nonviolence—is not even necessary. If protests over legitimate social ills or wounded religious pride can be hijacked by outside extremist proselytizers and manned by former Iraqi insurgents, violence of the sort that topples governments could yet register across Europe. The prospect of guerrilla fighting in the streets of Paris or Milan may seem laughable now to the average Westerner. Then again, few would have seriously believed, back in 2001, that terrorists would manage to topple the World Trade Center (WTC), attack the Pentagon, and inflict lethal carnage on the transportation systems of Madrid and London all in a span of less than four years.

The most worrying dimension of future terrorist trends may, however, be the specter of technology, which haunts the Balkans, Europe, and, indeed, the whole world. The Internet has been acknowledged as a vital terrorist tool since at least 9/11, when the al Qaeda hijackers corresponded online in planning their attacks. The Sarajevo arrests of late 2005 drew attention not only for their Balkan dimension, but for the fact that they had involved a small group of plotters from around the world, most of whom had never met, communicating online. Of course, Western intelligence was well aware of it and destroyed the virtual cell before it could act, largely through covert Internet operations of its own.[33] Nevertheless, this virtual, decentralized aspect of the phenomenon is very significant for the future. As a U.S. military official notes, "The internet allows the establishment of a worldwide insurgency by non-state actors...Insurgents or terrorists seldom need to come together to maintain a functional organization."[34] In Britain, MI5 chief Dame Eliza Manningham-Buller stated that "more and more people are moving from passive sympathy towards active terrorism through being radicalised or indoctrinated by friends, families, in organised training events here and overseas, by images on television, through chatrooms and websites on the internet."[35]

The danger of small pockets of the Balkans emerging as global threats becomes infinitely more likely in consideration of ever-improving modern technology and communications possibilities. As in Bosnia, Kosovo, and Macedonia, the Islamic charity network, Web sites, and chat groups have allowed a numerically insignificant group of radical Muslims to plan logistical operations, coordinated travel, and potential terrorist attacks in total secrecy with their collaborators around the world. Islamic radical sponsors are aware of the importance of the Internet for indoctrination efforts. It would be naïve to imagine that the schools founded by the Saudis and others for IT development are meant simply to give their students e-mail and word processing skills. Indeed, reveals Zoran Mitevski, "the Iranians are using video webcasts to beam lecturers from Iran into the Novi Pazar [Sandzak] Islamic university. This has two benefits: one, it is cheaper, two, it solves the potential problem that these Iranian proselytizers might encounter with getting visas into Europe."[36] Speaking at an October 2003 event in California for the so-called Internet Islamic University, Safet Catovic, former Bosnian diplomat and leader of the curious August 2001 "Jihad Camp" in Pennsylvania, exulted that "we need not travel to foreign lands to meet renowned Islamic scholars but can access them through our personal computers."[37]

Indeed, while Wahhabis and other fundamentalists may rail against modern global culture, they, of course, make full use of its technological achievements for the achievement of their own goals. Terrorists are already starting to employ the same hostile tactics as have long been used by organized crime syndicates, governments, and even corporations to expedite a myriad of goals including financial profit, espionage, and generally wreaking havoc. As such, the methods used by tomorrow's terrorists to wage a virtual jihad are shared by a wide range of malevolent parties and, while governments and the technology industries scramble to combat them, such security threats can and will manifest in unexpected and crippling ways for a modern, globalizing society that relies heavily on technology.

More than ever, regular improvements in consumer technology, and corresponding decreases in price, mean that the gap is closing between the capacities of governments and terrorists. What was once the exclusive property of intelligence services has become readily available to the general public. Prices for surveillance and countersurveillance equipment, for example, continue to fall, becoming affordable to a wider range of individuals. And by liaising with private security companies, of which the Balkans has an increasing number, Islamic extremists can also gain access to even more expensive and high-quality equipment. In short, it no longer takes millions to plot and execute a destructive terrorist attack, whether a virtual or a tangible one.

Given these realities, experts like Loretta Napoleoni are pessimistic about a future in which terrorists have an increasingly affordable range of technological means with which to wreak havoc. "With technology and globalization, terrorism today is much more dangerous today than it was just a few decades ago, when Marxist-Communist terror groups were the main threat," says Napoleoni. "And terrorism is much cheaper than ever before, making it easier to bomb, say, an embassy or a subway." Napoleoni affirms the hypothesis that future on-site terrorist attacks might be created and carried out without any of the actual plotters actually having met. Through e-mail, chat groups, free Internet telephony, and SMS text messages, multiple plotters can communicate anonymously, cheaply, and simultaneously.

Former CIA agent Philip Giraldi agrees, adding, "I am confident that internet terrorism is here to stay and that there will be attacks where the implementers and planners are linked only electronically." In fact, Giraldi adds, "the London attacks of [2005] may have been more-or-less of that type in that the possible role of an outside implementer is somewhat debated. The problem for the terrorist is establishing the bona fides of the guy on the other side of the electronic divide —he could easily be a security officer doing a dangle operation." In fact, this is precisely what occurred when pseudo-jihadi police infiltrators were able to bring down the multinational network around Mirsad Bektasovic in 2005.[38] However, the terrorists cannot be expected to lose every time, and other intelligence sources note that, even in undeveloped Balkan states like Albania, extremist Web sites are making increasingly sophisticated use of cryptography, hidden directories, and other means of concealing their actions.

When it comes to technology, however, of even greater concern to Western security services today is the threat of large-scale cyber attacks against vital industries, plots that, once again, no longer require a great deal of money, expertise, or personnel. In general, the three major danger areas for the Internet today are attacks involving Web content (including audio/video, podcasts, and rss feeds), incidents involving electronic mail, and attacks on networks. An example of the first, Web site defacement, is one of the most common electronic attacks used by jihadis. During the global protests over the Danish cartoons of the Prophet Mohammad and the Pope's controversial comments on Islam, hundreds of Web sites deemed offensive to Islam were hacked and defaced or shut down. However, since such attacks are essentially symbolic and temporary, they constitute more of an irritant than an existential threat.

The potential to incur great physical damage through malevolent misuse of the Internet becomes most significant with attacks on networks, such as distributed denial of service (DDoS) attacks, in which groups of computers simultaneously flood the target computer with nonsensical traffic (millions of zeros and ones), thereby exhausting the line capacity and thus making the target computers and its networks unavailable to others, rendering both inoperable. According to a well-informed European network securities professional, such DDoS attacks are both common and frighteningly efficient. Through this means the Chinese military was allegedly able to crash one of the root servers of Verisign, the American Internet company that provides security for millions of online credit card purchases around the world—bringing 30 percent of Internet traffic to a halt for six hours in the process.

"Most dangerous today are the denial of service attacks geared toward vital industries," says this industry expert. "For example, take the power companies, the air transport industry and the financial industry. They all rely on the internet for essential day-to-day operations: respectively, buying, selling and processing energy; radar guidance, ticket sales, flight routing and planning; and the safe storage and movement of money. It does not take much imagination to see how devastating sudden shutdowns or manipulations of these processes could be."

The sort of "digital doomsday scenarios" that DDoS attacks are capable of bringing about are indeed startling. The power industry could be afflicted by sudden shutdowns of electricity grids, the overloading of nuclear power plants, and the reversing or manipulation of plant processing in petrochemical factories. As for the airline industry, radar could be reprogrammed or jammed, resulting in plane collisions, and the ticketing and scheduling systems could be shut down, resulting in a chaos-inducing stoppage of travel. Financial interests, meanwhile, could be hard hit by the manipulation of funds transfers as well as by the disabling of the communication networks Wall Street relies on to do business. A combination of any two or three of these at the same time, timed to coincide with protests, paramilitary operations, or other highly charged events, could spell devastation of blockbuster-film proportions.

"Certain DDoS attacks are considered very bad," the industry source maintains. "Taking over a satellite is one. Choking the international telephone system is considered another one of the worst possible outcomes." Indeed, online attackers could "completely incapacitate electronic conversation for a fairly long period, by injecting an attack on an international telephone exchange." Today's digital telephony breaks voice communication into data packets. These data packets are separated from each other and routed across exchanges located everywhere in the world, before being reassembled by means of a tag at their place of destination. A telephone conversation between two people in Los Angeles and Paris might be routed via Brazil or New York or Beijing. A DDoS attack anywhere along the network thus has far-reaching implications. Worst of all, it requires no particular skill. The potential troublemaker "doesn't even need to know how to insert malicious code into a telephone exchange. The only thing he needs to do is to make sure that all traffic stops, that line capacities are completely choked."

There are numerous online threats in addition to DDoS attacks from simple spam, email "phishing" (whereby personal data are requested under a fraudulent pretext), spyware (which can surreptitiously remove, add, or modify data on the attacked computer), bot-net attacks, port attacks, and viruses of all sorts. While most often the motive for cyber attacks remains financial (as with the Ukrainian hackers who stole $100 million from a major multinational bank after illegally accessing thousands of credit card details), such a virtual war is becoming more appetizing to the next generation of young, tech-savvy terrorists. The terrorist attacks of 9/11 were meant to inflict a symbolic wound on Western global society, by devastating the most visible physical manifestations of that economic power (the Twin Towers) and the military authority that more or less enforces it (the Pentagon). Yet this symbolic attack on a few buildings, merely the successful conclusion of an operation that had been dreamt up in the 1980s and carried out (though unsuccessfully) in the 1993 WTC bombing, is already obsolete; it belongs to the maximal terrorist imagination of an earlier time. Today, via technology, multiple 9/11's are possible simultaneously, without the need for physical hijackers, large training camps, or much in the way of state sponsorship.

"Could a prepared team of terrorists in, let's say Albania, bring Heathrow [Airport] air traffic to a standstill in a few minutes, by deploying a PC with some aggressive software? Yes, without a doubt this can happen now," says the network securities expert. "There's no immediate need to attack any airplane. One simply cuts off the power, fewer radios work, fewer radars work, passengers get in disarray, planes are not fueled—a compounded range of effects ending in a calamity. Insert a thunderstorm in a weather forecast where there is no thunder at all. The human factor will bring doubt in the mind of a pilot. Let's divert a couple 100 yards left or higher. Yet another pilot sees it as a nonsense thunderstorm, and just keeps on flying. The hampered but not incapacitated VHF radio can only bring another party into the discussion with more confusion. An inserted radar blip where there is actually nothing will add to it. These minor attack components in and by themselves are not difficult to accomplish. It is just a matter of concerted efforts."

The fear of hijacked computer networks becoming a safe operational zone for terrorists—the virtual equivalent of what Afghanistan was to al Qaeda during the time of the Taliban—is another disturbing possible development. An industry Web site, Completewhois.com, keeps a running list of networks that have been taken over by criminal groups, from small-timers to the Russian mafia. "The bad dudes can do with these hijacked networks whatever they want," says the networks security expert. "Assume now that a 'Bad Ali' sitting in Sarajevo makes a deal—in return for $10 million to the hijackers, he gets a day's worth of use on the hostage network. What can he do with that? Let's say, cut the power to Rome, bringing chaos and about $250 million in losses, overheat a nuclear reactor, etc.... If a [DDoS] attack comes from let's say 5,000 different computers anywhere on the globe, one can potentially flatten the entire Internet with it. Young Islamic zealots today get trained in computers, learn how to hack with those, and in concert they become part of the new future army, if you will."

That said, there is one final question—regarding the prospective membership in this "future army"—that has immense ramifications for the future role of the Balkans in international terrorism. To be sure, its geographically ordained historic role as a transshipment corridor for illegal commodities will continue—even as the region falls ever more firmly into the grip of multinational corporations looking to fulfill the Balkans' potential as an energy corridor. Bulgaria, Greece, Albania, Macedonia, Serbia, and Romania are only some of the regional countries in which new oil and gas pipelines, and accompanying highways, are being planned. Indeed, behind the nationalist and national-alliance charade existing in the region, for the U.S., Russian, and European powers, the Balkans is less a patchwork of unique nations than a contiguous zone of operations in which topographical challenges outweigh political ones—something that is, come to think of it, not too far off from how the terrorists see the region themselves.

While the stated goal of Balkan energy corridor development may be positive (securing energy stability in local and Western countries), it also does entail the fact that more pipelines simply means more tangible territory that must be defended from terrorist attacks. As with the Internet and digital communications, an attack anywhere along the network debilitates the network. In places, the future collision of global Islam and global industry will meet head-on in remote places like southwestern Macedonia, where the long awaited AMBO (Albania-Macedonia-Bulgaria Oil) pipeline route is set to exit the country into Albania just north of one of the major covert centers of radical Islam in the country, a mountainous region also infested with cross-border drugs and weapons smuggling. The two parties have not yet been acquainted, but when they are, it will no doubt come as a shock to the many "experts" who have discounted the threat of radical Islam before even having examined the evidence. Indeed, most have scoffed at the idea of terrorist attacks in the Balkans as being beneath the interests of bin Laden and his ilk; however, bringing the region further along in its "Western integration" also means the risks, as well as the rewards, will be shared.

Where the question of the Balkans becomes critical to any assessment of the future membership of decentralized, loosely linked terrorist cells is, as has long been pointed out, the strategic value that Balkan Muslim terrorists—the so-called "white devils"—have over individuals of Arab or Southeast Asian descent for the jihad movement today. The undeniable tendency of Western countries towards racial stereotyping in the popular opinion that most Islamic terrorists are dark-skinned has been noted by the jihadis themselves as an argument for why Balkan Muslims (along with others, like Chechens and Western converts) would make ideal, undetectable jihadis, capable of operating and carrying out attacks undisturbed in Europe and America. Such logic was attested by Pakistani President Pervez Musharraf, who claimed that a thwarted al Qaeda plot to attack Heathrow Airport in 2002 had involved "European Muslims, including a number of white converts."[39]

Although he considers the Balkan terrorist threat "extremely limited" compared with that of Western Europe, French expert Claude Moniquet agrees that the risk of "white al Qaeda" members, even females, recruited from the Balkan Muslim communities is a very real one. "Such people could be used in terrorism in Italy, France, Germany or other countries with important 'Yugoslav' communities," he maintains, pointing out the December 2006 Italian police operation that resulted in the arrest of several Bosnian and Macedonian émigrés. In the Balkans, says Moniquet, "Bosnia is the most dangerous place and then Macedonia."[40]

For Philip Giraldi, "the recruitment of [white] Europeans as [terrorist] assets is a very real danger, particularly as those assets will have authentic documents that enable them to travel just about anywhere." He notes, "the intelligence services are aware of the problem, however, and are focusing on it." Among the practical obstacles to large-scale recruitment in the West, attests the former CIA agent, is that the security services' control of mosques has made it difficult for the jihadis to use mosques as recruiting centers. In the Balkans, however, this same degree of control has yet to be established and, in any case, the Dawa infrastructure is sufficiently broad—from youth groups, sports halls, schools, and cultural centers—that mosques are in any case not essential. With the proper grooming and attire, any Balkan Muslim could easily evade the scrutiny of Western security services on the lookout for Asian and Middle Eastern radicals.

In the end, one underlying, sovereign fact remains: that without a recruiting pool, terrorist groups cannot exist. Fundamentalist movements going against the grain of modern, global society and operating outside of their native environment, such as the Wahhabis in the Balkans, can only wither away and die out eventually if there is nothing to nurture them, ideologically and financially. Some Western observers and many Balkan Muslims believe this will be the case here as well, and we can only hope that they are proven right. Nevertheless, it does not depend solely on them. The development, or retardation, of Islamic extremism pits several regional and global forces together as if in a race. Urbanization and modernization shape and are shaped by demographic and economic trends. At the same time, Balkan political development is still being forged in the fires of state creation, heated narratives of national independence and tempered by the cool, faint future promise of European Union membership as the supposed remedy to all social, economic, and ethnic ills. Larger world events, such as wars, economic cycles, environmental concerns, immigration policy, technology, and more will also play an unpredictable and indirect role in the fate of radical Islam in the Balkans.

However, ahead of all of these in terms of relevance is the issue of whether, by one way or another, appreciable numbers of Balkan Muslims come to identify with the suffering of Muslims in the wider world, and to see attacks on the latter—which may actually worsen over the coming decade—as attacks on themselves too. Although we are still early on in the game, and though the rules may change for a number of reasons, it is impossible to deny that foreign proselytizers, waving lucre and spouting vitriol, have reprogrammed thousands of Balkan Muslims, making them more receptive to world views antithetical to Western civilization and, in some cases, to views that support the destruction of that civilization. The fact that small numbers of these Muslims have already participated in jihads and terrorist attacks around the world should come as a wake-up to Western policymakers who, unfortunately, seem to hear only what they want to hear.

Second, it is also well apparent that the universal stock of global sympathy the United States enjoyed on the morning of September 11, 2001, has long been thoroughly depleted, in some places more than in others. Already, Balkan Muslims have started to reappraise their opinions, taking a more mistrustful stance towards an America that has declared war on Muslims and on the European countries that continue to deport them and deny them visas. Further, the foreign Islamists' increasing success in making Balkan Muslims sympathize with the suffering of Muslims in Lebanon, Iraq, Palestine, Chechnya, and Afghanistan increase the risks that the former will become more active in future terrorist plots on the West. The pace with which these trends are coming together is striking. From the Albanian pastry chef who gleefully mocked the Bush administration and death of Americans in Iraq back in 2003 and to the Macedonian Muslim imam adamant on forcibly creating a caliphate in Europe, from the Bosnian student certain that Israel and the United States were behind every evil in the world and to the usually placid Serbian Muslim who vowed to become a suicide bomber should the United States invade Iran in 2006, this author has seen and heard many things that, when corroborated by the factual data disclosed in this book, would seem to indicate that perilous times lie ahead for the West in the battle with Islamic extremism—and that a big part of this threat involves the Balkans. The fact that through two decades of intervention, inattention, and criminal complicity the West has brought this scourge upon itself is, unfortunately, the most damning indictment of all.

Notes

INTRODUCTION

1. Stephen Grey and Don Van Natta, "Thirteen with the C.I.A. Sought by Italy in a Kidnapping," *New York Times,* June 25, 2005.

2. Craig Whitlock, "CIA Ruse Is Said to Have Damaged Probe in Milan," *Washington Post,* December 6, 2005.

3. Craig Whitlock, "Italians Detail Lavish CIA Operation," *Washington Post,* June 26, 2005.

4. John Hooper, "CIA Methods Exposed by Kidnap Inquiry," *Guardian,* July 2, 2005.

5. Ibid.

6. Craig Whitlock, "CIA Ruse is Said to Have Damaged Probe in Milan," *Washington Post,* December 6, 2005.

7. Phil Stewart, "Italy Eyes Rogue Spies, Not Agency, in CIA Kidnap," Reuters, July 11, 2006.

8. Craig Whitlock, "Italy Seeks Extradition of 22 CIA Operatives," *Washington Post,* November 12, 2005.

9. "Italian Probe of CIA Abduction Broadens to Domestic Spying Scandal and 'Black Propaganda' Misinformation Campaign by Italy Intel," www.democracynow.org (July 11, 2006).

CHAPTER 1

1. "Bosnia: 50 Al Qaeda Sympathizers Lose Citizenship," ADNKronos International, www.adnki.com (September 5, 2006).

2. A revealing account of how the Western media distorted the wars in Yugoslavia is veteran journalist Peter Brock's *Media Cleansing: Dirty Reporting. Journalism and Tragedy in Yugoslavia* (Los Angeles: GM Books, 2005).

3. The 20,000-strong SS Handzar Division was created on February 10, 1943, by Adolf Hitler and overseen by his second-in-command, Heinrich Himmler. An imam embedded within the ranks, Husejin Dzozo, captured the spirit of the day when he enthusiastically promised Herr Himmler that "we are prepared to lay down our lives in battle for the great leader Adolf Hitler and the New Europe." The Handzar Division's spiritual leader was the Grand Mufti of Jerusalem, Mohammad Amin al-Husseini, who ordered Muslims to "kill the Jews wherever you find them. This pleases God, history and religion." See Carl Savich, "Islam under the Swastika: The Grand Mufti and the Nazi Protectorate of Bosnia-Hercegovina, 1941–1945," www.serbianna.com. See also Vojin Joksimovich, "Alija Izetbegovic: A Retrospective Look at His Impact on Balkan Stability," International Strategic Studies Association, December 8, 2003.

4. Robert Fox, "Albanians and Afghans Fight for the Heirs to Bosnia's SS Past," *Daily Telegraph,* December 29, 1993.

5. Alija Izetbegovic, *Islamska deklaracija* [*The Islamic Declaration*] (Sarajevo: Mala Muslimanska Biblioteka, 1990). Italics added.

6. "Dubai Names Ex-Bosnian President as Islamic Personality of the Year," www.islamonline.net (November 21, 2001).

7. Author interview with Darko Trifunovic, October 2006.

8. "Al-Sirat Al-Mustaqeem: Interview with Sheikh al-Mujahideen Abu Abdel Aziz," *Al-Sirat Al Mustaqeem* [*The Straight Path*], no. 33 (August 1994). At time of writing the translated Arabic interview in English was available at the Web site www.seprin.com

9. J. Milton Burr and Robert O. Collins, *Alms for Jihad: Charity and Terrorism in the Islamic World* (Cambridge: Cambridge University Press, 2006), 133.

10. Ibid., 135–36.

11. Jürgen Elsässer, *Dzihad na Balkanu, Kako je dzihad stigao u Evropu* (Belgrade: Jasen, 2006), 53–55. Serbian translation of Jürgen Elsässer, *Wie der Dschihad nach Europa kam Gotteskrieger und Geheimdienste auf dem Balkan* (Vienna: Np Buchverlag, 2005).

12. Tim Judah, "German Spies Accused of Arming Bosnian Muslims," *Sunday Telegraph,* April 20, 1997.

13. Burr and Collins, *Alms for Jihad: Charity and Terrorism in the Islamic World,* 139–40.

14. Ibid., 141–42.

15. Ibid., 141–42.

16. Ibid., 138.

17. Frank Smyth and Jason Vest, "One Man's Private Jihad," *Village Voice,* August 18, 1998.

18. Cees Wiebes, *Intelligence and the War in Bosnia 1992–1995* (Münster: Lit Verlag, 2003), 159–66.

19. John Pomfret, "How Bosnia's Muslims Dodged Arms Embargo: Relief Agency Brokered Aid from Nations, Radical Groups," *Washington Post,* September 22, 1996.

20. "U.S. Had Options to Let Bosnia Get Arms, Avoid Iran," *Los Angeles Times,* July 14, 1996.

21. Bruno Lopandic, "Granic, Susak and Greguric Saved Galbraith," *Nacional* (Zagreb), no. 304, September 13, 2001.

22. Author interview with Jason Miko, December 2006.

23. Wiebes, *Intelligence and the War in Bosnia 1992–1995*, 208.

24. This 1994 mujahedin video, seen by the author, is held in the police archive of Bosnia's Republika Srpska.

25. See Evan Kohlmann, *Al-Qaida's Jihad in Europe: The Afghan-Bosnian Nework* (Oxford, UK: Berg, 2004); and Carl Savich, "Al Qaeda in Bosnia: Bosnian Muslims War Crimes Trial," www.serbianna.com

26. In August 1993, a Japanese photojournalist, Yasunari Mizuguchi, snapped shocking pictures of the roasted Serbs in the village of Milici. According to retired Professor of Linguistics Peter Maher, who met Mizuguchi and saw the photos in 1994, "The *New York Times* and other newspapers would not touch this, as it contradicted the Clinton administration's prevailing view of the Serbs as aggressors and the Muslims as innocent victims." Author interview with Peter Maher, October 2006.

27. Jeffrey Smith, "A Bosnian Village's Terrorist Ties," *Washington Post,* March 11, 2000.

28. "Clinton-Approved Iranian Arms Transfers Help Turn Bosnia into Militant Islamic Base," Congressional Press Release, U.S. Congress, January 16, 1997, www.globalresearch.ca

29. John Pomfret, "Bosnian Officials Involved in Arms Trade Tied to Radical States," *Washington Post,* September 22, 1996.

30. "High Muslim officials of the Bosnian foreign ministry agreed that it [the destruction of files linked to bin Laden] was the top priority. It was even more important than investigating a person responsible for granting a passport to the most wanted terrorist in the world." See "Bin Laden Was Granted Bosnian Passport," Agence France-Presse, September 24, 1999.

31. Hayder Mili, "Securing the Northern Frontier: Canada and the War on Terror," Jamestown Foundation, *Terrorism Monitor,* 3, no. 14 (July 15, 2005).

32. Craig Pyes, Josh Meyer, and William C. Rempe, "Terrorists Use Bosnia as Base and Sanctuary," *Los Angeles Times,* October 7, 2001.

33. See the National Commission on Terrorist Attacks upon the United States, Chapter 5, "Al Qaeda Aims at the American Homeland," www.9-11commission.gov

34. "Al Qaeda Video Takes Credit for 9/11," www.aljazeera.net (September 8, 2006).

35. "Bosnian Official Links with Terrorism, Including 9/11, Become Increasingly Apparent as Clinton, Clark Attempt to Justify Support of Bosnian Militants," *Defense & Foreign Affairs Daily,* September 17, 2003.

36. Akhtar M. Faruqui, "Dawn of a New Era in Islamic Education," www.pakistanlink.com (October 2003).

37. Andrew Purvis, "The Suspects: A Bosnian Subplot," *Time,* November 12, 2001.

38. See "Additional Background Information on Charities Designated under Executive Order 13224," available at the official Web site of the U.S. Treasury, www.ustreas.gov. See also *United States of America v. Benevolence International Foundation, Inc., and Enaam M. Arnaout a/k/a Abu Mahmoud a/k/a Abdel Samia,* Case No. 02 CR 414, www.findlaw.com

39. Darko Trifunovic, "Exclusive: Pattern of Bosnian and Other Links to Madrid Bombings Becoming Increasingly Clear," *Defense & Foreign Affairs,* June 21, 2005.

40. "Spain Asks Bosnia to Investigate Possible Link in Madrid Bombings," Radio Free Europe/Radio Liberty, April 9, 2004.

41. Rade Maroevic and Daniel Williams, "Terrorist Cells Find Foothold in Balkans; Arrests Point to Attacks Within Europe," *Washington Post,* December 1, 2005.

42. Ibid.

43. Ibid.

44. Author interview with Darko Trifunovic.

45. Rusmir Smajilhodzic, "Moderate Bosnian Muslims Fear Extremist Takeover," *National Post,* June 17, 2006.

46. Merima Spahic, "Tragichno predupregjenje" ["A Tragic Warning"], BETA (Belgrade), February 23, 2004, trans. www.media-diversity.org

47. Smajilhodzic, "Moderate Bosnian Muslims Fear Extremist Takeover."

48. Author interview with Anes Alic, November 2006.

49. "Bosni prijeti opasnost od vehabista," *Nacional* (Zagreb), August 14, 2006; excerpted as "Ex-Wahhabi Says Bosnia under Threat of Islamic Radicals," BBC Monitoring Europe, August 22, 2006.

50. Brian Whitmore, "Saudi 'charity' troubling to Bosnian Muslims," *Boston Globe,* January 28, 2002.

51. "Patterns of Global Terrorism 2005: Europe and Eurasia Overview," U.S. Department of State, available at official State Department Web site, www.state.gov

52. Risto Karajkov, "The Young and the Old: Radical Islam Takes Root in the Balkans," *Transitions Online,* www.tol.cz (May 3, 2006).

53. "Bosanski Wahabist kaze da mu je nugjeno para da unisti Katolichki spomenik u Maostaru" ["Bosnian Wahhabi Says that He Was Offered Money to Destroy a Catholic Monument in Mostar"], *Vecernji List* (Zagreb), July 19, 2006.

54. "Ex-Wahhabi Says Bosnia under Threat of Islamic Radicals."

55. M. Cubro, "Tužilaštvo BiH otvorilo istragu o poslovanju 'Organizacije preporoda islamske tradicije Kuvajt'" ["The Prosecutor of BiH Opened Investigation about dealing in 'Kuwait's Organization of Revival Islamic Heritage'"], Nezavisne Novine (Sarajevo), June 28, 2006.

56. See Christopher Deliso, "Has the UN Let a Blacklisted Islamic Charity Roam Free in Kosovo?" www.antiwar.com (September 15, 2005).

57. "Dzevad Galijashevic: Teshanj i Zavidovici su pravi Al Kaidin Centar" ["Dzevad Galijashevic: Teshanj and Zavidovici Are the Real al Qaeda Centers"], *Nezavisne Novine* (Sarajevo), November 25, 2006.

58. Mike O'Connor, "Police Official's Methods Raise Ethnic Fears in Bosnian Region," *New York Times,* June 16, 1996.

59. "Dzevad Galijashevic: Teshanj and Zavidovici Are the Real al Qaeda Centers."

60. See "Bosnian Muslims Move against Radicalization of Islam," Agence France-Presse, November 13, 2006.

61. "Vahabije—skrivena pretnja u BIH" ["Wahhabis—The Hidden Threat in BIH"], *Nezavisne Novine* (Sarajevo), November 5, 2006.

62. "Wahhabis Threaten Bosnia's Security," *B92* (Belgrade), www.b92.net, March 10, 2007.

63. D. Majstorovic, "Ko je najbliži saradnik nezvaničnog vođe vehabija u BiH Tunišanina Jusufa Barčića" ["The Tunisian Who Is the Closest Cooperator with the

Unofficial Leader of Wahhabis in Bosnia, Jusuf Barcic"], *Glas Srpske* (Banja Luka), March 5, 2007.

64. Anes Alic, "Wahhabism: from Vienna to Bosnia," *ISN Security Watch,* April 6, 2007.

65. "Tihic Thanks Qatar for Support to Bosnia," *The Peninsula* (Doha), June 10, 2006.

66. "Head of Bosnia's Islamic Community Urges Institutional Organisation of European Muslims," HINA News Agency (Zagreb), January 9, 2006.

67. "Bosnia: Muslim Leader Accuses Christians of Undermining State," ADNKronos, www.adnki.com (June 8, 2006).

68. Author interview with Anes Alic.

69. Author interview with Claude Moniquet, December 2006.

70. "Threat Assessment: Militancy in Bosnia and Herzegovina," *Jane's Intelligence Review,* August 1, 2006.

71. Author interview with U.S. military official, March 2006.

72. "Bosnia: 50 Al Qaeda Sympathizers Lose Citizenship."

73. Nebojsa Malic, "The Real Izetbegovic," www.antiwar.com, October 23, 2003.

74. Author interview with Jason Miko.

75. "Uhiceni trojica terorista Bosnjaka" ["Arrests of Three Bosnian Terrorists"], *Vecernji List* (Zagreb), December 2, 2006.

76. "Bh teroristi htjeli zatrovati pitku vodu" ["BH Terrorists Wanted to Poison Drinking Water"], *Vecernji List* (Zagreb), December 3, 2006.

77. "Pakistan Snatches Terror Pair from Germany," United Press International, March 12, 2007.

78. Evelyn Jamine, "Chemicals Stockpiled for 'Jihad on Sydney,'" *The Daily Telegraph* (Sydney), March 7, 2007.

CHAPTER 2

1. Fred Abrahams, "Albania," *Human Rights Watch,* 2, no. 33 (May 1997).

2. Teodor Misha, "Albania Denies Terrorist Links," Institute for War & Peace Reporting, September 26, 2001.

3. Miranda Vickers and James Pettifer, *Albania: From Anarchy to a Balkan Identity* (New York: New York University Press, 1997), 105.

4. Ibid., 102.

5. Aydin Babuna, "Albanian National Identity and Islam in the Post-Communist Era," *Perceptions: A Journal of International Affairs,* 8 (September–November 2003), Center for Strategic Research of the Turkish Ministry of Foreign Affairs. Available at the official Web site of the Turkish Ministry of Foreign Affairs, www.sam.gov.tr

6. Vickers and Pettifer, *Albania: From Anarchy to a Balkan Identity,* 104.

7. Grace Halsell, "Albania and the Muslim World," The Washington Report on Middle East Affairs, 1994.

8. Ibid.

9. J. Milton Burr and Robert O. Collins, *Alms for Jihad: Charity and Terrorism in the Islamic World* (Cambridge: Cambridge University Press, 2006), 147–49.

10. Franz Gustincich, "From Lenin to Bin Laden," *Gnosis: Online Italian Intelligence Magazine* (March 2005). Available at the official Web site of the Italian intelligence service, www.sisde.it

11. Damian Gjiknuri, "Albania's Counter-Terrorism Policy Options: Finding a Strategy of Common Sense" (U.S. Naval Postgraduate School thesis, Monterey, 2004), 12.

12. Ibid., 15.

13. Ibid., 13.

14. Vickers and Pettifer, *Albania: From Anarchy to a Balkan Identity,* 105.

15. Chris Stephens, "Bin Laden Opens European Terror Base in Albania," *Sunday Times,* November 29, 1998.

16. "Additional Al-Haramain Branches, Former Leader Designated by Treasury as Al Qaida Supporters," *U.S. Treasury Press Release* JS-1703, June 2, 2004. Available at the official Web site of the U.S. Treasury, www.ustreas.gov

17. Burr and Collins, *Alms for Jihad: Charity and Terrorism in the Islamic World,* 146.

18. See John K. Cooley, *Unholy Wars: Afghanistan, America and International Terrorism* (London: Pluto Press, 2000).

19. Burr and Collins, *Alms for Jihad: Charity and Terrorism in the Islamic World,* 146–47.

20. Tom Hundley and John Crewsdon, "Wife Was Left Behind with the Children," *Chicago Tribune,* July 3, 2005.

21. John Crewdson and Tom Huntley, "Abducted Imam Aided CIA Ally," *Chicago Tribune,* July 3, 2005.

22. Ibid.

23. Ibid.

24. Remzi Lani and Fabian Schmidt, "Albanian Foreign Policy Between Geography and History," *The International Spectator,* XXXIII, no. 2 (April–June 1998), Istituto Affair Internazionali.

25. Jane Meyer, "Outsourcing Torture," *The New Yorker,* February 7, 2005.

26. "Black Hole: The Fate of Islamists Rendered to Egypt," Part V, *Human Rights Watch,* May 2005.

27. Lani and Schmidt, "Albanian Foreign Policy Between Geography and History."

28. Yigal Chazan, "Albanian Mafias Find New Drug Routes Around Yugoslavia," *Christian Science Monitor,* October 20, 1994.

29. See Cooley, *Unholy Wars: Afghanistan, America and International Terrorism,* 127–61, for a comprehensive discussion of the issue.

30. Kendal Nazan, "Turkey's Pivotal Role in the International Drug Trade," *Le Monde Diplomatique,* July 1998.

31. Frank Viviano, "Drugs Paying for Conflict in Europe," *San Francisco Chronicle,* June 10, 1994.

32. Tim Judah, "Albanian Mafia Targets Drug Routes," *The Times,* October 18, 1994.

33. William Drozdiak, "Merchants of Death and Drugs; Porous Borders, Balkan War Bring Epidemics of Heroin Smuggling, Arms Sales," *Washington Post,* November 14, 1993.

34. "Crimes Committed in Italy Provide Funds for Kosovo Guerrillas," *Corriere della Sera,* January 19, 1999.

35. Andrew Gumbel, "The Gangster Regime We Fund," *The Independent,* February 14, 1997.

36. Fred Abrahams, "The Albanian House of Cards," *Dollars & Sense,* no. 212 (July–August 1997).

37. Fabian Schmidt, "Albania's Pharaoh and His Pyramids," Radio Free Europe/Radio Liberty, June 6, 2000.

38. See Brian Murphy, "KLA Volunteers Lack Experience," Associated Press, April 5, 1999.

39. Christophe Chiclet, "Rise of the Kosovar Freedom Fighters," *Le Monde Diplomatique,* May 1999.

40. Roger Faligot, "How Germany Backed KLA," *The European,* September 21, 1998.

41. "Balkan-Albania-Kosovo-Heroin-Jihad," Centre for Peace in the Balkans, May 2000.

42. "The Origins and Developments of Modern Islamist Organizations in the Balkans; New Terrorist Groups with Links to Old; Strong Involvement of Albanian, Turkish, and Northern Cyprus Governments," *Defense & Foreign Affairs Daily,* December 11, 2005.

43. Loretta Napoleoni, *Terror Incorporated: Tracing the Dollars Behind the Terror Networks* (New York: Seven Stories Press, 2004), 113.

44. Mirko Dakovic and Boro Miseljic, "Destabilizing the Balkans: US & Albanian Defense Cooperation in the 1990s," Independent Center for Geopolitical Studies JUGOIS-TOK, March 22, 2001, www.antiwar.com

45. As reported by Deutsche Press-Agentur on April 1, 1997.

46. Lani and Schmidt, "Albanian Foreign Policy Between Geography and History."

47. As reported by Agence France-Presse on October 26, 1997.

48. Ibid.

49. Andrew Higgins and Christopher Cooper, "CIA-Backed Team Used Brutal Means to Break Up Terrorist Cell in Albania," *Wall Street Journal,* November 20, 2001.

50. R. Jeffrey Smith, "US Probes Blasts' Possible Mideast Ties," *Washington Post,* August 12, 1998.

51. Barry Schweid, "NATO Braces for Wider Kosovo Fight," Associated Press, June 17, 1998.

52. "Kosovo Seen as New Islamic Bastion," *Jerusalem Post,* September 14, 1998.

53. Yossef Bodansky, "Italy Becomes Iran's New Base for Terrorist Operations," *Defense and Foreign Affairs Strategic Policy,* International Strategic Studies Association, February 1998.

54. Ibid.

55. "Unhealthy Climate in Kosovo as Guerrillas Gear Up for a Summer Confrontation," *Jane's International Defense Review,* February 1, 1999.

56. Tom Walker, "US Alarmed as Mujahidin Join Kosovo Rebels," *The Times,* September 29, 1998.

57. Brian Glyn Williams and Feyza Altindag, "Turkish Volunteers in Chechnya," Jamestown Foundation, *Terrorism Monitor,* no. 7 (April 7, 2005).

58. Philip Sherwell, "SAS Teams Move in to Help KLA 'Rise From the Ashes,'" *The Telegraph,* April 18, 1999.

59. On July 29, 2005, former U.S. Prosecutor John Loftus, speaking on a Fox News program said: "The US was used by Al-Muhajiroun for training of people to send to Kosovo. What ties all these cells together was, back in the late 1990s, the leaders all worked for British intelligence in Kosovo. Believe it or not, British intelligence actually hired some Al-Qaeda guys to help defend the Muslim rights in Albania and in Kosovo." See Michel Chossudovsky, "London 7/7 Terror Suspect Linked to British Intelligence?" Centre for Research on Globalization, www.globalresearch.ca (August 1, 2005).

60. See "Sheikh Muhammad Stubla, President of the Albanian Islamic Society in London: The Latest Massacres Warn of a New Genocide Targeting about 2 Million Muslims in Kosovo," *Nida'ul Magazine,* April–May 1998. The magazine's Web site has been

closed, but the article has been reprinted on the Web site of the Federation of American Scientists, www.fas.org

61. In mid-November 2003, the AIS suddenly closed its office at 233 Seven Sisters Road and relocated to West London, changing its name to Kosovo Albanian Islamic Society. A Muslim Association of Britain official believed that the group left because it could no longer pay its rent. (Author interview with MAB official, November 2003.)

62. In 2003, the FBI claimed that the London branch of Habibson's was also allowing U.S.-based terrorist sponsors to fund Hamas and connected charities in Kosovo and Bosnia. See "United States of America Vs. Abdurahman Muhammad Alamoudi," www.findlaw.com

63. "Pentagon Chief Cancels Albania Visit Over Terror Threat," CNN, July 15, 1999.

64. "Patterns of Global Terrorism, 1999," U.S. Department of State. Available at the official U.S. State Department Web site, www.state.gov

65. Frank Viviano, "Crest of a Human Wave: Illegal Immigrants Flood Albania To Be Smuggled Across Adriatic," *San Francisco Chronicle,* February 12, 1999.

66. Bill Gertz, "Hijackers Connected to Albanian Terrorist Cell," *Washington Times,* September 18, 2001.

67. "Berisha i dha nënshtetësinë krahut të djathtë të Bin Ladin" ["Berisha Gave Citizenship to bin Laden's Bunch"], www.gazeta-shqip.com (April 12, 2007).

68. "Treasury Designates Bin Laden, Qadi Associate," *U.S. Treasury Press Release* JS-2727, September 19, 2005. Available at the official Web site of the U.S. Treasury, www.ustreas.gov

69. As reported by Agence France-Presse, November 14, 1999.

70. David Pallister, "Head of Suspect Charity Denies Link to Bin Laden," *The Guardian,* October 16, 2001.

71. "Additional Al-Haramain Branches, Former Leader Designated by Treasury as Al Qaida Supporters."

72. Ibid.

73. "Kosovo SHIK, Directly Linked with Albanian SHIK Intelligence Organization, Prepares for 'Big Push' for Kosovo Independence," *Defense & Foreign Affairs,* January 16, 2006.

74. Risto Karajkov, "The Young and the Old: Radical Islam Takes Root in the Balkans," *Transitions Online,* www.tol.cz (May 3, 2006).

75. The historically contested region of Epiros straddles two countries. It is called Chameria by Albanians, Epiros by Greeks. Greeks refer to the cross-border area, where a Greek-speaking minority lives, as "Northern Epiros." For pan-Albanian idealists, "recovering" Chameria and uniting it with the motherland is an essential step in the formation of an Ethnic or Great Albania, which comprise Albanian-populated areas of Serbia, Macedonia, and Montenegro as well as Kosovo. Considering the political and military power of Greece, however, it is highly unlikely that Epiros will be annexed by Albania.

76. "The Origins and Developments of Modern Islamist Organizations in the Balkans; New Terrorist Groups with Links to Old; Strong Involvement of Albanian, Turkish, and Northern Cyprus Governments," *Defense & Foreign Affairs,* December 11, 2005.

77. MFA representatives, while they were quick to criticize their allegedly "unfair" depiction in the *Transitions Online* article to this author, did not respond to two requests for an interview to clarify their positions further.

78. The comments that incensed the Islamists were perhaps taken out of context; the president was speaking about religious tolerance among the Albanians. Nevertheless, he

caused a sensation by stating "that part of the Albanians which did not convert into Islam has in its tradition not simply fifteen centuries of Christianity, but two thousand years of Christianity...The Islamism in Albania is an Islam with a European face. As a rule it is a shallow Islamism. If you dig a little in every Albanian you can discover his Christian core." The original text of the speech can be found on the official Web site of the President of Albania, www.president.al

79. Llazar Semini, "Mother Teresa Statue Causes Friction," Associated Press, March 20, 2006.

80. Author interview with former MI6 officer, September 2006.

81. Josh White, "Lawyers Demand Release of Chinese Muslims," *Washington Post,* December 5, 2006.

82. Carol Rosenberg, "Pentagon Sends Guantánamo Captives to Albania," *Miami Herald,* November 17, 2006.

CHAPTER 3

1. "U.N. Police Fire Tear Gas at Protesters in Kosovo," Associated Press, November 28, 2006.

2. "U.N. in Kosovo Says 'Credible Threats' against Staff," Reuters, November 27, 2006.

3. Author interview with IOM official, March 2006.

4. Author interview with Tom Gambill, September 2006.

5. David Bamber and Chris Hastings, "KLA Raises Money in Britain for Arms," *The Sunday Telegraph,* April 23, 2000.

6. Kosovo Christians Targeted by Islamic Militants," *Charisma Magazine,* May 18, 2000.

7. Jolyon Naegele, "Yugoslavia: Saudi Wahhabi Aid Workers Bulldoze Balkan Monuments," Radio Free Europe/Radio Liberty, August 4, 2000.

8. Ibid.

9. Frank Brown, "Islam Builds a Future in Kosovo, One Mosque at a Time," Religious News Service, September 12, 2000.

10. Andras Riedlmayer, "Kosovo: The Destruction of Cultural Heritage," www.justiceforall.org (1999).

11. "Imam of a Kosovo Mosque Lauds Morocco's Backing," www.arabicnews.com, January 3, 2000.

12. David Binder, "A Troubled Dream," *Newsweek,* March 22, 2001.

13. Author interview with former NLA commander, August 2006.

14. Some of the alleged culprits named in various indictments of the war include the Albanian mafia, the U.S. government, and the then-Macedonian governing coalition, accused of having a secret plan to partition Macedonia along ethnic lines. More recently, with the restoration of that government to power in July 2006, a rival thesis has been circulated that states the NLA had a secret deal with the then-opposition Social Democratic Party (SDSM) to foment unrest and bring the leadership of both to power. While this indeed happened after the September 2002 elections, it is not possible to infer the cause from the effect. Like all Balkan conflicts, the Macedonian one is a complex story likely to never be told completely.

15. R. Jeffrey Smith, "Macedonian Guerrilla Group Forming in Kosovo Poses Threat of Expanded Conflict in Balkans," *Washington Post,* March 30, 2001.

16. "Macedonia on 'Brink of Abyss,'" BBC, May 7, 2001.

17. The treaty text is available at the official Web site of the Council of Europe, www.coe.int

18. "Iranian Gunrunners Detained in Kosovo," CNN, August 9, 2001.

19. Author interview with Macedonian intelligence officer, November 2005.

20. "Bin Laden's New Special Envoys," *Washington Times,* June 22, 2001.

21. Christian Jennings, "Fear over Islamic Terror Groups Using Macedonia as Base," *The Scotsman,* March 4, 2002.

22. Author interview with Goran Stojkov, October 2006.

23. "Kolezhot kaj Vejce go Izvrsile Mudjahedini," ["Massacre near Vejce was Done by Mujahedin"], A1 TV (Skopje), October 16, 2001.

24. Scott Taylor, "Bin Laden's Balkan Connections," *Ottawa Citizen,* December 15, 2001.

25. "Who Are Our Fundamentalists?" UNMIK Local Media Monitoring, October 30, 2001.

26. Author interview with Tom Gambill.

27. "In Kosovo Russian Peacekeepers Detain 30 Albanians Suspected As Terrorists," Pravda, January 4, 2002.

28. Jennings, "Fear over Islamic Terror Groups Using Macedonia as Base."

29. "UNMIK Warns Of Suicide-Bombers' Attacks," Tanjug, March 21, 2003.

30. Shaban Buza, "UN Suspension Move Angers Kosovo Ex-guerrillas," Reuters, December 3, 2003.

31. Author interview with Michael Stephen Harrison, October 2006.

32. Christopher Deliso, "The Internationals and the Mobs: Kosovo's Moment of Truth," www.antiwar.com (April 15, 2004).

33. "UN Administrators Flee 'Kristallnacht,'" B92 (Belgrade), March 17, 2004.

34. Matt Robinson and Christian Jennings, "Kosovo Clashes Were Planned, Says UN Official," *The Scotsman,* March 18, 2004.

35. Christopher Deliso, "An Uncertain Future for the Serbian Refugees of Kosovo," www.antiwar.com (April 7, 2004).

36. "Kosovo Clashes Orchestrated," BBC, March 20, 2004.

37. Deliso, "The Internationals and the Mobs: Kosovo's Moment of Truth."

38. Author interview with former German KFOR soldier, October 2006.

39. See "UNESCO Calls for Urgent Action to Protect Serbian Heritage in Kosovo," AFP, May 4, 2004, and Sherrie Gossett, "Church Desecration Video Serves as Jihad Fund-Raiser," www.cnsnews.com (August 11, 2005).

40. See Carl Savich, "Islam, Catholicism and Orthodoxy: The Civil War in Bosnia-Hercegovina, 1992–1995," Internet Library of Serb Culture, www.rastko.org.yu

41. Miroslav Filipovic, "Pricha o Ljubavi i Svetom Ratu" ["Story of Love and Holy War"], *Danas* (Belgrade), December 20, 1999, trans. www.ex-yupress.com

42. Mira Beham, "Kad Obaveshtajci Potpiruju" ["When Intelligence Officers Fan Flames"], *NIN* (Belgrade), November 25, 2004, trans. www.ex-yupress.com

43. Ibid.

44. Author interview with Sladjana Djuric, October 2006.

45. "Kosovo's U.N. Administration Praises Saudi Relief Committee," www.saudinf.org (May 25, 2004).

46. Isa Blumi, "Political Islam among the Albanians: Are the Taleban Coming to the Balkans?" Kosovar Institute for Policy and Research Development, June 2005.

47. Genc Morina, "Radical Islam: Wahhabism a Danger to Kosovo's Independence!" *Express* (Pristina), trans. available from Kosovo and Metohija Information Service, www.decani.org (October 15, 2006).

48. Ibid.

49. Author interview with American special police investigator, October 2006.

CHAPTER 4

1. Author interview with DBK agent, September 2006. See also Christopher Deliso, "Varieties of Religious Experience in a Macedonian Village," www.balkanalysis.com (September 27, 2006).

2. Alex Alexiev, "Tablighi Jamaat: Jihad's Stealthy Legions," *Middle East Quarterly* (February 2005). www.meforum.org

3. Susan Sachs, "A Muslim Missionary Group Draws New Scrutiny in U.S.," *New York Times,* July 14, 2003.

4. Ibid.

5. "The Radical with a Perfect Cover," *The Sunday Times,* August 20, 2006.

6. John K. Cooley, *Unholy Wars: Afghanistan, America and International Terrorism* (London: Pluto Press, 2000), 85.

7. B. Raman, "Harkat-ul-Mujahideen: An Update," South Asia Analysis Group, www.saag.org (March 20, 1999).

8. Christopher Deliso, "Fissures in Balkan Islam," *Christian Science Monitor,* February 14, 2006.

9. Paul Lewis, "Inside the Islamic Group Accused by MI5 and FBI," *Guardian,* August 19, 2006.

10. Christopher Deliso, "Vevchani and Labunishta: A Tale of Two Villages," *Hidden Europe Magazine,* May 2006, 4.

11. Author interview with DBK agent.

12. Author interview with EU PROXIMA officer, January 2005.

13. Irina Gelevska, Interview with Claude Moniquet, www.realitymacedonia.org.mk (December 12, 2004).

14. Christopher Deliso, "Fissures in Balkan Islam," *Christian Science Monitor,* February 14, 2006.

15. Author interview with Claude Moniquet, December 2006.

16. "Malaysian, EU-Rejected Islamists Penetrate Macedonia," www.balkanalysis.com (September 28, 2005).

17. Author interview with Zoran Mitevski, November 2006.

18. Christopher Deliso, "In Macedonia, New Concerns over Rural Fundamentalism," www.balkanalysis.com (October 2, 2006).

19. "Mujahedin Camps Spotted in Mountains Below Skopje, Newspaper Claims," www.balkanalysis.com (September 18, 2005).

20. Author interview with Zoran Mitevski.

21. Author interview with Taxhedin Bislimi, December 2005.

22. Risto Karajkov, "Macedonia: Big Rush in the Islamic Community," www.worldpress.org (September 26, 2005).

23. Ibid.

24. Author interview with Abdurahim Yashari, December 2005.

25. Emil Zafirovski, "Protesti Poradi Karikaturi so Muxamed" ["Protests because of the Caricatures of Muhammad"], *Vreme* (Skopje), February 11, 2006.

26. "Albanian Leaders Present Platforms before Debate, as Campaign Looms," www.balkanalysis.com (February 27, 2006).

27. Author interview with Struga imam, September 2006.

28. Author interview with Struga woman, September 2006.

29. Hany Salah, "Macedonian, Bosnian Pilgrims Increase," IslamOnline, www.islamonline.org, December 28, 2005.

30. "Sheik Yousef Al-Qaradhawi Responds to Prophet Muhammad's Caricature: Whoever Is Angered and Does Not Rage in Anger Is a Jackass; We Are Not a Nation of Jackasses," Middle East Media Research Institute, www.memritv.org, February 3, 2006.

31. Author interview with French former peacekeeper, June 2005.

32. "Fundamentalisti Izleguvat so Prviot Mrak" ["Fundamentalists Come Out at Dusk"], *Vest* (Skopje), December 7, 2004.

33. "Skopje Investigators Wary of Salafi Influence," www.balkanalysis.com, July 5, 2004.

34. Author e-mail correspondence with Russian Embassy spokesman, January 2006.

35. Author interview with Tetovo intelligence officer, September 2006.

36. "Kosovo Sparks Euro Violence," AFP, November 17, 2006.

37. See "Ohrid Wahhabis Kill Man in Botched Exorcism," www.balkanalysis.com, February 13, 2007.

38. Author interview with Claude Moniquet.

39. Author interviews with Macedonian military intelligence officer, September and December 2006.

40. "Terrorismo: 'Rete' da Balcani a Jihad, Basi in Italia/ANSA Perquisizioni in 4 Regioni, Riflettori su Internet e DVD" ["Terrorism: 'Network' from the Balkans to Jihad, Bases in Italy/ANSA Searches in 4 Regions, Reflected on Internet and DVD," ANSA (Trieste), December 1, 2006.

CHAPTER 5

1. Sandro Contenta, "Turks Blast Pope on Eve of Arrival," *Toronto Star,* November 27, 2006.

2. See Spiros Vrionis, *The Mechanism of Catastrophe: The Turkish Pogrom of September 6–7 1955, and the Destruction of the Greek Community of Istanbul* (New York: GreekWorks.com Inc., 2005).

3. Mehmet Kalyoncu, "Turkey: Why a Coup, Hard or Soft, is Unlikely in 2007," www.balkanalysis.com (December 2, 2006).

4. Ibid.

5. See M. Hakan Yavuz and John L. Esposito, eds., *Turkish Islam and the Secular State: The Gülen Movement* (Syracuse, NY: Syracuse University Press, 2003).

6. Johnny Dymond, "Turk to Lead World Muslim Group," BBC, June 16, 2004.

7. Author interview with Emre Yilmaz, October 2006.

8. "Ciller: Every Demand Met in the Fight against Terrorism," *Hurriyet* (Istanbul), February 11, 2000, trans. Turkish Directorate General of Press and Information, Office of the Prime Minister, www.byegm.gov.tr

9. Stephen Kinzer, *Crescent and Star: Turkey Between Two Worlds* (New York: Farrar, Strauss and Giroux, 2002), 100.

10. Author interview with Emre Yilmaz.

11. See Daniele Ganser, *NATO's Secret Armies* (London: Frank Cass, 2004).

12. Martin A. Lee, "Turkish Dirty War Revealed, but Papal Shooting Still Obscured," *Los Angeles Times,* April 12, 1998.

13. Ibid.

14. Kendal Nezan, "Turkey's Pivotal Role in the International Drug Trade," *Le Monde Diplomatique,* July 1998.

15. Sibel Edmonds, "The Hijacking of a Nation, Part 2: The Auctioning of Former Statesmen and Dime a Dozen Generals," www.nswbc.org (November 29, 2006).

16. Ian Cobain, "Feared Clan Who Made Themselves at Home in Britain," *The Guardian,* March 28, 2006.

17. Adrian Gatton, "The Susurluk Legacy," *DrugLink Magazine,* November–December 2006.

18. Nezan, "Turkey's Pivotal Role in the International Drug Trade."

19. Lee, "Turkish Dirty War Revealed, but Papal Shooting Still Obscured."

20. Ibid.

21. Nezan, "Turkey's Pivotal Role in the International Drug Trade."

22. See Lutz Kleveman, *The New Great Game: Blood and Oil in Central Asia* (New York: Atlantic Monthly Press, 2003).

23. George Monbiot, "A Discreet Deal in the Pipeline: Nato Mocked Those Who Claimed There was a Plan for Caspian Oil," *The Guardian,* February 15, 2001.

24. Author interview with Sibel Edmonds, October 2006.

25. Ali Isingor, "Istanbul: Gateway to a Holy War," CNN, 2000.

26. "Flying in the Wrong Direction," *The Economist,* May 4, 2006.

27. "The Origins and Developments of Modern Islamist Organizations in the Balkans; New Terrorist Groups With Links to Old; Strong Involvement of Albanian, Turkish, and Northern Cyprus Governments," *Defense & Foreign Affairs Daily,* December 11, 2005.

28. Ekaterina Terzieva, "Headscarf Dilemma Puzzles Bulgaria," Institute for War & Peace Reporting, August 31, 2006.

29. Dana Steinberg, "The Miniskirt and the Veil: Aid and Islam in Bulgaria," *Centerpoint* (Washington, DC: Woodrow Wilson International Center for Scholars, January 2006).

30. "Radical Islam Ungrounded in Bulgaria: Arabian Scholar," *Focus News* (Sofia), www.focus-fen.net, February 21, 2007.

31. "Radical Islamic Group Busted in Bulgaria," B92 (Belgrade), www.b92.net, February 22, 2007.

32. Yana Buhrer Tavanier, "Mysterious Mosques and Schools," *Transitions Online,* www.tol.cz (January 27, 2005).

33. Yana Buhrer Tavanier, "The Schools That Aren't Schools," *Transitions Online,* www.tol.cz (February 3, 2005).

34. "Religious Orders," *Turkish Daily News,* September 24, 2006.

35. Tavanier, "The Schools That Aren't Schools."

36. Author interview with former Gülen student in Macedonia, September 2006.

37. Author interview with senior Turkish diplomat in Skopje, August 2004.

38. See "Behind the Turkish Boycott in Macedonia: Interview with Kenan Hasipi," www.balkanalysis.com (February 24, 2005).

39. See Christopher Deliso, "Letter from Macedonia," *Moment Magazine,* October 2006, 56–59.

40. Ibid.

41. "Islam in Kosovo," *UNMIK On Air,* January 10, 2003.

42. "Georgievski: Xhaferi and I Had No Deal to Divide Macedonia," www.balkanalysis.com (June 3, 2005).

43. Rossen Vassilev, "Bulgaria's Demographic Crisis: Underlying Causes and Some Short-Term Implications," *Southeast European Politics* VI, no. I, (July 2005): 14–27.

44. Yana Moyseeva, "Passport to Bulgaria," *The Sofia Echo*, www.sofiaecho.com (November 20, 2006).

45. Krenar Gashi, "Investigation: Ex-Policemen Run Kosovo Passport Scam," Institute for War & Peace Reporting, December 1, 2006.

CHAPTER 6

1. Author interview with Philip Giraldi, November 2006.

2. Author interview with Darko Trifunovic, October 2006.

3. Author interview with Michael Steven Harrison, October 2006.

4. Author interviews with Tom Gambill, August 2005.

5. Steve Rodan, "Kosovo Seen as New Islamic Bastion," *The Jerusalem Post,* September 14, 1998.

6. See Victor Malarek, *The Natashas: Inside the New Global Sex Trade* (New York: Arcade Publishing, 2004), 228–255.

7. Ibid.

8. Christopher Deliso, "Has the UN Let a Blacklisted Islamic Charity Roam Free in Kosovo?" www.antiwar.com (September 15, 2005).

9. Ibid.

10. Ibid.

11. Ibid.

12. "Concern Charity Channelling Funds to Hamas," *Lateline,* Australian Broadcasting Company, September 22, 2003.

13. Eric Silver, "Charity Cash for Palestinian Poor Was Siphoned to Suicide Bombers," *The Independent,* November 28, 2005.

14. "Old Rivalries behind Kosovo Intelligence Plan," *Jane's Intelligence Digest,* September 15, 2006.

15. Author interview with American intelligence expert, November 2006.

16. Author interview with American soldier in Kosovo, October 2006.

17. Author interview with American special police investigator, October 2006.

18. Author interview with Macedonian military intelligence officer, December 2006.

19. Brian Knowlton, "Report Assails Collusion in Europe with CIA," *International Herald-Tribune,* November 29, 2006.

20. Wayne Madsen, "Intelligence Whispers," www.waynemadsenreport.com (January 8, 2006).

21. Jeffrey Fleishman, "Man's Claims May Be a Look at Dark Side of War on Terror," *Los Angeles Times,* April 12, 2005.

22. Jerry Markon, "Lawsuit against CIA Is Dismissed," *Washington Post,* May 19, 2006.

23. Neil A. Lewis, "Man Mistakenly Abducted by C.I.A. Seeks Redress," *New York Times,* November 29, 2006.

24. Mike Nartker, "Macedonian Missile Efforts Trigger U.S. Sanctions," *Global Security Newswire,* December 29, 2003.

25. Mike Nartker, "13 Firms Sanctioned for Alleged Aid to Iranian WMD, Missile Programs," *Global Security Newswire,* April 5, 2004.

26. Author interview with Blagoja Samakoski, November 2006.

27. Ibid.

28. Author interview with Jason Miko, December 2006.

29. Zarar Khan, "Al-Qaeda Link Suspected in Karachi Attack on Consulate," *The Scotsman,* December 6, 2002.

30. "'Foreign Militants' Killed in Macedonia," BBC, March 2, 2002.

31. Nicholas Wood, "Macedonia's 'Mujahideen'—Immigrants or Terrorists?" BBC, March 20, 2002.

32. "Macedonia Faked 'Militant' Raid," BBC, April 30, 2004.

33. Biljana Stavrova and Robert Alagjozovski, "Crimes and Misdemeanors," *Transitions Online,* www.tol.cz (May 20, 2005).

34. Scott Taylor, *Diary of an Uncivil War: The Violent Aftermath of the Kosovo Conflict* (Ottawa: Esprit de Corps Books, 2002), 127.

35. Author interview with Zoran Mitevski, November 2006.

36. Taylor, *Diary of an Uncivil War: The Violent Aftermath of the Kosovo Conflict,* 166.

37. "Slovenia & Terrorism: Hello, Operator?" www.aimpress.ch (September 28, 2001).

38. "Pardew ja osuetil akcijata na MV" ["Pardew Thwarted the Ministry of Interior's Plan"], *Dnevnik* (Skopje), November 14, 2001.

39. Author interview with former MI6 officer, November 2006.

40. Ibid.

41. Author interview with American special police investigator.

42. Author interview with Claude Moniquet, December 2006.

43. Author interview with Philip Giraldi.

CHAPTER 7

1. Detailed information on Ms. Edmonds' case can be found in several interviews with the author and others, as well as media articles gathered on her Web site, www.justacitizen.org. Leadoff vignette comes from author interview with Sibel Edmonds, October 2006.

2. Loretta Napoleoni, *Terror Incorporated* (New York: Seven Stories Press, 2005), 203.

3. Steve Kroft, "Addicted to Heroin," *60 Minutes,* October 16, 2005.

4. Carlotta Gall, "Opium Harvest at Record Level in Afghanistan," *New York Times,* September 3, 2006.

5. Tim McGirk, "Terrorism's Harvest," *Time Magazine Asia,* August 2, 2004.

6. "Heroin," Interpol Drugs Sub-directorate report, December 8, 2005. Available on the official Interpol Web site, www.interpol.int

7. Sibel Edmonds, "The Hijacking of a Nation, Part 2: The Auctioning of Former Statesmen and Dime a Dozen Generals," www.nswbc.org (November 29, 2006).

8. "Political 'Interests' Saved Kosovo's Thugs: Interview with Detective Stu Kellock," www.balkanalysis.com (January 13, 2006).

9. Author interview with Darko Trifunovic, November 2006.

10. "Kosovo Albanian Implicated in Norway Terror," www.serbianna.com (September 27, 2006).

11. Genc Morina, "Wahhabism a Danger to Kosovo's Independence!" *Express* (Pristina), October 15, 2006.

12. Author interview with Dusan Janjic, October 2006.

13. McGirk, "Terrorism's Harvest."

14. Author interview with Sibel Edmonds.

15. Hugh Griffiths and Gordana Igric, "Djukanovic Smuggling Claims Persist," Institute for War and Peace Reporting, July 23, 2003.

16. "Montenegro: Parliament Votes in New Government," ADN Kronos, www.adnki.com (November 10, 2006).

17. "Political 'Interests' Saved Kosovo's Thugs: Interview with Detective Stu Kellock."

18. Christopher Deliso, "The Black Hole of Europe: Kosovo Interventionists Cover Up their Crimes," www.antiwar.com (November 14, 2006).

19. "Remarks by the President to AFSCME Biennial Convention," http://clinton4.nara.gov/WH/New/html/19990323-1110.html (March 23, 1999).

20. See Carl Savich and Christopher Deliso, "International Intervention in Macedonia, 1903–1909· The Mürzsteg Reforms," www.balkanalysis.com (March 13, 2006).

21. Author interview with Darko Trifunovic.

22. "Serbia's Sandzak: Still Forgotten," International Crisis Group, April 8, 2005.

23. Paolo Pontoniere, "In Italy, Al Qaeda Turns to Organized Crime for Protection," www.newamericamedia.org (October 21, 2005).

24. Ibid.

25. Gregory Katz, "Terrorists Said To Be Getting Aid in Balkans," *Houston Chronicle,* December 27, 2005.

26. Ibid.

27. Frank Viviano, "Crest of a Human Wave: Illegal Immigrants Flood Albania To Be Smuggled Across Adriatic," *San Francisco Chronicle,* February 12, 1999.

28. Andi Balla, "Albania Bans Speedboats to Curb Trafficking," Institute for War & Peace Reporting, April 12, 2006.

29. For example, see "Landmine Deaths on Greek Border," BBC, September 29, 2003, and "Boat Carrying Illegal Migrants Capsizes in Aegean; 1 Dead, 2 Missing," Associated Press, November 19, 2006.

30. "Greece Picks Up 170 Illegal Aliens," Associated Press, December 27, 2001.

31. Ian Burrell, "Albanian Mafia Takes Control of Soho Vice Scene," *The Independent,* June 18, 2001.

32. Author interview with Anes Alic, November 2006.

33. Author interview with Zoran Mitevski, November 2006.

34. "Malaysian, EU-Rejected Islamists Penetrate Macedonia," www.balkanalysis.com, September 28, 2005.

35. Author interview with Sibel Edmonds.

36. Christopher Deliso, "An Interview with Sibel Edmonds," www.antiwar.com, July 1, 2004.

37. Matha Akeel, "Turkish Court Lifts Freeze on Yassin Al-Qadi's Assets," www.arabnews.com, August 9, 2006.

38. Author interview with Sibel Edmonds.

39. Recounted in Napoleoni, *Terror Incorporated*, 7.

40. Jeff Crogan, "Another FBI Agent Blows the Whistle," www.laweekly.com (July 31, 2002).

41. Napoleoni, *Terror Incorporated*, 202.

42. "Intelligence Matters," *Mother Jones*, November 23, 2004.

43. Napoleoni, *Terror Incorporated*, 201.

44. Ibid., 207.

CHAPTER 8

1. "Muslimanski ekstremisti sudarili se sa lokalnim vernicima u Novom Pazaru" ["Muslim Extremists Clash with Local Faithful in Novi Pazar"], BETA (Belgrade), November 6, 2006.

2. Author interview with Marko Lopusina, October 2006.

3. "For Some Bosnian Muslims in Serbia, Ethno-music is Simply Satanic," www.balkanalysis.com (June 5, 2006).

4. "Sandžačke vehabije svojim ženama odrezuju klitoris kako ne bi uživale u seksu i privlačile druge muškarce" ["Sandzak Wahhabis Cutting the Clitorises of Their Own Wives So As To Not Enjoy Sex and Attract Other Men"], *Kurir* (Belgrade), October 25, 2006.

5. "Vehabizam prihvata neprosvijecena omladina" ["Uneducated Youth Embrace Wahhabism"], *Vijesti* (Podgorica), October 14, 2006.

6. "Some Groups in Rozaje Look Like Wahhabis," *Dan* (Podgorica), November 11, 2006; excerpted as "Wahhabis in Montenegro Are Armed—Military Analyst," BBC Monitoring Europe, November 12, 2006.

7. M. Sekulovic, "Oružjem 'jačaju' islam" ["With Weapons They 'Strengthen' Islam"], *Večernje Novosti* (Belgrade), October 12, 2006.

8. See "Terrorism in the Balkans: Enter Sandzak?" www.balkanalysis.com (October 24, 2003). A report published in 2005 by interventionist think tank, the International Crisis Group, while noting the rise of Wahhabism in Sandzak, downplayed the threat, dismissing it as an "internal matter." See "Serbia's Sandzak: Still Forgotten," International Crisis Group, April 8, 2005.

9. "Politicised Islam Grows in Serbia's Sandzak," *Jane's Intelligence Digest*, April 1, 2006.

10. "Serbia: Muslims in Sandzak Region Strive for Autonomy," ADNKronos, www.adnki.com (October 23, 2006).

11. "Serbian Police Crack Down on Alleged Muslim Terrorist Group, Arrest 4," Associated Press, March 17, 2007.

12. "Serbia's Sandzak: Still Forgotten."

13. According to the International Crisis Group report, the Islamic Community-supported schools in the Sandzak "have better facilities than the secular schools, particularly in information technology, and a far lower teacher/pupil ratio. The educational activities are largely supported by diaspora Bosniaks, Middle-Eastern donors and nouveau riche local businessmen." See "Serbia's Sandzak: Still Forgotten."

14. Amela Bajrovic, "Politician's Murder Raises Tensions in Sandzak," Institute for War and Peace Reporting, September 14, 2006.

15. See Lawrence Wright, "The Master Plan," *The New Yorker,* September 11, 2006.

16. Author interview with Darko Trifunovic, October 2006.

17. "Serbia's Sandzak: Still Forgotten."

18. Author interview with U.S. military official, October 2006.

19. Based on author interviews, July 2006.

20. Sean O'Neill and Daniel McGrory, "Blasts Destroyed UK Terror Theories," *The Times,* December 29, 2005.

21. "Dzevad Galijashevic: Teshanj i Zavidovici su pravi Al Kaidin Centar" ["Dzevad Galijashevic: Teshanj and Zavidovici are the real al Qaeda Centers"], *Nezavisne Novine* (Sarajevo), November 25, 2006.

22. Author interview with former MI6 officer, October 2006.

23. Author interview with Philip Giraldi, November 2006.

24. Philip Giraldi, "The Jihadi War," *The American Conservative,* September 22, 2003.

25. Author interview with Loretta Napoleoni.

26. "Declassified Key Judgments of the National Intelligence Estimate—Trends in Global Terrorism: Implications for the United States," April 2006. Available at the official Web site of the U.S. Director of National Intelligence, www.dni.gov

27. Mark Mazzetti, "Spy Agencies Say Iraq War Worsens Terrorism Threat," *New York Times,* September 24, 2006.

28. Anna Badkhen, "Foreign Jihadists Seen as Key to Spike in Afghan Attacks," *San Francisco Chronicle,* September 25, 2006.

29. Gregory Katz, "Terrorists Said To Be Getting Aid in Balkans," *Houston Chronicle,* December 27, 2005.

30. Author interview with Philip Giraldi.

31. Richard Norton-Taylor, "MI5: 30 Terror Plots Being Planned in UK," *The Guardian,* November 10, 2006.

32. Arnaud de Borchgrave, "Multicultural Boondoggle," *Washington Times,* April 12, 2007.

33. Daniel McGrory, "British Computer Whiz-kid Exports Terror via Internet," *The Times,* June 7, 2006.

34. Todd A. Megill, "The Dark Fruit of Globalization: Hostile Use of the Internet," *Strategic Challenges for Counterinsurgency and the Global War on Terrorism,* ed. Williamson Murray (Strategic Studies Institute of the U.S. Army War College, September 2006), 224. Text available at the official Web site of the Strategic Studies Institute of the U.S. Army War College, www.strategicstudiesinstitute.army.mil

35. Norton-Taylor, "MI5: 30 Terror Plots Being Planned in UK."

36. Author interview with Zoran Mitevski.

37. Akhtar M. Faruqui, "Dawn of a New Era in Islamic Education," www.pakistanlink.com (October 2003).

38. See McGrory, "British Computer Whiz-kid Exports Terror via Internet."

39. Daniel McGrory, "America Paid Us To Hand Over al Qaeda Suspects," *The Times,* September 25, 2006.

40. Author interview with Claude Moniquet, December 2006.

Bibliography

Articles Without Named Authors

"Additional Al-Haramain Branches, Former Leader Designated by Treasury as Al Qaida Supporters." *U.S. Treasury Press Release* JS-1703, June 2, 2004. Available at the official Web site of the U.S. Treasury, www.ustreas.gov

"Albanian Leaders Present Platforms before Debate, as Campaign Looms." www.balkanalysis.com, February 27, 2006.

"Al Qaeda Video Takes Credit for 9/11." www.aljazeera.net, September 8, 2006.

"Al-Sirat Al-Mustaqeem: Interview with Sheikh al-Mujahideen Abu Abdel Aziz." *Al-Sirat Al Mustaqeem* [*The Straight Path*], no. 33, August 1994. Translation available at www.seprin.com

"Balkan-Albania-Kosovo-Heroin-Jihad." Centre for Peace in the Balkans, May 2000.

"Behind the Turkish Boycott in Macedonia: Interview with Kenan Hasipi." www.balkanalysis.com, February 24, 2005.

"Berisha i dha nënshtetësinë krahut të djathtë të Bin Ladin" ["Berisha Gave Citizenship to bin Laden's Bunch"]. www.gazeta-shqip.com, April 12, 2007.

"BH teroristi htjeli zatrovati pitku vodu" ["BH Terrorists Wanted to Poison Drinking Water"]. *Vecernji List* (Zagreb), December 3, 2006.

"Bin Laden's New Special Envoys." *Washington Times,* June 22, 2001.

"Bin Laden Was Granted Bosnian Passport." Agence France-Presse, September 24, 1999.

"Black Hole: The Fate of Islamists Rendered to Egypt," Part V. Human Rights Watch, May 2005.

"Boat Carrying Illegal Migrants Capsizes in Aegean; 1 Dead, 2 Missing." Associated Press, November 19, 2006.

"Bosanski Wahabist kaze da mu je nugjeno para da unisti Katolichki spomenik u Maos-taru" ["Bosnian Wahhabi Says that He Was Offered Money to Destroy a Catholic Monument in Mostar"]. *Vecernji List* (Zagreb), July 19, 2006.

"Bosnia: 50 Al Qacda Sympathizers Lose Citizenship." ADNKronos International, www.adnki.com, September 5, 2006.

"Bosnia: Muslim Leader Accuses Christians of Undermining State." ADNKronos, www.adnki.com, June 8, 2006.

"Bosnian Muslims Move against Radicalization of Islam." Agence France-Presse, November 13, 2006.

"Bosnian Official Links With Terrorism, Including 9/11, Become Increasingly Apparent as Clinton, Clark Attempt to Justify Support of Bosnian Militants." *Defense & Foreign Affairs Daily,* September 17, 2003.

"Bosni prijeti opasnost od vehabista." *Nacional* (Zagreb), August 14, 2006; excerpted as "Ex-Wahhabi Says Bosnia under Threat of Islamic Radicals." BBC Monitoring Europe, August 22, 2006.

"Ciller: Every Demand Met in the Fight against Terrorism." *Hurriyet* (Istanbul), February 11, 2000. Trans. Turkish Directorate General of Press and Information, Office of the Prime Minister. Available at www.byegm.gov.tr

"Clinton-Approved Iranian Arms Transfers Help Turn Bosnia into Militant Islamic Base." Congressional Press Release, U.S. Congress, January 16, 1997. Available at www.globalresearch.ca

"Concern Charity Channelling Funds to Hamas." *Lateline,* Australian Broadcasting Company, September 22, 2003.

"Crimes Committed in Italy Provide Funds for Kosovo Guerrillas." *Corriere della Sera,* January 19, 1999.

"Declassified Key Judgments of the National Intelligence Estimate—Trends in Global Terrorism: Implications for the United States." April 2006. Available at the official Web site of the U.S. Director of National Intelligence, www.dni.gov

"Dubai Names Ex-Bosnian President as Islamic Personality of the Year." www.islamonline.net, November 21, 2001.

"Flying in the Wrong Direction." *The Economist,* May 4, 2006.

"'Foreign Militants' Killed in Macedonia." BBC, March 2, 2002.

"For Some Bosnian Muslims in Serbia, Ethno-music Is Simply Satanic." www.balkanalysis.com, June 5, 2006.

"Fundamentalisti Izleguvat so Prviot Mrak" ["Fundamentalists Come Out at Dusk"]. *Vest* (Skopje), December 7, 2004.

"Galijashevic, Dzevad: Teshanj i Zavidovici su pravi Al Kaidin Centar" ["Dzevad Galija-shevic: Teshanj and Zavidovici Are the Real al Qaeda Centers"]. *Nezavisne Novine* (Sarajevo), November 25, 2006.

"Georgievski: Xhaferi and I Had No Deal to Divide Macedonia." www.balkanalysis.com, June 3, 2005.

"Greece Picks Up 170 Illegal Aliens." Associated Press, December 27, 2001.

"Head of Bosnia's Islamic Community Urges Institutional Organisation of European Mus-lims." HINA News Agency (Zagreb), January 9, 2006.

"Heroin." Interpol Drugs Sub-directorate report, December 8, 2005. Available on the offi-cial Interpol Web site, www.interpol.int

"Imam of a Kosovo Mosque Lauds Morocco's Backing." www.arabicnews.com, January 3, 2000.

"In Kosovo Russian Peacekeepers Detain 30 Albanians Suspected As Terrorists." Pravda, January 4, 2002.

"Intelligence Matters." *Mother Jones,* November 23, 2004.

"Iranian Gunrunners Detained In Kosovo." CNN, August 9, 2001.

"Islam in Kosovo." *UNMIK On Air* (Pristina), January 10, 2003.

"Italian Probe of CIA Abduction Broadens to Domestic Spying Scandal and 'Black Propaganda' Misinformation Campaign by Italy Intel." www.democracynow.org, July 11, 2006.

"Kolezhot kaj Vejce go Izvrsile Mudjahedini" ["Massacre near Vejce was Done by Mujahedin"]. A1 TV (Skopje), October 16, 2001.

"Kosovo Albanian Implicated in Norway Terror." www.serbianna.com, September 27, 2006.

"Kosovo Christians Targeted by Islamic Militants." *Charisma Magazine,* May 18, 2000.

"Kosovo Clashes Orchestrated." BBC, March 20, 2004.

"Kosovo Seen as New Islamic Bastion." *Jerusalem Post,* September 14, 1998.

"Kosovo SHIK, Directly Linked with Albanian SHIK Intelligence Organization, Prepares for 'Big Push' for Kosovo Independence." *Defense & Foreign Affairs,* January 16, 2006.

"Kosovo Sparks Euro Violence." AFP, November 17, 2006.

"Kosovo's U.N. Administration Praises Saudi Relief Committee." www.saudinf.org, May 25, 2004.

"Landmine Deaths on Greek Border." BBC, September 29, 2003.

"Macedonia Faked 'Militant' Raid." BBC, April 30, 2004.

"Macedonia on 'Brink of Abyss.'" BBC, May 7, 2001.

"Malaysian, EU-Rejected Islamists Penetrate Macedonia." www.balkanalysis.com, September 28, 2005.

"Montenegro: Parliament Votes in New Government." ADN Kronos, www.adnki.com, November 10, 2006.

"Mujahedin Camps Spotted in Mountains Below Skopje, Newspaper Claims." www.balkanalysis.com, September 18, 2005.

"Muslimanski ekstremisti sudarili se sa lokalnim vernicima u Novom Pazaru" ["Muslim Extremists Clash with Local Faithful in Novi Pazar"]. BETA (Belgrade), November 6, 2006.

"Ohrid Wahhabis Kill Man in Botched Exorcism." www.balkanalysis.com, February 13, 2007.

"Old Rivalries behind Kosovo Intelligence Plan." *Jane's Intelligence Digest,* September 15, 2006.

"The Origins and Developments of Modern Islamist Organizations in the Balkans; New Terrorist Groups With Links to Old; Strong Involvement of Albanian, Turkish, and Northern Cyprus Governments." *Defense & Foreign Affairs Daily*, December 11, 2005.

"Pakistan Snatches Terror Pair from Germany." United Press International, March 12, 2007.

"Patterns of Global Terrorism, 1999." U.S. Department of State. Available at the official U.S. State Department Web site, www.state.gov

"Patterns of Global Terrorism 2005: Europe and Eurasia Overview." U.S. Department of State. Available at official State Department Web site, www.state.gov

"Pentagon Chief Cancels Albania Visit Over Terror Threat." CNN, July 15, 1999.

"Political 'Interests' Saved Kosovo's Thugs: Interview with Detective Stu Kellock." www.balkanalysis.com, January 13, 2006.

"Politicised Islam Grows in Serbia's Sandzak." *Jane's Intelligence Digest,* April 1, 2006.

"Radical Islamic Group Busted in Bulgaria." *B92* (Belgrade), www.b92.net, February 22, 2007.

"Radical Islam Ungrounded in Bulgaria: Arabian Scholar." *Focus News* (Sofia), www. focus-fen.net, February 21, 2007.

"The Radical with a Perfect Cover." *The Sunday Times,* August 20, 2006

"Religious Orders." *Turkish Daily News,* September 24, 2006.

"Remarks by the President to AFSCME Biennial Convention." Available at http://clinton4.nara.gov/WH/New/html/19990323-1110.html, March 23, 1999.

"Sandžačke vehabije svojim ženama odrezuju klitoris kako ne bi uživale u seksu i privlačile druge muškarce" ["Sandzak Wahhabis Cutting the Clitorises of Their Own Wives So As To Not Enjoy Sex and Attract Other Men"]. *Kurir* (Belgrade), October 25, 2006.

"Serbia: Muslims in Sandzak Region Strive for Autonomy." ADNKronos, www.adnki.com, October 23, 2006.

"Serbia's Sandzak: Still Forgotten." International Crisis Group, April 8, 2005.

"Sheikh Muhammad Stubla, President of the Albanian Islamic Society in London: The Latest Massacres Warn of a New Genocide Targeting about 2 Million Muslims in Kosovo." *Nida'ul Magazine,* April–May 1998. Available on the Web site of the Federation of American Scientists, www.fas.org

"Sheik Yousef Al-Qaradhawi Responds to Prophet Muhammad's Caricature: Whoever Is Angered and Does Not Rage in Anger Is a Jackass; We Are Not a Nation of Jackasses." Middle East Media Research Institute, www.memritv.org, February 3, 2006.

"Skopje Investigators Wary of Salafi Influence." www.balkanalysis.com, July 5, 2004.

"Slovenia & Terrorism: Hello, Operator?" www.aimpress.ch, September 28, 2001.

"Some Groups in Rozaje Look Like Wahhabis." *Dan* (Podgorica), November 11, 2006; excerpted as "Wahhabis in Montenegro Are Armed—Military Analyst." BBC Monitoring Europe, November 12, 2006.

"Spain Asks Bosnia to Investigate Possible Link in Madrid Bombings." Radio Free Europe/Radio Liberty, April 9, 2004.

"Terrorism in the Balkans: Enter Sandzak?" www.balkanalysis.com, October 24, 2003.

"Terrorismo: 'Rete' da Balcani a Jihad, Basi in Italia/ANSA Perquisizioni in 4 Regioni, Riflettori su Internet e DVD" ["Terrorism: 'Network' from the Balkans to Jihad, Bases in Italy/ANSA Searches in 4 Regions, Reflected on Internet and DVD"]. ANSA (Trieste), December 1, 2006.

"Threat Assessment: Militancy in Bosnia and Herzegovina." *Jane's Intelligence Review,* August 1, 2006.

"Tihic Thanks Qatar for Support to Bosnia." *The Peninsula* (Doha), June 10, 2006.

"Treasury Designates Bin Laden, Qadi Associate." *U.S. Treasury Press Release* JS-2727, September 19, 2005. Available at the official Web site of the U.S. Treasury, www.ustreas.gov

"Uhiceni trojica terorista Bosnjaka" ["Arrests of Three Bosnian Terrorists"]. *Vecernji List* (Zagreb), December 2, 2006.

"UN Administrators Flee 'Kristallnacht.'" B92 (Belgrade), March 17, 2004.

"UNESCO Calls for Urgent Action to Protect Serbian Heritage in Kosovo." AFP, May 4, 2004.

"Unhealthy Climate in Kosovo as Guerrillas Gear Up for a Summer Confrontation." *Jane's International Defense Review,* February 1, 1999.

"U.N. in Kosovo Says 'Credible Threats' against Staff." Reuters, November 27, 2006.

United States of America v. Benevolence International Foundation, Inc., and Enaam M. Arnaout a/k/a Abu Mahmoud a/k/a Abdel Samia. Case No. 02 CR 414. Available at www.findlaw.com

"UNMIK Warns Of Suicide-Bombers' Attacks." Tanjug (Belgrade), March 21, 2003.

"U.N. Police Fire Tear Gas at Protesters in Kosovo." Associated Press, November 28, 2006.

"U.S. Had Options to Let Bosnia Get Arms, Avoid Iran." *Los Angeles Times,* July 14, 1996.

"Vahabije—skrivena pretnja u BIH" ["Wahhabis—The Hidden Threat in BIH"]. *Nezavisne Novine* (Sarajevo), November 5, 2006.

"Vehabizam prihvata neprosvijecena omladina" ["Uneducated Youth Embrace Wahhabism"]. *Vijesti* (Podgorica), October 14, 2006.

"Wahhabis Threaten Bosnia's Security." *B92* (Belgrade), www.b92.net, March 10, 2007.

"Who Are Our Fundamentalists?" UNMIK Local Media Monitoring (Pristina), October 30, 2001.

Articles by Authors' Names

Abrahams, Fred. "Albania," *Human Rights Watch* 2, no. 33 (May 1997).

Abrahams, Fred. "The Albanian House of Cards," *Dollars & Sense* no. 212 (July–August 1997).

Akeel, Matha. "Turkish Court Lifts Freeze on Yassin Al-Qadi's Assets." www.arabnews.com (August 9, 2006).

Alexiev, Alex. "Tablighi Jamaat: Jihad's Stealthy Legions." *Middle East Quarterly* (February 2005). www.meforum.org

Alic, Anes. "Wahhabism: from Vienna to Bosnia." *ISN Security Watch,* April 6, 2007.

Babuna, Aydin. "Albanian National Identity and Islam in the Post-Communist Era." *Perceptions: a Journal of International Affairs* 8 (September–November 2003), Center for Strategic Research of the Turkish Ministry of Foreign Affairs. Available at the official Web site of the Turkish Ministry of Foreign Affairs, www.sam.gov.tr

Badkhen, Anna. "Foreign Jihadists Seen as Key to Spike in Afghan Attacks." *San Francisco Chronicle,* September 25, 2006.

Bajrovic, Amela. "Politician's Murder Raises Tensions in Sandzak." Institute for War and Peace Reporting, September 14, 2006.

Balla, Andi. "Albania Bans Speedboats to Curb Trafficking." Institute for War and Peace Reporting, April 12, 2006.

Bamber, David, and Chris Hastings. "KLA Raises Money in Britain for Arms." *The Sunday Telegraph,* April 23, 2000.

Beham, Mira. "Kad Obaveshtajci Potpiruju" ["When Intelligence Officers Fan Flames"]. *NIN* (Belgrade), November 25, 2004. Translation available at www.ex-yupress.com

Binder, David. "A Troubled Dream." *Newsweek,* March 22, 2001.

Blumi, Isa. "Political Islam among the Albanians: Are the Taleban Coming to the Balkans?" Kosovar Institute for Policy and Research Development, June 2005.

Bodansky, Yossef. "Italy Becomes Iran's New Base for Terrorist Operations." *Defense and Foreign Affairs Strategic Policy,* International Strategic Studies Association, February 1998.

de Borchgrave, Arnaud. "Multicultural Boondoggle." *Washington Times,* April 12, 2007.

Brock, Peter. *Media Cleansing: Dirty Reporting. Journalism and Tragedy in Yugoslavia.* Los Angeles: GM Books, 2005.

Brown, Frank. "Islam Builds a Future in Kosovo, One Mosque at a Time." Religious News Service, September 12, 2000.

Burr, J. Milton, and Robert O. Collins. *Alms for Jihad: Charity and Terrorism in the Islamic World.* Cambridge: Cambridge University Press, 2006.

Burrell, Ian. "Albanian Mafia Takes Control of Soho Vice Scene." *The Independent,* June 18, 2001.

Buza, Shaban. "UN Suspension Move Angers Kosovo Ex-guerrillas." Reuters, December 3, 2003.

Chazan, Yigal. "Albanian Mafias Find New Drug Routes Around Yugoslavia." *Christian Science Monitor,* October 20, 1994.

Chiclet, Christophe. "Rise of the Kosovar Freedom Fighters." *Le Monde Diplomatique* (May 1999).

Chossudovsky, Michel. "London 7/7 Terror Suspect Linked to British Intelligence?" Centre for Research on Globalization, www.globalresearch.ca (August 1, 2005).

Cobain, Ian. "Feared Clan Who Made Themselves at Home in Britain." *The Guardian,* March 28, 2006.

Contenta, Sandro. "Turks Blast Pope on Eve of Arrival." *Toronto Star,* November 27, 2006.

Cooley, John K. *Unholy Wars: Afghanistan, America and International Terrorism.* London: Pluto Press, 2000.

Crewdson, John, and Tom Huntley. "Abducted Imam Aided CIA Ally." *Chicago Tribune,* July 3, 2005.

Crogan, Jeff. "Another FBI Agent Blows the Whistle." www.laweekly.com (July 31, 2002).

Cubro, M. "Tužilaštvo BiH otvorilo istragu o poslovanju 'Organizacije preporoda islamske tradicije Kuvajt'" ["The Prosecutor of BiH Opened Investigation about Dealing in 'Kuwait's Organization of Revival Islamic Heritage'"]. *Nezavisne Novine* (Sarajevo), June 28, 2006.

Dakovic, Mirko, and Boro Miseljic. "Destabilizing the Balkans: US & Albanian Defense Cooperation in the 1990s." Independent Center for Geopolitical Studies JUGOISTOK, March 22, 2001. Available at www.antiwar.com

Deliso, Christopher. "The Black Hole of Europe: Kosovo Interventionists Cover Up their Crimes." www.antiwar.com (November 14, 2006).

Deliso, Christopher. "In Macedonia, New Concerns over Rural Fundamentalism." www.balkanalysis.com (October 2, 2006).

Deliso, Christopher. "The Internationals and the Mobs: Kosovo's Moment of Truth." www.antiwar.com (April 15, 2004).

Deliso, Christopher. "An Interview with Sibel Edmonds." www.antiwar.com (July 1, 2004).

Deliso, Christopher. "Fissures in Balkan Islam." *Christian Science Monitor,* February 14, 2006.

Deliso, Christopher. "Has the UN Let a Blacklisted Islamic Charity Roam Free in Kosovo?" www.antiwar.com (September 15, 2005).

Deliso, Christopher. "Letter from Macedonia." *Moment Magazine* (Washington) (October 2006).

Deliso, Christopher. "An Uncertain Future for the Serbian Refugees of Kosovo." www.antiwar.com (April 7, 2004).

Deliso, Christopher. "Varieties of Religious Experience in a Macedonian Village." www.balkanalysis.com (September 27, 2006).

Deliso, Christopher. "Vevchani and Labunishta: A Tale of Two Villages." *Hidden Europe Magazine* (May 2006).

Drozdiak, William. "Merchants of Death and Drugs; Porous Borders, Balkan War Bring Epidemics of Heroin Smuggling, Arms Sales." *Washington Post,* November 14, 1993.

Dymond, Johnny. "Turk to Lead World Muslim Group." BBC, June 16, 2004.

Edmonds, Sibel. "The Hijacking of a Nation, Part 2: The Auctioning of Former Statesmen and Dime a Dozen Generals." www.nswbc.org (November 29, 2006).

Elsässer, Jürgen. *Dzihad na Balkanu, Kako je dzihad stigao u Evropu.* Belgrade: Jasen, 2006. Serbian translation of Jürgen Elsässer. *Wie der Dschihad nach Europa kam Gotteskrieger und Geheimdienste auf dem Balkan.* Vienna: Np Buchverlag, 2005.

Faligot, Roger. "How Germany Backed KLA." *The European,* September 21, 1998.

Faruqui, Akhtar M. "Dawn of a New Era in Islamic Education." www.pakistanlink.com (October 2003).

Filipovic, Miroslav. "Pricha o Ljubavi i Svetom Ratu" ["Story of Love and Holy War"]. *Danas* (Belgrade), December 20, 1999. Translation at www.ex-yupress.com

Fleishman, Jeffrey. "Man's Claims May Be a Look at Dark Side of War on Terror." *Los Angeles Times,* April 12, 2005.

Fox, Robert. "Albanians and Afghans Fight for the Heirs to Bosnia's SS Past." *Daily Telegraph,* December 29, 1993.

Gall, Carlotta. "Opium Harvest at Record Level in Afghanistan." *New York Times,* September 3, 2006.

Ganser, Daniele. *NATO's Secret Armies.* London: Frank Cass, 2004.

Gashi, Krenar. "Investigation: Ex-Policemen Run Kosovo Passport Scam." Institute for War & Peace Reporting, December 1, 2006.

Gelevska, Irina. "Interview with Claude Moniquet." www.realitymacedonia.org.mk (December 12, 2004).

Gertz, Bill. "Hijackers Connected to Albanian Terrorist Cell." *Washington Times,* September 18, 2001.

Giraldi, Philip. "The Jihadi War." *The American Conservative,* September 22, 2003.

Gjiknuri, Damian. "Albania's Counter-Terrorism Policy Options: Finding a Strategy of Common Sense." U.S. Naval Postgraduate School Thesis, Monterey, 2004.

Glyn Williams, Brian, and Feyza Altindag. "Turkish Volunteers in Chechnya." Jamestown Foundation, *Terrorism Monitor* 3, no. 7 (April 7, 2005).

Grey, Stephen, and Don Van Natta. "Thirteen with the C.I.A. Sought by Italy in a Kidnapping." *New York Times,* June 25, 2005.

Griffiths, Hugh, and Gordana Igric. "Djukanovic Smuggling Claims Persist." Institute for War and Peace Reporting, July 23, 2003.

Gumbel, Andrew. "The Gangster Regime We Fund." *The Independent,* February 14, 1997.

Gustincich, Franz. "From Lenin to Bin Laden." *Gnosis: Online Italian Intelligence Magazine* (March 2005). Available at the official Web site of the Italian intelligence service, www.sisde.it

Halsell, Grace. "Albania and the Muslim World." The Washington Report on Middle East Affairs, 1994.

Higgins, Andrew, and Christopher Cooper. "CIA-Backed Team Used Brutal Means to Break Up Terrorist Cell in Albania." *Wall Street Journal,* November 20, 2001.

Hooper, John. "CIA Methods Exposed by Kidnap Inquiry." *Guardian,* July 2, 2005.

Hundley, Tom, and John Crewsdon. "Wife Was Left Behind with the Children." *Chicago Tribune,* July 3, 2005.

Isingor, Ali. "Istanbul: Gateway to a Holy War." CNN, 2000.

Izetbegovic, Alija. *Islamska deklaracija* [*The Islamic Declaration*]. Mala Muslimanska Biblioteka (Sarajevo), 1990.

Jamine, Evelyn. "Chemicals Stockpiled for 'Jihad on Sydney.'" *The Daily Telegraph* (Sydney), March 7, 2007.

Jennings, Christian. "Fear over Islamic Terror Groups Using Macedonia as Base." *The Scotsman,* March 4, 2002.

Judah, Tim. "Albanian Mafia Targets Drug Routes." *The Times,* October 18, 1994.

Judah, Tim. "German Spies Accused of Arming Bosnian Muslims." *Sunday Telegraph,* April 20, 1997.

Kalyoncu, Mehmet. "Turkey: Why a Coup, Hard or Soft, is Unlikely in 2007." www.balkanalysis.com (December 2, 2006).

Karajkov, Risto. "Macedonia: Big Rush in the Islamic Community." www.worldpress.org (September 26, 2005).

Karajkov, Risto. "The Young and the Old: Radical Islam Takes Root in the Balkans." *Transitions Online,* www.tol.cz (May 3, 2006).

Katz, Gregory. "Terrorists Said To Be Getting Aid in Balkans." *Houston Chronicle,* December 27, 2005.

Khan, Zarar. "Al-Qaeda Link Suspected in Karachi Attack on Consulate." *The Scotsman,* December 6, 2002.

Kinzer, Stephen. *Crescent and Star: Turkey Between Two Worlds.* New York: Farrar, Strauss and Giroux, 2002.

Kleveman, Lutz. *The New Great Game: Blood and Oil in Central Asia.* New York: Atlantic Monthly Press, 2003.

Knowlton, Brian. "Report Assails Collusion in Europe with CIA." *International Herald-Tribune,* November 29, 2006.

Kroft, Steve. "Addicted to Heroin." *60 Minutes,* October 16, 2005.

Lani, Remzi, and Fabian Schmidt. "Albanian Foreign Policy Between Geography and History." *The International Spectator* XXXIII, no. 2 (April–June 1998), Istituto Affair Internazionali.

Lee, Martin A. "Turkish Dirty War Revealed, but Papal Shooting Still Obscured." *Los Angeles Times,* April 12, 1998.

Lewis, Neil A. "Man Mistakenly Abducted by C.I.A. Seeks Redress." *New York Times,* November 29, 2006.

Lewis, Paul. "Inside the Islamic Group Accused by MI5 and FBI." *Guardian,* August 19, 2006.

Lopandic, Bruno. "Granic, Susak and Greguric Saved Galbraith." *Nacional* (Zagreb), no. 304, September 13, 2001.

Madsen, Wayne. "Intelligence Whispers." www.waynemadsenreport.com (January 8, 2006).

Majstorovic, D. "Ko je najbliži saradnik nezvaničnog vođe vehabija u BiH Tunišanina Jusufa Barčića" ["The Tunisian Who Is the Closest Cooperator with the Unofficial Leader of Wahhabis in Bosnia, Jusuf Barcic"]. *Glas Srpske* (Banja Luka), March 5, 2007.

Malarek, Victor. *The Natashas: Inside the New Global Sex Trade.* New York: Arcade Publishing, 2004.

Malic, Nebojsa. "The Real Izetbegovic." www.antiwar.com (October 23, 2003).

Markon, Jerry. "Lawsuit against CIA Is Dismissed." *Washington Post,* May 19, 2006.

Maroevic, Rade, and Daniel Williams. "Terrorist Cells Find Foothold in Balkans; Arrests Point to Attacks Within Europe." *Washington Post,* December 1, 2005.

Mazzetti, Mark. "Spy Agencies Say Iraq War Worsens Terrorism Threat." *New York Times,* September 24, 2006.

McGirk, Tim. "Terrorism's Harvest." *Time Magazine Asia* (August 2, 2004).

McGrory, Daniel. "America Paid Us To Hand Over al Qaeda Suspects." *The Times,* September 25, 2006.

McGrory, Daniel. "British Computer Whiz-kid Exports Terror via Internet." *The Times,* June 7, 2006.

Meyer, Jane. "Outsourcing Torture." *The New Yorker,* February 7, 2005.

Mili, Hayder. "Securing the Northern Frontier: Canada and the War on Terror." Jamestown Foundation, *Terrorism Monitor* 3, no. 14 (July 15, 2005).

Misha, Teodor. "Albania Denies Terrorist Links." Institute for War & Peace Reporting, September 26, 2001.

Monbiot, George. "A Discreet Deal in the Pipeline: Nato Mocked Those Who Claimed There was a Plan for Caspian Oil." *The Guardian,* February 15, 2001.

Morina, Genc. "Radical Islam: Wahhabism a Danger to Kosovo's Independence!" *Express* (Pristina). Translation available from Kosovo and Metohija Information Service, www.decani.org (October 15, 2006).

Moyseeva, Yana. "Passport to Bulgaria." *The Sofia Echo.* www.sofiaecho.com (November 20, 2006).

Murphy, Brian. "KLA Volunteers Lack Experience." Associated Press, April 5, 1999.

Naegele, Jolyon. "Yugoslavia: Saudi Wahhabi Aid Workers Bulldoze Balkan Monuments." Radio Free Europe/Radio Liberty, August 4, 2000.

Napoleoni, Loretta. *Terror Incorporated: Tracing the Dollars behind the Terror Networks.* New York: Seven Stories Press, 2004.

Nartker, Mike. "13 Firms Sanctioned for Alleged Aid to Iranian WMD, Missile Programs." *Global Security Newswire,* April 5, 2004.

Nartker, Mike. "Macedonian Missile Efforts Trigger U.S. Sanctions." *Global Security Newswire,* December 29, 2003.

The National Commission on Terrorist Attacks upon the United States. "Al Qaeda Aims at the American Homeland," Chapter 5. Available at www.9-11commission.gov

Nazan, Kendal. "Turkey's Pivotal Role in the International Drug Trade." *Le Monde Diplomatique,* July 1998.

Norton-Taylor, Richard. "MI5: 30 Terror Plots Being Planned in UK." *The Guardian,* November 10, 2006.

O'Connor, Mike. "Police Official's Methods Raise Ethnic Fears in Bosnian Region." *New York Times,* June 16, 1996.

O'Neill, Sean, and Daniel McGrory. "Blasts Destroyed UK Terror Theories." *The Times,* December 29, 2005.

Pallister, David. "Head of Suspect Charity Denies Link to Bin Laden." *The Guardian,* October 16, 2001.

Pomfret, John. "Bosnian Officials Involved in Arms Trade Tied to Radical States." *Washington Post,* September 22, 1996.

Pomfret, John. "How Bosnia's Muslims Dodged Arms Embargo: Relief Agency Brokered Aid from Nations, Radical Groups." *Washington Post,* September 22, 1996.

Pontoniere, Paolo. "In Italy, Al Qaeda Turns to Organized Crime for Protection." www.newamericamedia.org (October 21, 2005).

Purvis, Andrew. "The Suspects: A Bosnian Subplot." *Time,* November 12, 2001.

Pyes, Craig, Josh Meyer, and William C. Rempe. "Terrorists Use Bosnia as Base and Sanctuary." *Los Angeles Times,* October 7, 2001.

Raman, B. "Harkat-ul-Mujahideen: An Update." South Asia Analysis Group, www.saag.org (March 20, 1999).

Riedlmayer, Andras. "Kosovo: The Destruction of Cultural Heritage." www.justiceforall.org (1999).

Robinson, Matt, and Christian Jennings. "Kosovo Clashes Were Planned, Says UN Official." *The Scotsman,* March 18, 2004.

Rodan, Steve. "Kosovo Seen as New Islamic Bastion." *The Jerusalem Post,* September 14, 1998.

Rosenberg, Carol. "Pentagon Sends Guantánamo Captives to Albania." *Miami Herald,* November 17, 2006.

Sachs, Susan. "A Muslim Missionary Group Draws New Scrutiny in U.S." *New York Times,* July 14, 2003.

Salah, Hany. "Macedonian, Bosnian Pilgrims Increase." IslamOnline, www.islamonline.org, December 28, 2005.

Savich, Carl. "Al Qaeda in Bosnia: Bosnian Muslims War Crimes Trial." www.serbianna.com

Savich, Carl. "Islam, Catholicism and Orthodoxy: The Civil War in Bosnia-Hercegovina, 1992–1995." Internet Library of Serb Culture. Available at www.rastko.org.yu

Savich, Carl, and Christopher Deliso. "International Intervention in Macedonia, 1903–1909: the Mürzsteg Reforms." www.balkanalysis.com (March 13, 2006).

Schmidt, Fabian. "Albania's Pharaoh and His Pyramids." Radio Free Europe/Radio Liberty, June 6, 2000.

Schweid, Barry. "NATO Braces for Wider Kosovo Fight." Associated Press, June 17, 1998.

Sekulovic, M. "Oružjem 'jačaju' islam." ["With Weapons They 'Strengthen' Islam"]. *Večernje Novosti* (Belgrade), October 12, 2006.

Semini, Llazar. "Mother Teresa Statue Causes Friction." Associated Press, March 20, 2006.

Sherwell, Philip. "SAS Teams Move in to Help KLA 'Rise From the Ashes.'" *The Telegraph,* April 18, 1999.

Silver, Eric. "Charity Cash for Palestinian Poor Was Siphoned to Suicide Bombers." *The Independent,* November 28, 2005.

Smajilhodzic, Rusmir. "Moderate Bosnian Muslims Fear Extremist Takeover." *National Post,* June 17, 2006.

Smith, Jeffrey. "A Bosnian Village's Terrorist Ties." *Washington Post,* March 11, 2000.

Smith, R. Jeffrey. "Macedonian Guerrilla Group Forming in Kosovo Poses Threat of Expanded Conflict in Balkans." *Washington Post,* March 30, 2001.

Smith, R. Jeffrey. "US Probes Blasts' Possible Mideast Ties." *Washington Post,* August 12, 1998.

Smyth, Frank, and Jason Vest. "One Man's Private Jihad." *Village Voice,* August 18, 1998.

Spahic, Merima. "Tragichno predupregjenje" ["A Tragic Warning"]. BETA (Belgrade), February 23, 2004. Translation at www.media-diversity.org

Stavrova, Biljana, and Robert Alagjozovski. "Crimes and Misdemeanors." *Transitions Online.* www.tol.cz (May 20, 2005).

Steinberg, Dana. "The Miniskirt and the Veil: Aid and Islam in Bulgaria." *Centerpoint.* Washington, DC: Woodrow Wilson International Center for Scholars, January 2006.

Stephens, Chris. "Bin Laden Opens European Terror Base in Albania." *Sunday Times,* November 29, 1998.

Stewart, Phil. "Italy Eyes Rogue Spies, Not Agency, in CIA Kidnap." Reuters, July 11, 2006.

Tavanier, Yana Buhrer. "Mysterious Mosques and Schools." *Transitions Online.* www.tol.cz (January 27, 2005).

Tavanier, Yana Buhrer. "The Schools That Aren't Schools." *Transitions Online.* www.tol.cz (February 3, 2005).

Taylor, Scott. "Bin Laden's Balkan Connections." *Ottawa Citizen,* December 15, 2001.

Taylor, Scott. *Diary of an Uncivil War: The Violent Aftermath of the Kosovo Conflict.* Ottawa: Esprit de Corps Books, 2002.

Terzieva, Ekaterina. "Headscarf Dilemma Puzzles Bulgaria." Institute for War & Peace Reporting, August 31, 2006.

Trifunovic, Darko. "Exclusive: Pattern of Bosnian and Other Links to Madrid Bombings Becoming Increasingly Clear." *Defense & Foreign Affairs,* June 21, 2005.

Vassilev, Rossen. "Bulgaria's Demographic Crisis: Underlying Causes and Some Short-Term Implications." *Southeast European Politics* VI, no. I, July 2005: 14–27.

Vickers, Miranda, and James Pettifer. *Albania: From Anarchy to a Balkan Identity.* New York: New York University Press, 1997.

Viviano, Frank. "Crest of a Human Wave: Illegal Immigrants Flood Albania to Be Smuggled Across Adriatic." *San Francisco Chronicle,* February 12, 1999.

Viviano, Frank. "Drugs Paying for Conflict in Europe." *San Francisco Chronicle,* June 10, 1994.

Vrionis, Spiros. *The Mechanism of Catastrophe: The Turkish Pogrom of September 6–7, 1955, and the Destruction of the Greek Community of Istanbul.* New York: GreekWorks.com Inc., 2005.

Walker, Tom. "US Alarmed as Mujahidin Join Kosovo Rebels." *The Times* (London), September 29, 1998.

White, Josh. "Lawyers Demand Release of Chinese Muslims." *Washington Post,* December 5, 2006.

Whitlock, Craig. "CIA Ruse is Said to Have Damaged Probe in Milan." *Washington Post,* December 6, 2005.

Whitlock, Craig. "Italians Detail Lavish CIA Operation." *Washington Post,* June 26, 2005.

Whitlock, Craig. "Italy Seeks Extradition of 22 CIA Operatives." *Washington Post,* November 12, 2005.

Whitmore, Brian. "Saudi 'Charity' Troubling to Bosnian Muslims." *Boston Globe,* January 28, 2002.

Wiebes, Cees. *Intelligence and the War in Bosnia 1992–1995.* Münster: Lit Verlag, 2003.

Wood, Nicholas. "Macedonia's 'Mujahideen'—Immigrants or Terrorists?" BBC, March 20, 2002.

Wright, Lawrence. "The Master Plan." *The New Yorker,* September 11, 2006.

Yavuz, M. Hakan, and John L. Esposito, eds. *Turkish Islam and the Secular State: The Gülen Movement.* Syracuse, NY: Syracuse University Press, 2003.

Zafirovski, Emil. "Protesti Poradi Karikaturi so Muxamed" ["Protests because of the Caricatures of Muhammad"]. *Vreme* (Skopje), February 11, 2006.

Index

About the Author

CHRISTOPHER DELISO, an American journalist and travel writer based in the Balkans, has been investigating radical Islamic trends in the region for the past six years, in the process discovering emerging threats and groups that had been obscurely or completely unknown to the outside world. Deliso, who holds a master's degree in Byzantine Studies from Oxford University, is director of Balkanalysis.com, a leading independent Balkan news Web site. He also serves as field analyst for the Economics Intelligence Unit, London, on Macedonian politics. His freelance articles on Balkan politics, economics, and security issues have been published widely in the mainstream and alternative media in America and abroad.